S

KO SAMUI
& THE ANDAMAN COAST

SUZANNE NAM

Contents

KO SAMUI AND THE ANDAMAN COAST

THE LOWER SOUTHERN GULF

Visit the lower southern Gulf of Thailand for the idyllic islands of the Samui Archipelago, off-the-beaten-path beaches on the mainland, and some charming small historical cities where you can learn about the culture and history of the region.

White sandy beaches, coconut trees, and green rolling hills, as well as excellent diving, make the Samui Archipelago islands off the coast of Surat Thani a top choice if you're looking for a beach vacation in Thailand. Although some mistakenly consider the Samui Archipelago second-best when compared with the Andaman coast, the region has plenty to offer that you won't find on the other side of the Kra Isthmus. The landscapes are not as dramatic as the karst cliffs that pepper Phuket, Krabi, and Trang, but thanks to an abundance of coconut trees and a softer, more rolling topography, the islands are greener and lusher. The resorts can be as posh as those on the Andaman coast, and at the cheaper end, the selection is better. The rainy season is much shorter, lasting from only mid-October–mid-December. Plus, the Ang Thong National Marine Park, comprising 40 islands, is much less touched by tourism than any of the marine national parks in the Andaman region.

The islands of Ko Samui, Ko Pha-Ngan, and Ko Tao, sometimes called the pearls of the gulf, were once considered a backpacker haven, but at least Ko Samui is moving upscale, with five-star resorts and plenty of indulgent spas. Ko Pha-Ngan, just north of Ko Samui, has more luxury lodgings every year but is still one of the few popular islands left in the country where

HIGHLIGHTS

◖ **Mu Ko Ang Thong National Marine Park:** These lush, green islands near the Samui Archipelago are easy to visit on a day trip and offer snorkeling, kayaking, and camping (page 15).

◖ **Lamai Beach, Ko Samui:** This pretty beach on Thailand's popular resort island offer everything you could ever want, including soft sand, peace and quiet, and five-star resorts (page 18).

◖ **Nakhon Si Thammarat:** The coolest city you've never heard of is the center of Thai Buddhism, and it offers plenty of culture, great food, and not a lot of other travelers (page 43).

◖ **Khanom and Sichon:** These are two relatively undiscovered beaches with clear, clean, warm water, soft sand, and friendly people (page 47).

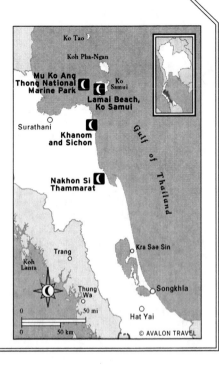

LOOK FOR ◖ TO FIND RECOMMENDED SIGHTS, ACTIVITIES, DINING, AND LODGING.

designer suitcases might get some funny looks among fellow travelers and cheap bungalows remain the norm.

If you want to get away from the crowds of travelers and the indulgent atmosphere you'll find on Samui or the party atmosphere on Ko Pha-Ngan, visit some of the mainland beaches north of Nakhon Si Thammarat. Although they aren't as slick and foreigner-friendly as the more popular beach spots, the natural landscape is mostly unmarred by development, and the area still retains the typically Thai culture that's often harder to see in more popular destinations.

South of Nakhon Si Thammarat, the coast along the Gulf of Thailand changes significantly. You'll still find stretches of beach and plenty of friendly people, but once you enter Songkhla Province, Islam begins to be more

apparent. Hat Yai, the area's economic hub, attracts hordes of visitors, but mostly people from Malaysia, who come for shopping and to take advantage of Thailand's more permissive culture. This makes it a very interesting place to people-watch, if you happen to be passing through, although it's probably not going to be a primary destination for most.

PLANNING YOUR TIME

Many visitors to the gulf spend all of their time on Ko Samui, and it's easy to do so with direct flights to the island from Bangkok. On Ko Samui you'll find there are few cultural and historical sights to visit, as the island has really only developed around the travelers that have come to visit in recent decades, but there are plenty of beach activities to fill your time. If you plan on seeing more than one of

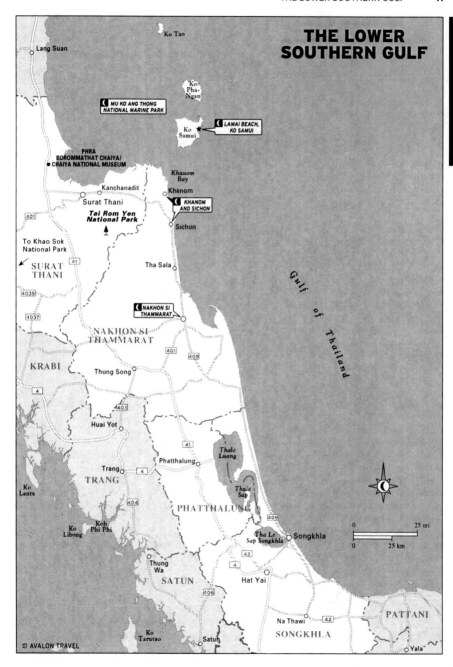

fishing boat off of Ko Samui

© SUZANNE NAM

the islands in the archipelago, give yourself at least a week, especially if you want to get some diving in. Hopping from Ko Samui to Ko Pha-Ngan to Ko Tao is simple but time-consuming, and there are frequent ferry boats between the islands.

If you're flying into nearby Surat Thani and taking a ferry to one of the islands, expect to spend about half a day getting from the airport to the ferry pier and then to the island itself. It's not as convenient as flying into Ko Samui, but you may save yourself quite a few thousand baht. There are only two airlines—Bangkok Airways and Thai Airways—that fly into Ko Samui from Bangkok. Bangkok Airways, which owns the Samui airport, is known for great service and convenient flight schedules, but not cheap prices. Since Thai Airways started flying to Samui a few years ago, many thought prices would go down. So far, they haven't, so travelers on a budget usually opt to take one of the low-cost carriers to Surat Thani and transfer from there.

If you're planning on a visit to the cities of Nakhon Si Thammarat or Songkhla, you can easily see most of the important sights in a day

or two, leaving plenty of extra time to relax on one of the beaches up north. With direct flights on Nok Air to Nakhon Si Thammarat, it's surprisingly easy to get to the city or nearby Songkhla without spending hours transferring from one place to another.

Although Islam and Buddhism have coexisted in this part of the country for centuries with few problems, sectarian violence currently gripping Yala, Pattani, and Narathiwat has recently spilled over into parts of Songkhla. Hat Yai, the province's capital, has had multiple bomb attacks in the past decade that have targeted hotels, pubs, and shopping centers. The violence so far has been limited to Hat Yai and has been very sporadic, but it's something that cannot be ignored if you're traveling to this part of the country. There have been no incidents, however, in any of the popular tourist spots and no indication that there is a threat of violence there.

HISTORY
Although these days the mainland cities in this part of the country look more like semi-industrialized towns and transport hubs for travelers

moving onto the beaches and islands, Surat Thani was once the seat of the Srivijaya empire in Thailand. Though little is known about the lost empire, historians speculate that it existed from somewhere between the third and fifth centuries to the 13th century. The center of the Srivijaya empire's power was on the island of Sumatra, in present-day Indonesia, but the empire spread throughout the Indonesian archipelago and northward, encompassing the Malay Peninsula up to present-day Surat Thani. Although the kingdom was Hindu, Buddhist, and then Muslim, remains from the Surat Thani area are Mahayana Buddhist, and there are temple ruins in the city of Chaiya, outside of Surat Thani, as well as the Chaiya National Museum.

In some sense, Thailand became its own kingdom in the 13th century when the region became ruled by Thai people instead of outsiders, but the country as it is known today did not exist until the 20th century. Southeast Asia had for centuries been under the influence of innumerable empires bearing little relation to current national borders, and it was the Anglo-Siamese Treaty of 1909 that put the last pieces of the puzzle (at least in the south) together for the Kingdom of Siam. It was then that Siam got the provinces of Satun, Songkhla, Pattani, Narathiwat, and Yala in exchange for giving up claims to provinces farther south that are now part of Malaysia. While the country as a whole identifies with the Kingdoms of Sukhothai and Ayutthaya, the south has always had a somewhat different history.

Since the Srivijaya period, Nakhon Si Thammarat emerged as its own kingdom of sorts, existing independently but paying tribute to the Sukhothai and then Ayutthaya Kingdoms. By the 18th century, the region was ruled by the Kingdom of Siam, although at least with respect to Songkhla, that rule was challenged until the 1909 treaty.

Nakhon Si Thammarat has become an important city for Buddhists, and you'll see plenty of *wats* if you visit. Just south, in Songkhla, the predominant religion is Islam.

The island of Samui was first officially recorded by the Chinese around 1500 in ancient maps but was probably settled more than 1,000 years ago by mariners from Hainan in southwest China. While the mainland was a part of the Srivijaya Kingdom, Samui and neighboring islands were not a significant part of the kingdom. Until the 1970s, Ko Samui was just a simple island relying on ample coconut trees and fishing for commerce. During World War II, Ko Samui was briefly occupied by the Japanese, but otherwise it stayed below the radar.

Three decades later, the island and neighboring Ko Pha-Ngan arrived on the backpacker trail and slowly grew from quiet tropical refuges to international tourist destinations.

Ko Samui and the Samui Archipelago เกาะสมุย

Once just a quiet island happily going about its business farming coconuts, Ko Samui is now one of the most popular vacation spots in Thailand. Filled with palm trees and rimmed by white sandy beaches, the island has all the ingredients necessary for a gorgeous holiday retreat. If you're arriving by plane to Ko Samui, the moment you step off the airplane and onto the tarmac you'll understand what the island is all about. There's no steel or glass at the international airport. Instead, it's a group of thatch-roofed huts where you check in and pick up your luggage. To get to and from the planes, passengers are taken by open-air buses akin to large golf carts. If you're arriving by ferry from the mainland, you'll get to enjoy the spectacular view of the surrounding islands during the 90-minute ride.

The island is not all huts and coconut trees, however. Since its debut as a budget destination, Samui has grown up. Although there are still beach bungalows to be found, there is also

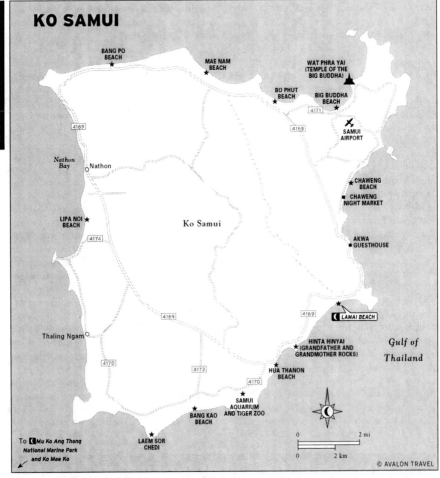

KO SAMUI

BANG PO BEACH

MAE NAM BEACH

WAT PHRA YAI (TEMPLE OF THE BIG BUDDHA)

BO PHUT BEACH

BIG BUDDHA BEACH

4171

4169

4169

SAMUI AIRPORT

Nathon Bay

Nathon

CHAWENG BEACH

CHAWENG NIGHT MARKET

LIPA NOI BEACH

4174

Ko Samui

AKWA GUESTHOUSE

4169

4169

LAMAI BEACH

Thaling Ngam

Gulf of Thailand

HINTA HINYAI (GRANDFATHER AND GRANDMOTHER ROCKS)

4170

4173

HUA THANON BEACH

4170

SAMUI AQUARIUM AND TIGER ZOO

BANG KAO BEACH

To Mu Ko Ang Thong National Marine Park and Ko Mae Ko

LAEM SOR CHEDI

0   2 mi

0   2 km

© AVALON TRAVEL

a large selection of five-star resorts as well as lots of spas and retreats and a dining scene that gets better every year. Thanks to a ring road that circles the entire island, there's plenty of built-up infrastructure, and you'll have easy access to things such as medical care and rental cars. Every beach has at least one Internet café, and many hotels and cafés in more built-up beach areas have Wi-Fi. The development hasn't come without a price. Although the beaches are still beautiful, parts of the island can seem like a messy, incoherently developed mass of cheap concrete buildings and tangled power lines. Covering nearly 260 square kilometers, Samui is a large island and can sometimes feel like a small city instead of desert paradise.

Just north of Samui, Ko Pha-Ngan is still mostly a backpacker haven, with a good selection of inexpensive places to stay and plenty of cheap drinks and all-night partying. The island's famous full moon parties, which seem

© SUZANNE NAM

small islands off the northern tip of Ko Samui

to take place every weekend regardless of the lunar phase, are what has given Ko Pha-Ngan this reputation, although there are more high-end resorts opening up and attracting a different type of independent traveler. The physical landscape of the island, with gentle hills covered in trees and white sandy beaches, is as beautiful as Samui, and perhaps even more so, as it's less developed. Part of this is certainly due to the fact that there are no flights to the island. If you are visiting Pha-Ngan, you'll need to take a ferry boat from Surat Thani or Ko Samui, making it a good choice if you have the luxury of time but not money. Ko Tao, the northernmost main island in the archipelago, is still largely a base for divers but shares the same topography as its larger neighbors.

SIGHTS
◖ Mu Ko Ang Thong National Marine Park
อุทยานแห่งชาติหมู่เกาะอ่างทอง
This national park, spanning a cluster of more than 40 small islands in the Samui

Archipelago, is the gem of the region. The relatively small, amazingly green islands are really limestone mountains rising out of the sea, so there are plenty of caves and interesting rock formations to explore while you're there, as well as a handful of sandy beaches, rare birds, and macaques.

What really sets this group of islands apart is that they are virtually undeveloped and uninhabited, something you won't see on the Andaman coast. Before being declared a national park in 1980, the area was used by the Royal Thai Navy, and thus there are no bungalow developments or other commercial activity to disturb the natural environment. Getting to the islands is not a problem, though: There are plenty of tour companies on Samui and in Surat Thani who do daily day trips.

If you're into snorkeling or scuba, this is probably not the place for you, however. The water can be less than crystal clear, and there is only limited coral. This has nothing to do with the cleanliness of the water in the gulf; it's just that the islands are located in relatively shallow

© SUZANNE NAM

islands within Mu Ko Ang Thong National Marine Park

waters, and sediment that runs off from mainland rivers into the gulf doesn't settle quickly. If you're planning on visiting the park, remember that it is closed for most of November–December because of the monsoon season.

The national park headquarters are on the island of **Ko Wua Talap,** and this is a great place to start your tour of the islands (many guided tours stop here for a couple of hours). In addition to a white-sand beach right in front of the headquarters, there is also a hiking trail to a lookout point with a fantastic view of the surrounding islands. If you take the hike, expect to spend at least an hour going up and down, and do not attempt it in flip-flops. At certain points the trail becomes very steep (and very slippery if it has recently rained), and you'll need to rely on the ropes to pull yourself up. Although there are no commercial accommodations on any of the islands in the park, there are simple but charming fan-cooled bungalows and a campground on Ko Wua Talap as well as a drinks concession and a small restaurant.

Ko Mae Ko also has a nice beach to spend some time on, but if you're visiting this island, make sure to hike up to Thale Nai, a large emerald-green saltwater lake in the middle of rising cliffs. Much of the path is lined with stairs, which can be very steep at times, and as long as you go slowly, the 10-minute climb is fine even for moderately active people. For clear water, sandy beaches, and good snorkeling by the shore, **Ko Samsoa,** just across from Ko Mae Ko, is also a nice island on which to spend some time. If you're on a tour, you'll be provided with snorkel gear, though many boats don't bring fins.

Most visitors to the national marine park start from Ko Samui, where there are a number of tour operators that do the trip.

Samui Aquarium and Tiger Zoo
พิพิธภัณฑ์สัตว์น้ำสมุยและสวนเสือ
The aquarium and zoo (33/2 Mu 2, Maret, tel. 07/742-4017, www.samuiorchid.com, 9 A.M.–5 P.M. daily, 250B) are part of the private Samui Orchid Resort, and the animals are there as entertainment, not part of a conservation effort or scientific endeavor. In the tanks you'll see lots of colorful coral as well as exotic tropical fish and even a couple of sharks. In the cages are tigers, monkeys, and birds, and you

can even have your picture taken with one of the tigers if you're brave enough.

Wat Phra Yai (Temple of the Big Buddha)
วัดพระใหญ่

At the northern tip of the island is Wat Phra Yai, an outdoor temple with an immense 10-meter golden statue of Buddha. Although it's right near the eponymous Big Buddha Beach, it's a very peaceful place to visit and hear the resident monks pray and get a nice panoramic view of the surrounding area, especially at sunset (since you'll have to climb quite a few stairs to get to the Buddha). When you visit, you have to toll the bells surrounding the Buddha for good luck. If you're anywhere in the area, you won't be able to miss the big Buddha on the mountain. To get here, you'll need to take Route 4171 heading east, or arrange a ride with an off-duty *song thaew*.

HinTa HinYai (Grandfather and Grandmother Rocks)
หินตาหินยาย

Near Lamai Beach, HinTa HinYai is a very famous natural phenomena—strange rocks look like human sex organs when viewed from a certain angle. The locals discreetly refer to them as grandfather and grandmother. When you visit, make sure to bring a camera to capture the view. When you're done, make sure to buy some *kalamae* from one of the nearby vendors. It's a type of Thai toffee and it's creamy, not too sweet, and comes packaged in little triangles. The rocks are just a couple of kilometers south of Lamai Beach off of the ring road. If you are on Lamai, you can either walk there or catch a *song thaew* the short distance (make sure to tell the driver you are going to HinTa HinYai).

Laem Sor Chedi
เจดีย์แหลมสอ

On the southern tip of the island is Laem Sor Chedi, a seldom visited, peaceful place with a large, ornate *chedi* right adjacent to the beach. Although you won't find much to do here,

that's sort of the point. Next to the *chedi* is a small forest clearing often referred to as the meditation forest, where visitors can go and sit and ponder existence (you can even arrange to spend a few days at the *wat* learning how to meditate, but you'll need to work that out in person with the resident abbot). Laem Sor Chedi is about 1.5 kilometers off the main Ring Road around the island, so it is possible to take a *song thaew* and then walk the rest of the way. You can also take a taxi, but if you do not want to walk the 1.5 kilometers back to the main road, consider asking the driver to wait for you. The round-trip will cost you around 500B depending on which beach you are coming from. If you are driving, on the way to the *chedi* is a secret viewpoint. All of the signs are in Thai, so to get there your best bet is to enlist the help of a local (taking a taxi might be even better). You'll have to follow the turnoff to the Rattanakosin Chedi, up an extremely steep road to a beautiful viewpoint where you can see the southern part of the island.

BEACHES
East Coast

Chaweng Beach, on the island's east coast, is the most famous beach in Samui, and it always draws more than its fair share of visitors, especially those traveling from other countries. The beach itself is a beautiful, long strip of light, soft sand backed by palm trees, and the water is warm, clear, and generally calm. Although Chaweng is one continuous bay, it's broken into three different sections—North Chaweng, Central Chaweng and Chaweng Noi, and Coral Cove just below it. There's a reef just offshore that serves to break most incoming waves. During high season, you can't avoid feeling a little hustle and bustle here, and visitors flock to the numerous resorts that line the beach. It's the most built-up area on the island, which makes it a very convenient place to stay, and in addition to the bungalows you'll find fronting the shore, there are also lots of restaurants and vendors. The main road runs parallel to the shore just behind the beach, and it feels more like a little city than

busy Chaweng Beach

a quiet beach town. Here you'll see lots of familiar brands, such as McDonald's, Pizza Hut, and Starbucks. In fact, it might be hard to notice you're in Thailand at all, as most of the signs are in English.

◖ LAMAI BEACH
Lamai Beach, just south of Chaweng, is the island's second most popular beach. In Thai, Lamai means "sweet" and "smooth," and that's a good description of Lamai Beach. Although Chaweng Beach has the softest sand and arguably the best view, Lamai is a close second. It's also second to Chaweng in terms of development and, for lots of visitors, represents a happy medium between development and seclusion. There is a good selection of resorts and ample places to eat, but it's also a bit more *sabai* than its neighbor to the north. There are still plenty of conveniences here, though, as central Lamai just behind the beach is full of shops and restaurants. The beach itself is typical of Samui—a gently curving bay, bathwater-temperature water, and lots of surrounding coconut

trees swaying in the wind. Lamai Beach has rougher water, as there's no reef to break the waves as they come in. At the southern end of the beach is the strange rock formation HinTa HinYai, which draws daily crowds of visitors.

South Coast
Hua Thanon and **Bang Kao** beaches on the south of the island are the least developed on Samui. Some of this part of the coast is rocky, although there are plenty of places were you can comfortably spread out a towel or open a beach chair and enjoy the peace and quiet. There are not many accommodations on this part of the island, but the few that are here are quite nice and have private beaches. The village at Hua Thanon is a picture-perfect, charming little Muslim fishing village with a small market that adds to the overall beauty of the physical surroundings.

West Coast
The west coast of the island is dominated by **Nathon Bay,** where most ferries from Ko Pha-

DETOX RETREATS

The colonic-irrigation trend is still popular in Thailand, and Ko Samui has more than a handful of spas offering the service as part of a multiday detox program. The programs vary from spa to spa, but in general, participants consume only water, fruit juice, special low-calorie shakes, and vitamin supplements for the duration. In addition to twice-daily colonics, the spas offer meditation, yoga classes, and massage.

Colonics have been viewed with skepticism by the traditional medical community, but there are thousands of people from across the globe who flock to Samui's spas every year for their detox programs, hoping to get a little healthier and maybe drop a few kilograms in the process. Whether it works in the long term is up for debate, but people who've spent a week at one of the island's detox retreats say they come away feeling good.

Although the focus of many spas is colonic detox, and many require fasting as part of the program, they also offer regular retreats with healthy low-calorie meals, meditation, and yoga.

Absolute Yoga, one of the upscale yoga studios in Bangkok, has a spa called **Absolute Yoga & The Love Kitchen** (Fisherman's Village, Bo Phut Beach, tel. 07/743-0290, www.absoluteyogasamui.com) offering a variety of programs from weekend detox retreats to 10-day intensive programs that include yoga, meditation, and colonics. Some of the programs involve juice fasting, but they also have programs where you dine on vegetarian food from their Love Kitchen. The programs run around 1,400B per day, which includes food and classes. If you're not interested in the detox regimen, you can buy an unlimited yoga pass for a week for just 1,500B. The resort itself is a charming, boutique-style small hotel with colorful but elegant guest rooms and a nice swimming pool.

The **Spa Resorts** (Lamai Beach, tel. 07/742-4666, www.thespa resorts.net) has been around for more than 15 years and has a number of programs centered on detox and cleansing as well as meditation and yoga. The program runs around 1,500B per day, not including accommodations. The spa also has a basic bungalow resort with a nice swimming pool and gardens. The vegetarian menu at the spa is one of the best on the island.

Ngan and Surat Thani arrive. The town of Nathon is definitely worth some time, as it's home to many of the local residents of the island and offers a chance to see what life is like in Thailand, but bear in mind that Nathon is the business end of Samui, and the beach itself is much less beautiful than what you'll find at Lamai, Chaweng, or Big Buddha Beaches.

South of Nathon Bay are two wonderful small beaches. **Lipa Noi Beach** is nestled amidst coconut trees. The water is shallow for quite a way offshore, making it a great place for kids to play. There are a few cheap bungalows and resorts here, and a handful of places to eat, but otherwise it's a very quiet, almost sleepy beach area. May through November, the water is too shallow for swimming except at high tide. **Thaling Ngam** is a small, secluded beach backed by cliffs and ubiquitous coconut trees. The scenery is beautiful, but parts of the beach are rocky and the sand has lots of coral fragments, so it's not as soft as other beaches on the island.

North Coast

On the northern part of the island, the largest stretch of beach is at **Bang Po Beach.** This four-kilometer-long beach has clear water, soft, light sand, and coconut trees as well as a coral reef just off the coast. It's backed by green hills and has a beautiful, secluded feeling. Despite all the draws, the beach is generally quite quiet, and there are only a handful of resorts and visitor amenities in the area. If you're looking to do a lot of swimming, this is not a great spot, as the water is very shallow until you pass the reef, and this may be why it's less popular. It's a good beach for snorkeling, however, since the reef is in shallow water, and you'll usually see at least a handful of people out looking at the reef and marinelife.

Mae Nam Beach, Bo Phut Beach, and **Big Buddha Beach** (also called Bangrak Beach) are all adjacent to each other on the northern coast, and some consider this the best part of the island. Each of the beaches is in a softly curving cove, and although there's no view of either sunset or sunrise, the beach, the water, and the surrounding greenery are beautiful. There are a handful of inexpensive bungalows here along with some of the nicest resorts on the island and some trendy, upscale places to eat. Although not nearly as busy as Chaweng Beach, there are still dive shops and travel agencies if you're looking to schedule an excursion. Some spots on these beaches won't be easily swimmable April–November due to seasonal tides that make the water too shallow. Mae Nam Beach is the quietest of the three and could be a great choice if you want to feel like you're in a quiet area but have access to more of the action. Plus it has the best selection of cheap bungalows. Bo Phut Beach is particularly charming, especially due to the adjacent fishing village with charming wooden shophouses. If you're looking to Jet Ski, it's one of the places on the island you can rent a Jet Ski on the beach. If you're looking for peace and quiet, however, all the activity can be annoying. Big Buddha Beach, right near the airport, has the most action. Although it's named after the large golden Buddha that sits on a nearby hill overlooking the island, it's not quite the tranquil spot the name would imply. There are scores of cheap bungalows here, and the beach tends to attract a younger crowd. Although there are no discos or true nightclubs, there are plenty of bars with live music lining the beach at night.

SHOPPING

Most of the tourist shopping you'll find on the island is in the street stalls surrounding the beaches, which sell everything from sarongs to kitchenware made of coconut shells. If you're looking to drop a few baht, find that you've forgotten your flip-flops, or want casual and

inexpensive beachwear, the best bet is Chaweng Beach. The nearby roads are lined with stalls and small shops, and it's an especially vibrant and bustling scene after dark. It's sometimes referred to as the **Chaweng Night Market,** although it is technically open all day too. When you buy, make sure to barter, as prices tend to start high. Although there are some more upscale shops in Chaweng as well, prices are generally not that competitive if you're comparing them to what you'll find in Bangkok, or in any major city around the world, for that matter.

The shopping scene for necessities is a little better. Chaweng has a **Tops Market** with international and local groceries, and there are similar shops in Lamai. The **Tesco Lotus** on the ring road between Bo Phut Beach and Chaweng Beach has everything from household appliances to staple groceries, plus fresh meat and produce. It's in a mall surrounded by smaller local shops, pharmacies, restaurants, and a movie theater.

SPORTS AND RECREATION
Kayaking and Snorkeling Tours

Day tours to Ang Thong National Marine Park or neighboring Ko Tao and Ko Nang Yuan are some of the most popular activities for visitors to Samui. There are a handful of companies offering these tours, which almost always include either snorkeling or kayaking. Some also include elephant trekking. Tickets are almost always sold through tour agents scattered across the island. Tours are very similar to one another and competitively priced, so expect to pay 1,200–1,500B for a day tour. Even though many brochures have prices printed on them, agents will almost always offer at least a 10 percent discount, so ask if you haven't been offered it. Also make sure to look over the tour brochure and ask the travel agent what your tour includes. Each usually includes pickup from your hotel or guesthouse; you'll be dropped of at the pier, where you'll board either a **speedboat** or a **ferry** with other passengers. Speedboat tours have the benefit of less time in transit and are a little more adventurous, but a ride on a larger boat allows for more relaxing and lounging. Regardless of the type of vessel, you'll be given a light breakfast (coffee and fruit or pastry) and you'll also be served lunch either onboard or on one of the islands you'll stop at. Make sure to bring a swimsuit, towel, and good shoes for hiking, as many tours include stops on islands with good viewpoints.

Samui Island Tour (349 Mu 3, Ang Thong, tel. 07/742-1506, www.samui-islandtour.com) offers daily tours of Ang Thong National Marine Park on large ferries, with stops at Ko Mae Ko and Ko Wua Talap (national park headquarters). They also offer kayaking with a guide on their tours. Expect to pay 400–500B extra to use their kayaks.

Seahawk Speedboat (14/1 Mu 2, Chaweng Beach, tel. 07/723-1597) offers speedboat tours of both Ang Thong National Marine Park and the islands surrounding Ko Tao. The marine park tours are similar to those offered by Samui Island Tours with the addition of a stop at Ko Paluay, where you can snorkel or use one of their kayaks. Their Ko Tao day tour takes you to Ko Tao for snorkeling, then to Ko Nang Yuan (the three connected islands) for sunbathing and sightseeing.

Another speedboat tour is **Grand Sea Discovery** (187 Mu 1, Mae Nam Beach, tel. 07/742-7001, www.grandseatours.com), which offers tours to Ko Tao and Ko Nang Yaun, Ang Thong National Marine Park, or Ko Pha-Ngan. Their Ko Tao trip follows basically the same route as Seahawk Speedboat's, and their marine park tour is similar to that of Samui Island Tour. They also offer a one-day tour of Ko Pha-Ngan, where you'll do some sightseeing, visit an elephant camp, have lunch, and swim and snorkel.

Sea Safari by Speed Boat (tel. 07/742-5563, www.islandsafaritour.com) offers a typical tour of Ang Thong National Marine Park, which includes sea canoeing, but also adds elephant trekking or ATV biking in the afternoon, making for a long but full day.

Island Tours

If you're interested in staying on dry land, there are also a few outfits offering island tours. **Sita**

Tour 2000 (9/13 Mu 2, Chaweng Beach, tel. 07/748-4834) offers half-day tours of the island's sights, and includes stops at the Big Buddha, HinTa HinYai rocks, and even a monkey show. These trips cost less than 500B for a half day, but they do not include meals, and since the island's sights and attractions aren't all that spectacular, they are probably best left for a rainy day. **Mr. Ung's Safari** (52/4 Mu 3, Chaweng Beach, tel. 07/723-0114, www.ung-safari.com) offers full-day tours of the island's sights but throws in some trekking, four-wheeling, and elephant rides.

Boating

Lately Samui has become a popular place for sailors—not the type on shore leave from long journeys abroad but the jet-set kind who like to travel in multimillion-dollar yachts. Much of this popularity may be due to the **Samui Regatta** (www.samuiregatta.com), an annual five-day sailboat race held in late May–early June, pulling in competitors from all over the world. If you find yourself without your own boat on Samui, there are a handful of sailboat rental agencies, including **Samui Ocean Sports** (Chaweng Regent Beach Resort, 155/4 Mu 2, Bo Phut Beach, tel. 08/1940-1999, www.sailing-in-samui.com) and **Sunsail Thailand** (www.sunsailthailand.com). If you're lucky enough to be staying at the posh Anantara Resort, they have a number of craft available for rent, including Hobbies and Lasers, as well as sailing lessons and other sailing activities.

ACCOMMODATIONS
Under 1,500B

For a quintessential beach bungalow experience, try **New Huts** (Lamai Beach, tel. 08/9729-8489, 200B). Here you'll get a small, very basic wooden bungalow just a few steps above a shack and share a basic bath with other travelers. Oh, and there's no air-conditioning, but for 200B it's hard to complain, especially considering the location a short walk from a nice part of Lamai Beach. If you can't get a room here, **Beer's House Beach Bungalows** (161/4 Mu 4, Lamai Beach, tel. 07/723-0467, www.beerhousebungalow.com, 600B) is another excellent option in the budget category. Here most of the bungalows have private baths with coldwater showers, and there is a small restaurant on the premises.

While there are plenty of beach bungalows in the 400–500B range on Mae Nam Beach, **Moon Huts** (67/2 Mu 1, Mae Nam, tel. 07/742-5247, www.moonhutsamui.com, 500B) tend to be a little cleaner and nicer than the competition. At this price they won't deliver luxury, but you will get a private bath, fresh sheets, and a spotless guest room a short walk from the beach and the property's bar-restaurant. Nicer bungalows on the beach have air-conditioning instead of fans; expect to pay around 1,000B for these. There are also large two-bedroom family bungalows available.

The **Akwa Guesthouse** (28/12 Chaweng Beach Rd., tel. 08/4660-0551, 800B) is head and shoulders above the typical guesthouse experience in Thailand, and if you're looking for an edgy, comfortable place on Samui, and there happens to be a room available, you can't go wrong here. The guesthouse, just a two-minute walk from quieter northern Chaweng Beach, is clean, funky, and inexpensive, and the management and staff are excellent. The guest rooms are all decorated with pop art prints and colorful, thoughtfully placed furnishings, starkly contrasting against the white-duvet-covered beds. There's free Wi-Fi throughout, and standard guest rooms come equipped with DVD and MP3 players; some have nicely decorated wooden decks too. If you want to have an urban palace in the middle of the tropics, the 65-square-meter penthouse is also available, and it has an amazing deck. The downstairs restaurant, which offers very reasonably priced Thai and Western dishes all day, has the same design theme and friendly attitude. Aside from the fabulous decor, reasonable prices, and good food, everyone who works at the Akwa is sincere and will go out of their way to make your stay memorable, from arranging airport transfers to setting up excursions. Although there's no pool here and it doesn't have the typical resort amenities, this is the type of place you

rarely find in touristy areas and one you'll want to return to again after your first stay.

Beachfront bungalows are tough to find in this price range on this beach, but **Thong Ta Kian Villa** (Thong Ta Kien Bay, 146 Mu 4, Maret, tel. 07/723-0978, 1,300B) offers some exceptionally clean, large, stand-alone guest rooms. Design is simple, and this is certainly not a resort, but extras such as air-conditioning, small fridges to keep your beer cold, and TVs put this property well above the typical beach bungalow offerings.

Though not right on the beach, **Cocooning Hotel and Tapas Bar** (6/11 Mu 1, Bo Phut Beach, tel. 07/742-7150, www.cocooninghotelsamui.com, 1,000B) is a lovely, intimate, well-designed guesthouse with some of the prettiest guest rooms you'll find on the island. There are only a handful of guest rooms here, and each has its own color and design theme against a backdrop of white walls and modern concrete flooring. This is not a resort, and it's quite small, so the only amenities available are a very small swimming pool and a tapas bar serving drinks and light snacks. Still, the property has a very chic European feel to it, probably thanks to the French owner.

Ampha Place Hotel (67/59 Mu 1, Mae Nam, tel. 07/733-2129, www.samui-amphahotel.com, 1,200B) has cheap, clean guest rooms just 10 minutes on foot from Mae Nam Beach. Ampha Place is a no-frills property but isn't old or run-down. Guest rooms are small but surprisingly well-equipped, have small balconies, and are accented with Thai decor. There is also a small but pretty swimming pool in the middle of the property.

NovaSamui Resort (147/3 Mu 2, Chaweng, tel. 07/723-0864, www.novasamui.com, 1,200B) has cheap, clean guest rooms, a large swimming pool, and nicely maintained common areas. Although the NovaSamui has some resort-level amenities, it's not a luxury resort, and it's not right on the water, but just a short walk from Chaweng Beach. For about one-third of the price, however, it's an excellent choice.

Like other Ibis properties in Thailand and all over the world, **The Ibis Bophut** (197/1

Mu 1, Bo Phut Beach, tel. 02/659-2888, www. ibishotel.com, 1,400B) offers guests a good location and spotlessly clean, reliable guest rooms and common areas. Guest rooms at this large hotel are very small, but the bar, restaurant, and large pool area give guests plenty of other options for hanging out. There are also family rooms available with bunk beds for kids, although they are also small.

Marina Villa (124 Mu 3, Lamai Beach, tel. 07/742-4426, www.marinavillasamui.com, 1,400B), right on Lamai Beach, is a small, pleasant, family-friendly resort with comfortable, clean guest rooms and a good location. This is not a luxury resort but does have two swimming pools and a restaurant.

1,500-3,000B

Choeng Mon Beach Hotel (24/3 Mu 5, Choeng Mon Beach, Bo Phut, tel. 07/742-5372, www.choengmon.com, 1,500B), on Choeng Mon Beach just northeast of Bo Phut Beach, is a somewhat generic midsize tourist hotel but has amenities and facilities, including a swimming pool, a small gym, and a restaurant that make it a good value for guests who want resort perks but do not want to pay resort prices for them. Guest rooms at this beachfront property are clean, simple, and comfortable. Larger groups can also rent one of their bungalows.

A good location and reasonably priced guest rooms are what make **Samui Hacienda** (98/2/1 Mu 1, Bo Phut Beach, tel. 07/724-5943, www. samui-hacienda.com, 1,800B) such a good value. Guest rooms, many of which have beach views, are simple but clean and comfortable, and the whole property is well maintained. The design theme—a fusion of Mediterranean and Thai styles—surprisingly does not seem out of place in Bo Phut. There is a very small rooftop pool, not big enough to get any exercise but a wonderful place for a cocktail or just to cool off.

The **Lamai Wanta** (124/264 Mu 3, Lamai Beach, tel. 07/742-4550, www.lamaiwanta. com, 1,800B) is right on Lamai Beach and has modern, comfortable, well-maintained guest rooms and a small but very pretty pool overlooking the ocean. There are both traditional hotel rooms and stand-alone villas, some with two bedrooms. The location, just walking distance from Lamai's restaurants, is convenient, but the hotel is big enough that it still feels quiet and private.

Montien House (5 Mu 2, Chaweng Beach, tel. 07/742-2169, www.montienhouse.com, 2,500B) is another great property on Chaweng if you're looking for a resort environment but don't want to pay five-star prices. The Montien is right on the beach but far enough away from the center that you'll be able to enjoy some peace and quiet. There's a lovely small pool and a beachside restaurant, and the traditional Thai-style grounds are well maintained. The standard guest rooms are clean and well maintained, if a little Spartan. The beachfront guest rooms, housed in small cottages, are a little more expensive but feel a little more luxurious and are great for small families.

The guest rooms and villas at **The Waterfront Boutique Hotel** (71/2 Mu 1, Bo Phut Beach, tel. 07/742-7165, www.thewaterfrontbophut.com, 2,900B) are simple and unpretentious, and the setting right next to the beach, with the requisite coconut trees shading the sun, is as good as it gets. What sets this property apart is the relaxed environment, the friendly staff, and the great value for the money. There's a pool and also a small restaurant on the premises where you can enjoy a complimentary fresh-cooked breakfast and Wi-Fi, but it's not quite luxurious enough to be a boutique hotel. It is, however, a very family-friendly place—there are larger suites available as well as babysitting services.

Another inexpensive gem on Chaweng is **Tango Beach Resort** (119 Mu 2, North Chaweng Beach, www.tangobeachsamui.com, 2,700B). This is not five-star luxury, but nonetheless it's an amazing value for the price. The small resort has pretty, simple grounds with a nice, if small, swimming pool, a beachfront bar and restaurant, and their own chair-and-towel service on the sand. The guest rooms are surprisingly well furnished in a modern

Thai style, and some even have views of the ocean. Baths are on par with more expensive resorts and feature rain showerheads and glass bowl sinks. The hotel is located in northern Chaweng, which is a more relaxed and quiet area of the beach, although it's not as easy to swim here because there are sandbars at low tide. If you're looking to get to the bustling center, expect a 15-minute walk or five-minute motorcycle ride.

The Maryoo Hotel Samui (99/99 Mu 2, North Chaweng Rd., tel. 07/760-1102, www. maryoosamui.com, 2,700B), a modern mid-size hotel near Chaweng Beach, has very clean, comfortable guest rooms and a big, beautiful swimming pool. There is also an average Thai restaurant and a spa on the property. This won't be the right choice for those looking for lots of personality, but those who want cleanliness and comfort at a reasonable price will find it a great value.

3,000-4,500B

Villa Nalinnadda (99/1-4 Mu 1, Maret, tel. 07/723-3131, www.nalinnadda.com, 3,500B) is a small luxury boutique hotel on Lamai Beach that seems like it was expressly designed for honeymoons and romantic getaways. All of the eight bright, airy guest rooms on the property face the ocean, they'll serve you breakfast in bed whenever you want it, and the guest rooms also come equipped with private whirlpool tubs. There's also a definite Greek Mediterranean feeling to the property, thanks to the bright white buildings, but you won't forget that you're still in Thailand. The beach it's on is very quiet, but if you travel down to the center of Lamai Beach, you can find some more action.

Over 4,500B

The **⟨ Anantara Samui** (101/3 Bo Phut Bay, tel. 07/742-8300, www.anantara.com, 6,000B) has all the luxury, style, and generous Thai hospitality that has made Samui famous the world over. The grounds are perfectly manicured and filled with exotic details such as fire torches and reproductions of ancient sculptures. The

pool area, with a large infinity pool that seems to spill out into the Gulf of Thailand, and the main lobby look like the grounds of a royal palace. The guest rooms are modern and luxurious, and there's also an indulgent spa and lots of great restaurants to eat and drink at. The staff is professional and friendly. If you're looking for a place to splash out, perhaps for a honeymoon or an anniversary, you will not be disappointed here. The Anantara offers lots of the typical activities and excursions, but they also have windsurfing lessons on Bo Phut Bay as well as sailboat rental.

The **Scent Hotel** (58/1 Mu 4, Bo Phut Beach, tel. 07/796-2198, www.thescenthotel. com, 6,000B), a high-end, intimate boutique hotel right on the beach, has beautifully furnished guest rooms with European or Asian decor (you can specify, depending on availability). Regardless of decor, guest rooms are spacious and many have balconies with enough space to dine. The common areas are not large, but all guest rooms open onto the property's pleasant beachfront infinity pool and are reminiscent of an old Chinese shophouse.

If you want to stay in a large resort hotel with lots of amenities and facilities as well as nicely appointed guest rooms, the **Centara Grand** (38/2 Mu 3, Chaweng Beach, tel. 07/723-0500, www.centarahotelsresorts.com, 6,500B) is a great choice on Chaweng Beach. The resort has more than 200 guest rooms, so although it doesn't quite feel secluded, there is plenty of pool space, a beautiful full-service spa, and bars and restaurants on the premises. There are also tennis courts and even a small Jim Thompson Thai Silk outlet. The guest rooms are all modern Thai with dark hardwood flooring and private balconies. The property has just undergone refreshing and renovation, so the guest rooms and grounds feel new and fresh despite the fact that the resort has been around for a while. Although it's quiet and peaceful on the grounds, just outside on Chaweng Beach it can get crowded and noisy, especially during high season.

Napasai (65/10 Mu 10, Mae Nam Beach, tel. 07/742-9200, www.napasai.com, 10,000B), one of the Orient Express branded hotels, is also one of the island's most luxurious and indulgent properties. The villas and guest rooms are scattered among the surrounding hills and are spacious and private. Some also have kitchens where guests or staff can cook. Expansive common areas, including an infinity pool, a spa, two restaurants, and two bars, mean guests don't need to leave the property for anything if they don't want to.

The Library (14/1 Mu 2, Bo Phut Beach, tel. 07/742-2767, www.thelibrary.co.th, 12,600B) is centered around the property's immense, übertrendy library filled with books and magazines, but guests may find it hard to focus on anything other than the superb modern design of the resort. It's just too cool here. The buildings are white minimalist cubes, and the grounds are filled with modern sculpture. The best part is the red-tiled swimming pool. Inside the enormous guest rooms and suites, expect to find sleek wood furniture, lots of sunlight, and sparse decorations; they share the same clean, modern design as the rest of the resort. You'll still find the same types of amenities, such as a beachside restaurant and cozy lounge chairs on the beach, as you would in other similarly priced resorts.

Sila Evason Hideaway & Spa (9/10 Mu 5, Ban Plai Laem, Bo Phut Beach, tel. 07/724-5678, www.sixsenses.com/SixSensesSamui/, 17,000B) looks like it was built specifically with the jet-setting movie-star crowd in mind. The private thatched-roof villas come complete with personal butlers available to answer your every need. Each also has a small private dip pool and lounge area. And the views, which you can easily enjoy from the comfort of your bed, are amazing. The public parts of the property, including the large swimming pool and open-air restaurant, are equally swanky, although the style of the grounds and buildings is subdued, sleek, and modern.

FOOD
Whatever you're in the mood for, you won't go hungry on Ko Samui. The island seems to have an inordinate number of restaurants for its size.

Although there are plenty of uninspired, overpriced tourist restaurants, there are more and more excellent places to eat, whether you're looking for quick, inexpensive street food, international fare, or a special Thai meal in a romantic setting overlooking the ocean. On Ko Samui, it's important to remember that the quality of the food sometimes has no relationship to the appearance of the restaurant. Some of the best meals to be found are at very casual places that almost look like holes-in-the-wall. Although you'll find the most restaurants on and near busy Chaweng Beach, if you're looking for a place to enjoy a meal and watch the sunset, head to Nathon Beach on the west coast of the island.

Markets
The **Lamai Food Center,** about 2.5 kilometers from HinTa HinYai Rocks in front of the Wat Lamai School, has a handful of small casual restaurants with great inexpensive Thai food. This is a very relaxed local spot, so expect great food but not a lot of amenities. Many of these restaurants stay open till the wee hours of the morning. If you're in the mood for some *kanom chin* (rice noodles with curry), try **Sophita** (tel. 08/6954-8861, 9 A.M.–3 A.M. daily, 40B). For simple but hearty *guay teow* or *khao mu dang* (red pork with rice), try **Chakangraw Noodle** (tel. 08/9868-8515, 40B). If you're in the mood for freshly made seafood, **Chaophraya Seafood** (tel. 07/741-8117 or 08/6345-9647, 80B) has excellent *gang thot kratiem* (extralarge fried shrimp with garlic and pepper).

Right near Chaweng Beach, close to the Island Resort and Chaweng Villa Resort, is a food center with different food vendors where you can find fresh fruit, the typical selection of noodles and rice dishes, and lots of seafood.

Thai Food
If you're near Lamai Beach, stop at **Sabiang Lae** (tel. 07/723-3082, 10 A.M.–10 P.M. daily, 200B), between Lamai Beach and Ban Hua Thanon, for seafood Samui style. This casual open-air beachfront restaurant is a great place to watch the sunset and enjoy some *kung yai thot*

rad nam manao (fried lobster with lime juice) and *yum sabiang lae* (spicy seafood salad).

Bang Po Seafood (10 A.M.–10 P.M. daily, 300B) on Bang Po Beach is another great seafood restaurant with a similar atmosphere to Sabiang Lae. This is a popular spot among international and Thai visitors to the island, perhaps because of the *kei ji* appetizer they offer for free. It's a delicious blend of shrimp paste and coconut, and you won't find it anywhere in Bangkok.

Another great casual open-air spot for good, inexpensive food is **Sunset Restaurant** (Nathon 175/3, Mu 3, Tambon Ang Thong, tel. 07/742-1244, 4–10 P.M. daily, 300B) on Nathon Beach. Although it's not right on the beach, as the name implies, it's a great place to watch the sunset overlooking Nathon Pier, and the Thai food is fresh, fast, and cheap. Try the rice in coconut if you're looking for something hearty and not spicy; it's great comfort food. This is definitely a casual place to eat, so don't worry about showing up in flip-flops and a T-shirt.

K-Siri (4169 Mu 1, Bo Phut Ring Rd., no phone, 6–10 P.M. daily, 150B), a modest restaurant serving Thai seafood, is the perfect spot for those looking for a place to eat that's basic and simple but doesn't skimp on quality ingredients or preparation. The open-air restaurant, just a short walk from the beach, is a step above a basic shophouse (they even serve wine!) but is definitely pleasant enough for a casual dinner.

Fusion and International

If you're on Chaweng Beach for breakfast, head straight to **Akwa Guesthouse** (28/12 Chaweng Beach Rd., tel. 08/4660-0551, 7 A.M.–11 P.M. daily, 300B). Their breakfast combos are generous and delicious; no tiny slices of toast and hot dogs masquerading as sausages here. Instead, you'll get real sausage, fresh bread, omelets, pancakes, and even hash browns. All of that comes on one plate if you order the Canadian breakfast. Their imported coffee is also excellent, and the bright colors and friendly staff will definitely help wake you up.

Poppies (Chaweng Beach, tel. 07/742-2419, www.poppiessamui.com, 6:30 A.M.–midnight daily, 600B) has become something of an island sensation in the past decade, thanks to the elegant setting at the resort of the same name, the beach view, and the excellent food. The restaurant serves Thai and international dishes, and both sides of the menu offer innovative interpretations of standard fare. Try the *kai pad met mamuang* (stir-fried chicken with cashew nuts) or the roast-duck spring rolls if you're looking for something familiar with a creative twist. Or try the ostrich in panang curry for something really unexpected. Poppies also has an extensive selection of seafood and grilled meats as well as a very good vegetarian menu. The vegetarian green curry with pumpkin is excellent and something you won't be able to find meatless in many places.

Top Ten (98 Mu 2, Chaweng Beach Rd., tel. 07/723-0235, www.toptenrestaurantsamui. com, 5–11 P.M. daily, 400B), a nicely decorated, upscale modern restaurant, serves a mix of straight European flavors, fusion, and some standard Thai dishes, including a clever *tom yam* pasta. The restaurant wins on decor and service, and it's a great choice if you want to eat somewhere a little nicer than the typical Chaweng Beach restaurant.

Sala Thai (12/12, Mu 1, Tambon Mae Nam, tel. 07/742-5031 to 07/742-5038, 6–11 P.M. daily, 700B) is another excellent choice for an upscale Thai meal. The restaurant is part of the Santiburi Resort but attracts plenty of people who aren't staying there. The setting—traditional Thai architecture, lily ponds, pathways lit with tiki torches, and a luxuriant garden—is about as romantic as it gets. The food is mostly traditional Thai cuisine, and it's all expertly prepared and presented. The *tom yam kung* is as good as you'll find anywhere, as are other classic dishes such as *kai phat* (stir-fried chicken) and *pha kung* (spicy shrimp salad).

The chef at **Zazen** (Zazen Boutique Resort and Spa, 177 Mu 1, Bo Phut Beach, tel. 07/742-5085, 5–11 P.M. daily, 600B) mixes fresh local ingredients with foreign flavors to create interesting and innovative modern Thai and fusion cuisine. The elegant restaurant, with a nice view of the Gulf of Thailand, serves dishes such as five spices–marinated barracuda, sesame and wasabi–crusted shrimp, and *neua pla nam deng* (caramelized roasted fish) in addition to some traditional Thai and European favorites. For dessert, the banana flambé in Mekhong whiskey is both entertaining and palate-pleasing.

Betelnut (43/4-5 Mu 3, Soi Colibri, Chaweng Beach, tel. 07/741-3370, 6–11 P.M. daily, 700B) is a top contender for best restaurant on the island. The California-Thai fusion menu is filled with the dishes of crab cake, seared tuna, and duck breast you'll find at upscale international dining spots around the world. To spice things up a bit, the U.S.- and European-trained chef also features dishes such as New England clam chowder with green curry and softshell crab with mango and papaya salad. Although there are lots of culinary risks being taken in the kitchen, the food is too good to be gimmicky. The restaurant is light and airy, with plenty of modern art on the walls.

Another great choice for a special dinner on Chaweng Beach is **Eat Sense** (11 Mu 2, Chaweng Beach, tel. 07/741-4242, 11 A.M.–midnight daily, 700B). The upscale beachside restaurant has lots of seating with great views of the Gulf of Thailand, and there are plenty of little patios at different levels to make the large space feel a little more intimate. The cuisine is international, and there are lots of seafood dishes to choose from. The Thai food, which includes a variety of seafood dishes such as the classic *pla thot ta khrai* (fried whole fish with lemongrass, garlic, and lime juice) is definitely made for Western palates. If you're looking for something a little spicier, make sure to ask.

The cliff-top **Dr. Frogs** (103 Mu 3, Chaweng Beach Rd., tel. 07/741-3797, www.drfrogssamui.com, noon–2 A.M. daily, 400B), a Thai and Italian restaurant, has some of the nicest views on the island and for that reason alone is worth visiting for drinks or dinner. Food is well-prepared and presented, and while their pizzas may not remind you of your vacation

in Italy, considering the island location, they are pretty good. Pastas and seafood entrées are consistently delicious.

The dark wood furnishings, lounge music, and trendy patrons make **◖ Rice** (167/7 Mu 2, Chaweng Beach, tel. 07/723-1934, www.ricesamui.com, 6 P.M.–midnight daily, 400B) feel more like the type of Italian restaurant you'd find in a trendy city neighborhood instead of on the main strip in Chaweng Beach. The food is among the best European fare you'll find on Samui. In fact, the brick oven–baked pizza is unparalleled. Ditch the flip-flops, or you'll definitely feel underdressed.

The small, unpretentious, but well-put together **Barracuda** (216/2 Mu 2, Soi 4, Mae Nam Beach Rd., tel. 07/724-7287 or 07/792-1663, www.barracuda-restaurant.com, 6–11 P.M. daily, 400B) offers high-quality seafood dishes that take advantage of Thai flavors, such as lobster tortellini and salmon with a *tom yam* sauce, and other mostly Western fare. The interior feels more like a nice fish shack than a shophouse restaurant.

While combining Greek and Thai cuisine in one restaurant seems like a recipe for mediocrity, **Fi Kitchen & Bar** (75/1 Mu 1, Mae Nam Ring Rd., tel. 08/9607-2967, 6–11 P.M. daily, 300B) pulls off the combo surprisingly well, and it's a fun, casual place to go, especially if you're craving Greek food. Fresh vegetables and lots of flavor seem to be the hallmarks of the Greek dishes, and the small stand-alone restaurant, which opened in early 2011, already has a following among expatriate and vacationing Greeks on Samui.

The sexy, shabby chic **Boudoir** (Soi 1, Mae Nam Beach, tel. 08/5783-1031, 6 P.M.–midnight daily, 450B), offers casual French cuisine in a relaxing, fun atmosphere. This is a good place to go for inexpensive wine and cheese platters before dinner, although the full meals are also a great value.

Homesick for cheesecake, brownies, and a Western breakfast? Head to **Angela's Bakery and Café** (64/29 Mu 1, Mae Nam Beach, tel. 07/742-7396, 7 A.M.–3:30 P.M. daily, 150B) for some of the best desserts and baked goods on the island. The very basic restaurant has been around for years, and they even have bagels and lox and sandwiches, although those looking for Thai food will find a few dishes.

For well-prepared, great-tasting vegetarian food, **Radiance** (Spa Samui Resort, 71/7 Mu 3, Maret, tel. 07/723-0855, 7 A.M.–10 P.M. daily, 300B) is the best choice on the island and might even be the best in the country. The extensive menu has mostly meatless and vegan dishes made with lots of fresh fruits and vegetables, but it features a few fish and chicken meals too. It can be difficult to find vegetarian versions of most Thai dishes, but here the kitchen can make just about anything, including *tom kha* (coconut soup) and *tom yam* (spicy, sour soup) without any meat products. Spa Samui also has a large breakfast menu featuring items such as french toast made with homemade whole-grain bread and veggie sausages. There's even a large selection of raw dishes for raw foodists. This is a casual place, with open-air seating on the spa's verdant grounds.

A Cajun restaurant in the middle of a tropical island in Southeast Asia seems a little strange, but when you enter **Coco Blues** (161/9 Mu 2, Chaweng Beach Rd., tel. 07/741-4354, 5 P.M.–midnight daily, 300B) on Bo Phut Beach, it all makes sense. The spicy dishes, including blackened fish and Cajun crepes, taste just right in the heat, and the live blues music creates a decidedly comfortable atmosphere. The three-story restaurant opens onto the street and has New Orleans decor and vibe. If you've already eaten, drop in to listen to some music and have a draft beer or two.

For a casual beer and some barbecue, stop in to **Bill's Beach Bar** (near Hua Thanon Beach, just south of Lamai Beach, tel. 08/4778-9145, 9 A.M.–10 P.M. daily). Imagine an open-air beach shack, add running water, a mix of Thai-, Australian-, and Western-style grilled meats, and plenty of foreigners, and you'll get a good idea of what to expect here. The bar holds a barbecue party every Sunday for just 100B pp.

A pretty beachside location, nice Mediterranean fare, and a relaxing atmosphere make **Ad Hoc Beach Cafe** (11/5 Mu 1, Bo Phut Beach, tel. 07/742-5380, noon–11:30 P.M. daily, 450B) a perfect spot for a casual meal or a snack and cocktails while watching the sunset. The menu, mostly typical Italian dishes, is reliable and not too expensive, but it's the view that keeps people coming back.

The Farmer (1/26 Mu 4, Mae Nam Beach, tel. 07/744-7222, www.thefarmerrestaurantsamui.com, noon–11 P.M. daily, 550B), surrounded by paddy fields with mountains in the background, is one of Samui's nicest new restaurants. The interior of the large open-air restaurant is upscale but understated, so it doesn't compete with the beautiful view outside. The menu, mostly European dishes but including some Thai classics, spotlights local and organic produce. It's definitely worth the taxi ride.

INFORMATION AND SERVICES

The regional **Tourism Authority of Thailand office** (TAT, 5 Talat Mai Rd., Surat Thani, tel. 07/728-2828) is located on the mainland in Surat Thani, but you can call either the office or the TAT hotline (1672, 8 A.M.–8 P.M. daily) for information about ferry schedules and other travel-related issues.

Internet access is available at Internet cafés on most beaches. All large resorts and even many small guesthouses now offer at least Wi-Fi too.

GETTING THERE
Air

Samui has its own charming little airport owned by **Bangkok Airways** (www.bangkokair.com), which runs as many as 17 flights per day during high season. Although Bangkok Airways has just opened the airport to **Thai Airways,** they are only running limited flights, mostly for international passengers connecting in Bangkok and traveling on to the island, but between the two, if you are booking even a few days in advance and are flexible with your travel times, you should be able to get a flight. The big exception to this is during

Ko Samui's airport

high season, especially in December, when you should book as far in advance as possible. With limited competition, airfares to Samui from Bangkok are generally higher than for similar distances to other parts of the country, where budget airlines such as Nok Air can fly. Expect to pay 5,000–9,000B for a round-trip ticket to the island. The cheapest fares sell out quickly. If you're flying in from Bangkok, the flight is just over an hour.

Boat

If you have a little more time, it's easy to fly into Surat Thani on Nok Air or Air Asia and then take a fast boat to Samui. Flights to Surat Thani can cost as little as 3,000B round-trip with tax, and once you arrive at the Surat Thani airport, you can buy a combination bus-ferry ticket for around 300B that will take you from the airport to the pier, and then from the pier to the island. The **Pantip Ferry Company** (tel. 07/727-2906) has a booth in the Surat Thani airport. From the airport to the ferry pier is about 90 minutes; from the time you leave the

airport, expect the whole trip to take about 4.5 hours to your hotel.

Bus or Train

You can also take a bus from Bangkok's Southern Bus Terminal or an overnight train from Hua Lamphong to Surat Thani (actually Phun Phin, about 16 kilometers outside downtown Surat Thani). If you are coming by train, you'll need to take a bus to the Donsak pier from the station, and then transfer to the ferry. Whatever time of day or night you arrive, there will be touts selling combination bus-train tickets to the islands; they should cost no more than 300B. If you are taking a government bus from Bangkok, the ride to Surat Thani is around 12 hours, but you'll then have to get from downtown Surat Thani to the pier. You can either take a local bus, which you can get at the bus station, or a taxi to Donsak pier. The better way may be to take a Samui express bus from Bangkok, using one of the private bus companies that leave from the Southern Bus Terminal. These buses will travel directly to the pier, and some include the ferry ride in the price. **Transportation Co.** (tel. 07/742-0765) and **Sopon Tours** (tel. 07/742-0175) both run VIP buses to the ferry, and fares are under 700B for the trip.

GETTING AROUND

Ko Samui has frequent *song thaew* that circle the island's main road from early morning into the evening. There are no fixed stops, so if you want a ride, just give the driver a wave and then hop in the back. When you want to get off, press the buzzer in the back (it's usually on the ceiling) and then pay your fare after you get off. Fares are set, and rides cost 20–60B if you are going from beach to beach. For trips from the pier to Chaweng, expect to pay 110B, less if you are traveling to a closer beach. There are also plentiful taxis and motorcycle taxis on the popular beaches in the area (if you are staying somewhere more secluded, your guesthouse can call one for you).

KO PHA-NGAN
เกาะพะงัน

If you're looking for a beautiful island with nice beaches that's cheap and full of folks who want to party all night long, this is the spot to pick. Although Ko Pha-Ngan is physically similar to Ko Samui, except that it's about half the size and has smaller sandy beaches instead of Samui's large, sweeping ones, and is just a short ferry trip away, it definitely feels a world apart. You won't see as much development here, or even any main roads. Instead, the island is rimmed by stretches of clean white sand, and the interior mountainous rainforest is peppered with inexpensive bungalows and, more and more, secluded resorts.

Although there is one long strip of coast on the west side of the island, which gives the added benefit of beautiful sunsets, many of the beaches on Ko Pha-Ngan are set in small coves backed by cliffs and thick forest. The physical landscapes are truly beautiful, and they are often the more secluded-feeling areas, but they can be really tough to access. Weather and tidal conditions permitting, you can take a longtail

boat from one beach to another. Many of the roads leading to these beaches are dirt roads; there are some 4WD vehicles on the island that can take you, and many visitors also rent motorcycles to get from one beach to another. If you go that route, be aware that some of the dirt roads can be treacherous on two wheels, especially if it has been raining.

In many ways, Ko Pha-Ngan is a breath of fresh air since it's so much less developed than other popular spots in the region. It tends to attract visitors such as young backpackers and aging hippies, all looking to enjoy the beauty of the region without spending a lot of money. For better or worse, the island has become something of an international party zone, probably thanks to the many young travelers who visit every year. During high season, the all-night full moon parties have given way to half moon parties and black moon parties—any excuse to have a few drinks and dance around on the beach to music more fit for an urban rave than a tropical paradise. Don't bother wearing a watch, as the drinking tends to start as soon as the haze from the night before has cleared sufficiently to open a bottle of beer. If you're in the right mood, it can be a lot of fun, particularly because you can sleep your hangover off on one of the beautiful beaches come morning. If you're not into the scene, avoid Hat Rin, the island's party beach.

Beaches and Islands

The beaches in the northern part of the island on **Ao Chaloklum Bay** are the least desirable on the island. The sand is darker and a little coarser, and the tides make it difficult to swim unless you're doing so at high tide. It's also not a great place for snorkeling as most of the coral surrounding the bay is dead. It's not paradise, but it is home to a fishing village, so while you may not be able to enjoy the swimming too much, you will be able to hang out and watch the colorful longtail boats on the water. If you travel just a little east to **Hat Khom,** you'll find a prettier beach with some vibrant coral in relatively shallow water (great for snorkeling). This beach, however, is not easily swimmable at low

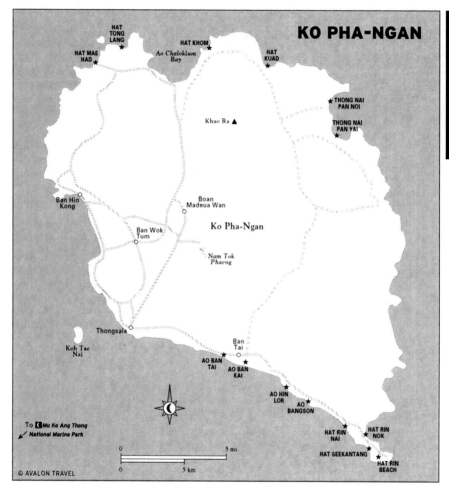

tide either. **Hat Kuad,** just to the west, is one of the island favorites. A wide swath of sand backed by green mountains and surrounded by a cove, it's one of the prettier beaches on the north side of the island. It's difficult to get to by land, so it's only crowded by those willing to take a longtail or endure a bumpy ride in a 4WD vehicle to get here. Although there's no coral, you can swim regardless of the tide thanks to a steep drop-off close to shore. **Hat Tong Lang** is in a small cove surrounded by leafy green foliage. There's a coral reef close to shore, and its presence creates a lagoon of sorts. This beach is also tough to access and hence calm and quiet. You can take a longtail boat from Chaloklum Bay, but if you go by land, the dirt road leading to the beach is pretty rough.

The east side of the island has just a handful of beautiful small beaches interspersed among the green hills and mountains. Thanks to the geography, there's a definite wild and natural

DIVING THE SAMUI ARCHIPELAGO

Although the water in the Gulf of Thailand is not as clear as what you'll find on the Andaman coast, there are still many excellent diving opportunities. Ko Tao is by far the most popular spot for diving, thanks to its proximity to some of the region's best diving sites.

SAIL ROCK

This rock pinnacle between Ko Tao and Ko Pha-Ngan is the region's most popular dive spot and is appropriate for all levels of divers. The pinnacle, which towers about nine meters above the surface, is a magnet for fish, so there's plenty of colorful marinelife to be spotted. The swim-through chimney, a cavernous tunnel through the pinnacle, is a must-do for anyone visiting Sail Rock.

CHUMPHON PINNACLE

Just under 10 kilometers northwest of Ko Tao is Chumphon Pinnacle, a very popular granite pinnacle that does not break the surface. The base is covered with colorful anemones and attracts plenty of large and small fish (including little clownfish, which everyone in the area refers to as "Nemos" after the Disney movie). Large whale sharks are often spotted here, as are leopard sharks.

SHARK ISLAND

Southeast of Ko Tao is a grouping of rocks surrounded by colorful coral and anemones. Snappers, rays, and angel fish congregate in the rocks and, as you might suspect from the name, so do sharks.

KO MA

Just north of Ko Pha-Ngan (actually connected to it by a strip of sand at low tide) is Ko Ma, which has some vibrant and healthy hard and soft coral as well as lots of colorful marinelife swimming around. Given its proximity to the main island and its suitability for divers of all levels, this is often where beginning divers are taken when they are getting certified.

KO NANG YUAN

The three interconnected islands also offer some nice snorkeling and diving opportunities. The coral reef attracts plenty of smaller fish (no sharks, though) and is a nice place for beginning divers and for snorkelers. Nang Yuan pinnacle, a small granite pinnacle below the surface, attracts larger fish who've come to feed.

DIVE SHOPS AND COURSES

There are many dive shops in the area, especially on Ko Tao, which has dozens. Safety records across Thailand's diving industry are good, but make sure to inspect equipment and talk to the instructors and dive masters you'll be with before signing up to make sure you're comfortable with them. Also ask about environmental awareness. PADI divers should follow a strict no-hands rule, but some dive shops have been known to be somewhat lax about it (touching or even brushing up against coral can damage it).

On Ko Tao, especially, many dive shops also have small guesthouses, and you'll get a discounted rate (sometimes just a few hundred baht) if you're taking lessons or going out on

---

feeling here. There's no coral on this side of the island, but if you happen to be awake in time, the sunrises are beautiful. **Thong Nai Pan Noi** and **Thong Nai Pan Yai** are the most popular beaches on the east side of the island, and there are some simple bungalows and a few more upscale resorts if you want to stay here. The two curved beaches are set in coves and have soft white sand. Thong Nai Pan Noi has a little

village with restaurants, bars, and a few places to spend money, while Thong Nai Pan Yai is a little less developed.

Hat Rin Beach in the southern part of Ko Pha-Ngan is the island's most popular. Located on a small peninsula on the southern tip of the island, Hat Rin is actually two bays—**Hat Rin Nok** and **Hat Rin Nai** (also called Hat Rin Sunrise and Hat Rin Sunset, since the beaches dives with them. Accommodations run the gamut from basic and clean to luxurious. You'll be surrounded by fellow divers if you choose to stay in one of these guesthouses.

There are also plenty of dive shops on Ko Samui and Ko Pha-Ngan who offer diving trips and equipment. You can also take 3–4-day PADI diving certification courses that can be arranged at any of the diving shops and schools listed below. Live-aboards tend to be less popular in this part of the country; instead, most diving is done on day trips or multiday trips where divers sleep in basic accommodations on one of the islands in Ang Thong National Park.

Ko Samui

- **Blue Planet Dive Centre** (119 Mu 2, Chaweng Beach, tel. 07/741-3106, www.blue-planetdivers.net)

- **Calypso Diving** (27/5 Chaweng Rd., Chaweng Beach, tel. 07/742-2437, www.calypso-diving.com)

- **Samui Diving Service** (80/3 Mu 3, Chaweng Beach, tel. 07/723-0053)

- **Samui Easy Divers** (locations on Bo Phut, Chaweng, Lamai, and Big Buddha Beaches, tel. 07/723-1190, www.easydivers-thailand.com)

- **SIDS-Samui International Diving School** (Malibu Beach Resort, Chaweng Beach, tel. 07/742-2386, www.planet-scuba.net)

- **Silent Divers** (101/7 Mu 2, Bo Phut Beach, tel. 07/742-2730, www.silentdivers.com)

Ko Pha-Ngan

- **Asia Divers Koh Phangan** (44/42 Mu 1, Thongsala Pier, tel. 07/737-7274, www.asia-divers.com)

- **Haad Yao Divers** (Sandy Bay Bungalows, Hat Yao, tel. 07/734-9119, www.haadyaodivers.com)

- **MTF Diving** (Weangthai Resort, Ban Tai Bay, tel. 07/737-7247, www.mtfdiving.com)

Ko Tao

- **Ban's Diving Center** (Sairee Beach, tel. 07/745-6466, www.amazingkohtao.com)

- **Blacktip Diving** (40/5 Mu 3, Tanote Bay, tel. 07/745-6488, www.blacktipdiving.com)

- **Buddha View Dive Resort** (45 Mu 3, Chalok Ban Kao, tel. 07/745-6074, www.buddhaview-diving.com)

- **Coral Grand Divers** (15/4 Mu 1, Sairee Beach, tel. 07/745-6431, www.coralgranddivers.com)

- **Crystal Dive Resort** (7/1 Mu 2, Mae Hat, tel. 07/745-6107, www.crystaldive.com)

- **Easy Divers – Koh Tao Island** (10/3 Mu 2, Mae Hat, also located on Ko Nang Yuan, tel. 07/745-6321, www.kohtaoeasydivers.com)

- **Sairee Hut Dive Resort** (14/45 Sairee Hut Resort, Mu 2, Sairee Beach, tel. 07/745-6815, www.saireehut.com)

- **SIDS-Planet Scuba Koh Tao** (9 Mu 2, Mae Hat, tel. 07/745-6110, www.planet-scuba.net)

---

face east and west, respectively). At the bottom of the peninsula is **Hat Seekantang,** a small, slightly quieter beach. All of the beaches on the peninsula have clean, light sand and clear water and are fringed with palm trees. Since they're so popular among travelers, there are plenty of bungalows and plenty of bars. Hat Rin Nok and Hat Rin Nai are home to the island's infamous full moon parties, so expect a lot of partying if you're hanging out or staying here.

Traveling up the west side of the island from the Hat Rin peninsula, there's a long stretch of beach broken only by an outcropping of verdant hills. Here you'll find **Ao Bangson, Ao Hin Lor, Ao Ban Kai,** and **Ao Ban Tai.** The beaches are long and look idyllic thanks to the coconut trees, views of Samui, and fishing boats on the water. The swimming is not always great, however. There's a coral reef just off the coast, and there are some sandbars that pop up at low tide, making it difficult to do more than walk or wade. Around Ao Ban Kai and Ao Ban Tai, you'll find lots of inexpensive to moderately priced bungalows as well as beach bars and restaurants.

Around the ferry pier at **Thongsala** is a stretch of beach more than five kilometers long with plenty of bungalows to choose from (and some of the cheapest on the island). Right at the beach, the land is mostly flat, and there are plenty of surrounding coconut trees that help create the tropical-paradise vibe. Perhaps because they're so close to the ferry, the bungalows tend to be cheaper and also to attract a younger crowd.

The upper western part of the island has a number of beaches close together, although separated by cliffs or hills and mostly accessible by dirt road. **Hat Yao** and **Ao Chao Phao** to the west are some of the most popular beaches on the island. The beaches are about a kilometer long, the sand is white, the western views spectacular, and the surrounding green hills an added bonus. Here you'll find a variety of accommodation options, from simple 200B-per-night bungalows with fans to more upscale small resorts.

Hat Mae Had is another beautiful white-sand beach fringed with coconut trees, but what really sets this beach apart is neighboring **Ko Ma,** a small island that's connected to the main island by a thin sandbar. The snorkeling around Ko Ma is great, as there is a lot of healthy coral and marinelife to look at, so it's also a popular dive site.

Sports and Recreation

If you're staying on Ko Pha-Ngan, expect to do quite a bit of hiking, unless you park yourself on the beach and don't leave till it's time to go home. Much of the island's interior is rugged, and some of it is rocky, so you'll need to be agile to get from one place to another. The island's highest peak is at **Khao Ra,** just over 600 meters above sea level. To hike there,

start in the village of **Ban Madeua Wan** in the center of the island. The trail will take you past **Namtok Phaeng** and lead to the top of the mountain, where there's a viewpoint from which you can see the whole island. The trail is steep at times and not always clearly marked, so use caution when climbing, and expect to spend a couple of hours going and coming back if you are in good physical shape.

The west side of the island has some coral reefs, sometimes just a few hundred meters from the coastline. The water is generally very shallow until the reefs, so you'll be able to see the reefs without having to swim out too deep.

The best diving in the area is around Ko Tao, but the west side of Ko Pha-Ngan has some good diving too. Most of the diving is relatively shallow, at around 15 meters, but there's plentiful hard and soft coral to see as well as lots of colorful marinelife swimming around. Local dive companies also do daily trips to dive sites around the region.

Accommodations

Most of what you'll find on Ko Pha-Ngan is casual beach bungalows and mid-priced small resorts. Unlike neighboring Ko Samui, the island isn't filled with luxurious amenities, although there are more small, high-end resorts opening every year. If you are on a tight budget and looking for simple accommodations, you'll be able to find something inexpensive and comfortable. If you want to get away from it all and enjoy a little luxury, there are a handful of resorts that are not in the middle of all of the action.

Coco Garden Bungalows (100/7 Mu 1, Bang Thai Beach, tel. 07/737-7721, www.cocogardens.com, 400B) is as good a bungalow resort as you're going to find on the island. The small compound is right next to a beautiful strip of the beach, the bungalows are cute and well maintained, and the interiors are furnished in a simple Thai style. Only a handful of the bungalows come with air-conditioning, so if that's a priority, book early and make sure you confirm you are not in a fan-only guest

FULL MOON PARTIES

While it's tempting to think that celebrating the full moon by dancing out on the sand is part of some ancient Thai ritual, the truth is that it's a relatively new tradition and one that's primarily fueled by foreign visitors.

No one can agree on exactly how the tradition was started, but as the prevailing legend would have it, the full moon parties that Ko Pha-Ngan has become famous for were started by a small group of backpackers who celebrated the full moon one night by throwing a party on Hat Rin. The party was such a success that on the night of the next full moon, they threw another party, and more visitors joined them, then another and another until the attendees packed the beach.

Whatever its origins, during peak season the full-moon parties on Hat Rin now attract thousands of partiers, and coming down to the beach for one of the outdoor all-night music-filled soirees is an unforgettable experience. There are DJs, fire-eaters, fireworks, and lots and lots of booze. The all-night outdoor raves also tend to feature illicit drugs of various sorts and sometimes undercover police.

seems to permeate the area. The beach is good for snorkeling, and the staff has snorkel sets available. There is a small restaurant attached, but if you're looking for more action, it'll be tough to get there—you have to travel about 15 minutes on an unpaved road to get back to civilization (the bungalow will arrange to pick you up at the pier and take you back when you depart). Better to pack a bunch of books and enjoy their cold beer without having to leave.

Seaview Bungalows Thansadet (Thansadet Beach, no phone, www.seaview.thansadet.com, 400B) is an excellent choice for cheap, clean bungalows. Thansadet Beach, south of Thong Nai Pan, is small, rugged, and secluded and has beautiful clear water. Fan-cooled bungalows are very basic wooden structures but have comfortable beds and modern baths (albeit with cold water only). Although there isn't lots to do on the beach, there is a small restaurant on the property, and most people come just to relax anyway.

The rustic but comfortable **Sunset Cove Resort** (Ao Chao Phao, www.phangansunset.com, 1,200B), on popular Ao Chao Phao on the west coast, has pretty, lush grounds, a great pool, and a fantastic location right on the beach. Guest rooms are clean, and though not opulent, are well-coordinated and calming. Staff are super friendly and helpful, and they set the tone everyone else at the resort seems to follow—happy and relaxed. There is a restaurant and bar on the property, but this is really more a place to chill out and have a few beers with friends while enjoying the view than to party.

Palita Lodge (119 Mu 6, Bang Thai Beach, tel. 07/737-5170, www.palitalodge.com, 2,000B) isn't a high-end resort but offers guests nearly every amenity that more expensive properties do, including a very pretty, well-maintained swimming pool as well as clean, stylish guest rooms with flat-screen TVs and minibars and spotless modern baths. The modern Thai style is subtle but consistent throughout the property. Palita Lodge is right on Hat Rin and in the middle of full moon madness, and it tends to attract partygoers.

room. There's a small, relaxed restaurant and bar on the premises serving inexpensive and well-made food and drink; if you're looking to enjoy some of the partying that goes on, you'll be close to the black moon and half moon parties on Hat Rin—but not so close that you won't be able to get some sleep if you want.

If you're on the island to enjoy the rugged beauty and peace and quiet, the **Coconut Beach Bungalows** (Hat Khom Beach, Chaloklum, no phone, 400B) on Hat Khom is an excellent choice. The bungalows are very simple and very cheap, and what they lack in amenities, such as hot water and air-conditioning, they make up for in the friendliness of the staff and the secluded, peaceful feeling that

The **Green Papaya Resort** (64/8 Mu 8, Salad Beach, tel. 07/737-4230, www.greenpapayaresort.com, 4,600B) is a beautifully designed small resort on the northwestern part of the island. The property is filled with modern Thai furnishings, a beautiful pool overlooking the ocean, a couple of restaurants, and not much else to distract you from the scenery or the sunsets. Most of the accommodations are in new wooden bungalows with all the amenities you could want inside, including large sleek baths, DVD players, and minibars. There are also two-bedroom family villas on this property.

Another option for a bit of remote luxury is the **Panviman Resort** (22/1 Mu 5, Thong Nai Pan Noi Bay, Bantai, tel. 07/744-5100, 4,500B) on Bantai. Like the Santhiya, it's in a location that's well away from the crowds and the partying, and it has a beautiful pool, restaurants, and a bar to keep you fed, quaffed, and entertained. The guest rooms are done in a Thai style, and the baths are large, well equipped, and nicely designed. This is a great resort for families since there are a few large family villas that can accommodate more than two people comfortably. Some of the guest rooms and villas are in the hills, so when booking, make sure to take that into consideration; the hillside rooms have a nicer view, but you'll need to climb some stairs to get to them.

For a more upscale Ko Pha-Ngan experience, try the **Santhiya Resort & Spa** (22/7 Mu 5, Thong Nai Pan Yai, tel. 07/742-8999, www.santhiya.com, 10,000B), which opened in 2006 and has some of the nicest guest rooms on the island. The resort is done in a traditional Thai style, with plenty of carved woodwork and colorful textiles as well as luxuriant grounds. The guest rooms are all nestled in the cliffs surrounding the beach, and the views are beautiful, although it can be difficult to get from one place to another, especially if you're in one of the higher-level guest rooms or you're not agile. The grounds, in the middle of lush tropical foliage, have multiple swimming pools, including one with a waterfall. For those who want to stay out of the sun, there is also a fitness center

and a library. The Santhiya offers reasonably priced guests transfer by catamaran or speedboat from Samui, which makes it considerably more convenient. The beach itself is not quite as smooth on your feet as others you'll find on the island, but if you're just there to sunbathe and kayak, it's not a problem.

Food
If you're looking for something authentically Thai, you'll probably be disappointed in the offerings on Ko Pha-Ngan. The island is so overrun by young Western travelers looking for pizza and falafel that it's nearly impossible to find great Thai food. Western food varies from mediocre to pretty good, and most of the restaurants are around "Chicken Corner" in Hat Rin, the area's crossroads.

The street parallel to Hat Rin Beach is full of places advertising foreign food of all types, but **Fair House Restaurant & Bar** (119/1 Hat Rin Rd., 9 A.M.–10:30 P.M. daily, 100B) has just about anything Western you could be missing. From potatoes (baked, mashed, or fried) to pasta dishes, steaks, bacon rolls, plus a wide selection of Thai options and even burritos, the menu here is massive, but the pizza is a winner. They also have some creative and appetizing salads on the menu (pumpkin-tofu), and drinks cover the rounds, from *lassis* to whiskey fruit shakes and cocktails. Try a carrot-honey *lassi.* The only downside to this casual spot is that you will have to endure season after season of the TV series *Friends,* although they sometimes play movies at nighttime.

In a location that's too convenient to be good, **Pia-Bia Restaurant** (Hat Rin Rd., 36 Mu 6, next to Sunrise Resort, 9:30 A.M.–11 P.M. daily, 100B) actually does get patrons returning for their tasty and satisfying meals. Better known as the "Family Guy restaurant," they play episodes of the U.S. comedy series *The Family Guy* continuously. The menu here is almost as extensive as Fair House's, with options for everyone. All of the following got seriously good reviews: shrimp pad thai, green curry chicken or seafood, and the *yam* salad with chicken: a Thai dish with plenty of chicken and a light spicy dressing. For Western fare, the burgers and hot sandwiches are popular. The large drink selection, including alcoholic drinks and shakes, will quench any thirst. Besides the food, it seems that no matter what the nationality, the crowd drawn to "Family Guy" is a friendly sort, and it is an overall pleasant dining experience, especially after a day in the sun.

The baked goods alone will force you to peek into **Nira's Deli Sandwich Bar & Restaurant** (right off Hat Rin Rd., on the way to Chicken Corner, sit-down meals 7 A.M.–11 P.M., bakery and deli 24 hours, 200B), just a few meters off the main drag. If you can tear your eyes away from the food on display, you will see the build-your-own-sandwich board. What better for a place that has the best bread in town? (We suspect they supply all other restaurants offering "fresh bread.") The options range from spreads—cheese, hummus, even Mexican salsa—to more hearty fillings such as boiled egg, smoked salmon, and even turkey. The deli shares dining space with their full-service restaurant, offering Thai food as well as thin-crust individual pizzas baked in the oven just behind the counter. Whatever you fancy, they have a delicious breakfast menu, and you don't have to be a vegetarian to order the vegetarian sandwich (scrambled eggs with tomato, onion, and cheese on your choice of bread). Nira's opens early, making it a great option before a ferry trip or if your night runs into morning. In their fridges they have premade sandwiches and foods and usually squares of deep-dish pizza at the bakery. They also sell their hummus and salsa. Even with all the sweets that make you forget about any other food you ate, this place definitely has a healthy vibe; whole grains and fresh fruit juices such as carrot-ginger abound.

If you're craving Middle Eastern food, **Paprika Mediterranean Restaurant** (Chicken Corner, 11 A.M.–10:30 P.M. daily, 150B) is as good as it gets. It's also why you'll hear mostly Hebrew chatter here. The service also sets this place apart, and they can pop out a delicious Israeli salad in three minutes. On Saturday they offer a special beef-tomato stew, but the hummus and falafel dishes are so good it can be difficult to order anything else. Paprika's also serves schnitzel (it comes out steaming hot) and *shawarma,* so everyone can be satisfied. There is Thai food on the menu too, but it is quite possible nobody has ever tried it. Perhaps the true reason this place always has customers is their 80B deal: a full pita with falafel and hummus and a fruit shake. The best of both regions? Judge for yourself.

Palita Lodge (119 Mu 6, Hat Rin, tel. 07/737-5170, 8 A.M.–10 P.M. daily, 150B) will make you wish your breakfast wasn't included in the cost of your accommodations. Their menu has seven different sets to choose from, such as eggs, porridge, or pancakes. Each set comes with a choice of hot drink (tea, chocolate, or fresh coffee), plus fresh fruit or juice. The fruit plate is a better option and very generous. If you want a traditional Thai breakfast, opt for the rice soup. There are also plenty of Thai and Western choices for lunch and dinner. It is a very pretty spot, a bit away from the main entrances to the beach, so it is surprisingly quiet without being out of the way. Digest afterward by their pool in the comfortable sun chairs.

The Lighthouse (Leela Beach, Hat Rin, 8 A.M.–11 P.M. daily, 200B) gets an A for atmosphere. The isolated corner it is located on is an easy walk from the hedonistic side of Hat Rin Beach, but it feels like it is the opposite side of the island. Perched on the very southern tip of Ko Pha-Ngan, the panorama-windowed eating-lounging area looks straight out to sea. If you go by beach, you walk to the end and then follow a lovely boardwalk that wraps around the corner of the island. Come lounge in the hammock and admire the view over fruit shakes; it has an atmosphere that feels like an afternoon nap. The scenery is especially beautiful at sunset, but at any point during the day, the peaceful atmosphere dissipates tension as well as any Thai massage. It has the familiar menu with Western and Thai options along with very hearty breakfasts, from porridge to a Thai stuffed omelet. The Thai food is the cheapest option, and you aren't charged extra for picking a back-road location. They have a choice of salads, plus a more obscure Western taste that found its way to the menu: the cheese plate—four different types of cheese (including brie) with salad. Order this if it's to your liking, with a glass of 100B wine, and looking out at the ocean, you may decide you have achieved the pinnacle of all Euro-Asian ideals.

Far up the hill, **Sunsmile Restaurant and Guesthouse** (Hat Rin Beach, 8 A.M.–9:30 P.M. daily, 100B) occupies a scenic spot overlooking Hat Rin Nok (Sunrise Beach). An everlasting breeze blows here. They definitely cater to backpackers, and you can either dine outside with the view or inside with a host of movies to choose from. It is a hike—at least a 10-minute walk up a heavily rutted rocky and sandy road—so if you need to escape and really just avoid people for a bit, this is the place. The curries and Thai food are very good deals. Western food is on the menu but is more limited. During full moon party weeks, it can be fun to watch the party from a distance and still be able to hear the music. The rest of the month, it's one of the quietest places in all of Hat Rin.

Getting There

The closest airport to Ko Pha-Ngan is on Samui, so if you want to spend as little time as possible getting to the beach, you can fly to the neighboring island and then take a ferry boat to Ko Pha-Ngan.

Since the island mostly attracts a younger crowd with tighter purse strings, most people arrive by boat from Surat Thani. If you're arriving in Surat Thani by air, you can buy a combination bus-ferry ticket right at the airport, and the whole trip should run around five hours. If you're coming to Surat Thani by train or bus from Bangkok, you'll need to make your way to the Donsak pier outside of town and then catch a ferry to Ko Pha-Ngan. The ferries that travel from Surat Thani to Samui then make their way to Ko Pha-Ngan; you'll spend another couple of hours on the ferry and pay an additional 150B on top of the

Samui fare. There is no direct ferry to Ko Pha-Ngan from Surat Thani—you have to stop in Samui first.

Getting Around

Ko Pha-Ngan is less built-up than Ko Samui but has some roads in place, and during the day there are *song thaew* running from the pier in Thongsala to other beaches. You should pay under 80B for most rides (unless you charter the *song thaew* to take you to a specific destination that is not on the route, in which case you'll need to negotiate a price). Many visitors also rent motorcycles or mountain bikes, both of which are available at most beaches. Expect to pay around 200B per day regardless of whether you're getting a pedal-powered or gas-powered bike.

KO TAO

เกาะเต่า

Ko Tao means turtle island, although that's not so much about its shape (it looks more like a kidney bean) as the fact that the waters around the island used to be filled with sea turtles. They've since mostly moved on, but there's still lots of amazing marinelife to explore around Ko Tao. The waters surrounding the island are relatively shallow and have little current, except during monsoon season. In fact, the island is one of the best launching points for scuba diving in the Gulf of Thailand and a great place to do some snorkeling right off the beach. The island is full of dive shops and dive schools, so if you're looking to get PADI certified, this is a great place to pick—courses tend to be a little cheaper than the rest of the country, and you can really shop around for the dive instructor you feel most comfortable with. In fact, the island issues more PADI certificates than any other spot in Thailand and most other spots in the world. If you visit, you'll find bungalow resorts and a few up-market offerings, and they are mostly geared toward divers. Every resort, up-market or otherwise, has a dive shop attached.

Even if you're not into diving, Ko Tao is a beautiful little island to enjoy the scenery and the beaches, although you might feel a bit like the odd man out. The island itself is surrounded by some stretches of sandy shore surrounded by rocky promontories and backed by shady palm trees. The center of the island is mostly jungly rain forest, although there's enough development here that you'll be able to find a post office and a few places to spend your money. Getting around the island, however, can be a little tough. It's a great place for hiking, but the road system is not well developed. If you're not staying near Mae Had (on the island's west coast, where the ferry arrives and departs), expect a long and bumpy ride, especially if you're going across the island. Despite the challenging transport, don't write off Ko Tao—its remoteness gives it a distinct *sabai* attitude.

Beaches and Islands

For a clear stretch of sandy beach, **Sairee Beach,** closest to the ferry pier, is your best bet on the island. The nearly 3.5-kilometer beach faces west, so you not only get the view of the mainland but beautiful sunsets too. This is the most populated beach on the island, and there is a good selection of accommodations and places to eat, although you could hardly call it overcrowded, even in high season. Since the island itself is so small—just a couple of kilometers across—it's a good base from which you can hike around the rest of the island. Just south of Sairee Beach and adjacent to it is **Mae Had,** where the ferry pier is located and probably the only part of the island that could ever legitimately be described as crowded or busy. The area right around the pier isn't optimal for relaxing, but to the south the beach gets nicer and there are some decent places to stay.

Aside from the long stretch of sand on Sairee Beach and Mae Had, the rest of Ko Tao is made up of about a dozen small bays on the north, east, and south of the island. Popular ones include **Hin Wong Bay** on the east coast and **Mango Bay** on the north coast. Both have spectacular views and excellent snorkeling and diving, but the beaches are often quite rocky. Neighboring **Ko Nang Yuan,** just off the

northeast coast of Ko Tao, is perhaps the coolest-looking island in the area. It's actually three separate small islands connected together by a thin stretch of sand you can walk across during low tide. The cluster of small islands also lends itself well to snorkeling and diving, as the interconnecting islands create three separate shallow bays that are mostly protected from strong currents. The beaches are also very shallow unless you walk out pretty far, making it a great place for families. If you're looking for something to do on land, the mountainous island is filled with boulders to climb and a couple of short hiking trails.

From Sairee Beach on Ko Tao you can charter a longtail boat to take you to Ko Nang Yuan for about 150B each way. During high season there are plenty of people going back and forth, so it won't be a problem to get a ride back to Ko Tao. During low season you should arrange a round-trip ride. There is also a ferry that runs from the main pier in Ko Tao once a day during high season; make sure to check at the pier for the current schedule and price. If you are coming from Ko Samui, you can take the ferry to Ko Tao, and then transfer to another boat (either a small ferry or longtail), but you may want to consider spending at least one night on Ko Tao if you're doing that, as you'll spend at least five hours traveling back and forth. There is one resort on the island, Three Paradise Islands, and if you're staying there, they'll help you arrange transport.

Accommodations and Food

For simple, rustic, charming bungalows, the **Sai Thong Resort & Spa** (Mu 2, Sai Nuan Beach, tel. 07/745-6868, 350B) cannot be beat. It's in a remote spot on the southwestern part of the island, so the only way to get there is either by boat taxi or a bumpy ride in a 4WD vehicle. Once you're there, the view to the Gulf of Thailand is gorgeous, as is the surrounding verdant scenery. The bungalows are very simple wooden shacks with mosquito netting and fans. There's a small restaurant that's open all day, and even Internet access, but no pool, and the spa has limited services. It's not a luxury choice, by any means, but if you're looking for that *Survivor* feeling on a budget, you'll be very satisfied here.

If you're just on the island to do some diving, **Khun Ying House** (15/19 Mu 1, Sairee Beach, tel. 08/0620-5527, 450B) is a cheap, clean, and comfortable hotel. The guest rooms are well maintained, although they aren't the most stylishly designed. Some have shared baths and fans, and you can use their kitchen facilities if you feel like cooking up a meal yourself. There are limited facilities here; it's definitely just a place to store your flippers and sleep.

Koh Tao Simple Life (Sairee Beach, tel. 07/745-6142, www.kohtaosimpleliferesort. com, 1,500B) has a good location on popular Sairee Beach, a big swimming pool, a popular restaurant and bar serving Thai and Western food, and nicely furnished, stylish, modern guest rooms. Despite the name, though, it's not a luxury resort and really more like a well-run midsize hotel.

The **Mango Bay Grand Resort** (11/3 Mu 2, Mae Had, tel. 07/745-6097, www.kohtao-mangobay.com, 1,500B) isn't quite grand, and it's not really a resort either, since there's no pool and limited facilities. Still, it's a great place because of its location and the clean and well-maintained bungalows perched on stilts on the rocks above the bay. The interiors of the bungalows are simple and clean, and each has comfortable beds and stunning views to the water. The interior design in the baths may cause you to wonder who picked the paint and tile colors, but everything is modern and works well despite the fact that it's not entirely fashionable. The snorkeling in the area is excellent when it's not monsoon season, and this alone might be reason to stay here. From the resort you can swim out to see excellent coral and other marinelife.

For small-resort luxury, the **Jamakhiri Spa & Resort** (19/1 Mu 3 Chalook, Ban Kao, tel. 07/745-6400, www.jamahkiri.com, 2,500B) is an exceptional property set on the rocks and just a few minutes' walk to the beach. The guest rooms are all large and well kept, with comfortable modern Thai-style furnishing and

hardwood floors. All have views to the Gulf of Thailand and large bay windows. There's a beautiful pool, a small spa, and even a fitness center, although unless it's pouring outside, there's really no reason to stay indoors. The resort seems to cascade down the rocks, which means there's quite a bit of walking involved if you're staying on one of the higher levels. As at many other secluded places on the island, you'll have to contend with difficult roads to reach the Jamakhiri, although the hotel will arrange transportation for you from the pier.

The small, upscale **Chintakiri Resort** (19/59 Mu 3 Chalook, Ban Kao, tel. 07/745-6391, www.chintakiriresort.com, 2,500B) has beautiful views of the Gulf of Thailand and clean, nicely furnished Thai-style bungalows. The property is built into the hills behind the beach on one of the island's southern bays near the Jamakhiri Spa & Resort, which makes for amazing views, lush landscaping, and a secluded feeling, but those with any mobility issues might have trouble getting up and down to their guest room. The infinity pool is not huge but also has a beautiful view, and since the property is so small, it rarely gets full.

Anankhira Boutique Villas (15/3 Mu 1, Sairee Beach, tel. 08/7719-7696, www.anan-khira.com, 3,500B) is a little more luxurious than the typical Sairee Beach accommodations. Each of the charming thatched-roof villas has a big bedroom, large outdoor lounging area, and its own small plunge pool. The style, which management calls "ecoconscious," is rustic but very clean and well-maintained. Those who want more space and privacy will find these an excellent value. The villas are not right on the beach, but they are a 10-minute walk away from the northern part of Sairee Beach.

If you want to stay on Ko Nang Yaun, the set of three islands joined by sandbars just off the coast of Ko Tao, your only choice is the **Three Paradise Island Resort,** sometimes also called the **Nang Yuan Island Dive Resort** (tel. 07/745-6088, www.nangyuan. com or www.3paradiseislands.com, 1,500B). The resort has accommodations scattered across the three islands, from simple fan bungalows to larger air-conditioned cottages. None of the options are luxurious, but there's a small restaurant and a dive shop, and staying on a private island might be worth giving up a few amenities.

Getting There

The only way to get to Ko Tao is by boat, either from Chumphon on the mainland or from Ko Samui and Ko Pha-Ngan, using the normal ferries. A high-speed ferry from Chumphon or Samui takes just under two hours and costs around 550B; an overnight ride on a cargo boat takes six hours and costs half the price. There are a number of different companies offering ferry services, including **Lomprayah High Speed Ferries** (www.lomprayah.com), **Ko Jaroen Car Ferry** (tel. 07/758-0030), **Seatran Ferry** (tel. 02/240-2582, www.seatrandiscovery.com), **Songserm Express Boat** (tel. 02/280-8073, www.songserm-expressboat.com) and the **Talay Sub Cargo Night Boat** (tel. 07/743-0531), and the schedules change from year to year, but from neighboring islands there are at least two boats per day each way.

Mainland Surat Thani   สุราษฎร์ธานี

Surat Thani isn't a place most tourists end up spending too much time, given the beautiful islands just offshore. It's more or less a run-of-the-mill city going about daily life despite the throngs of foreign visitors that pass through. But just outside the city is Chaiya, the former seat of the Srivijaya Empire, which has an excellent museum. There are also a couple of nearby national parks worth visiting if you are in the area.

TAI ROM YEN NATIONAL PARK
อุทยานแห่งชาติใต้ร่มเย็น

The Tai Rom Yen National Park (Amphoe Ban Na San, Surat Thani, tel. 07/734-4633, 8:30 A.M.–6 P.M. daily, 400B), covering part of the Nakhon Si Thammarat mountain range, is covered in dense forest, with beautiful waterfalls to visit and well-marked trails for hiking. The 22-step **Dard Fa Waterfall** is the region's largest, and one of the levels is a 75-meter cliff drop. To get here, you must drive to the base of the trail at the park headquarters (once you enter the park you'll see signs), where you can also pick up a map to get to **Khao Nong**, the highest point in the province at over 1,370 meters. In addition to the beautiful natural scenery, the park is also home to a couple of significant historical landmarks worth visiting.

In the 1970s and 1980s, the area was a communist-rebel stronghold, and there are a couple of former hideout camps that can now be visited. There are bungalows and a canteen at the park headquarters near the Dard Fa Waterfall.

Getting There

From Surat Thani there's a direct bus that will take you to the entrance of the park on Route 4009 (ask for buses headed south toward the Phin Phun train station; the 15-minute trip should cost around 20B), but once you arrive, it is impossible to get around the park without transportation. If you're driving, take Route 4009 south from Surat Thani about 24 kilometers to Ban Chiang Phra, then look for the signs for the national park.

KHAO SOK NATIONAL PARK
อุทยานแห่งชาติเขาสก

Khao Sok National Park (8:30 A.M.–6 P.M. daily, 400B) in Surat Thani Province is covered with rainforest, limestone cliffs, and lakes. It's the wettest national park in the country, thanks to an abundance of rain in the region, and it's also often referred to as the most beautiful. The frequent rainfall keeps the park lush and green, and there is plentiful exotic flora, including palm trees, fig trees, lots of bamboo, and vine trees. There's also the

Rafflesia. At nearly one meter wide, the flower is one of the largest in the world and is quite rare. You'll also find pitcher plants, which are large insect-eating plants shaped like pitchers to trap unsuspecting bugs. You can tour the park's waterfalls and caves and canoe on the Chong Kaeb Khao Ka Loh lake, the result of a dam built to generate hydroelectric power for the region.

Accommodations and Food

The park offers simple accommodations in dormitory-style rooms and very cool but basic floating huts near two of the ranger stations. The huts, which have beds but shared toilets, are only 400B per night but are popular with large tour groups and book up quickly; you must reserve your place in advance. The park's website (www.dnp.go.th) has instructions on reserving accommodations (click on "National Park Online Reservation" in the English version of the site). Near the ranger station are also a couple of small restaurants that are open for breakfast, lunch, and dinner. These canteens serve only Thai food, but it is fresh and inexpensive.

Getting There

If you are coming from Surat Thani, you can pick up a bus to the park's entrance. The bus ride takes an hour and costs 70B, but they only run two a day, one in the morning and one in the afternoon (make sure to check at the bus station for current schedules). Once you are in the park, as with all national parks in Thailand, you will have a very difficult time getting around unless you either plan on hitching rides with other visitors or renting a car. If you are driving on your own, the park's entrance is on Route 401, which runs east–west between Surat Thani and Takua Pa. The park is about 97 kilometers east of Surat Thani.

PHRA BOROMMATHAT CHAIYA AND THE CHAIYA NATIONAL MUSEUM
พระบรมธาตุไชยา และ
พิพิธภัณฑสถานแหงชาติไชยา

Located about 48 kilometers north of the city, Phra Borommathat Chaiya is an ancient *chedi* said to house relics of the Buddha. The *chedi* itself is small but has amazingly detailed carvings. It was probably built around 1,200 years ago during the Srivijaya Empire. On the grounds you'll also find the Chaiya National Museum (Raksanorakit Rd., Tambon Wiang, Amphoe Chaiya, tel. 07/743-1066, 9 A.M.–4 P.M. Wed.–Sun., 30B). This small gem of a museum has an excellent collection of prehistoric artifacts such as tools, pottery, and housewares found in the region as well as regional art from the sixth century to the present. Here you'll be able to see a large collection of Srivijaya art, mostly devotional figures of the Buddha, but also Hindu art such as sculptures of Vishnu from before Buddhism took hold in the region.

The museum also has a collection of items found in shipwrecks in the Gulf of Thailand, left by sailors from China and beyond.

Getting There

If you're driving, Chaiya is 48 kilometers north of Surat Thani on Route 41. To visit without a car, you can take one of the frequent *song thaew* that depart from Surat Thani's bus terminal during the day. The trip will take about 45 minutes and costs 50B.

Nakhon Si Thammarat Province จังหวัดนครศรีธรรมราช

The Nakhon Si Thammarat region might just be one of the best untouristed places to visit in Thailand. The city is well organized, easy to navigate, and filled with museums and *wats*. The beaches have the clean, warm waters of the Gulf of Thailand but none of the crowds, and the inland national parks are filled with fertile rainforests and scores of waterfalls. There's also an airport with direct flights from Bangkok, and you can pick up a ticket for a song on Nok Air. Best of all, if you enjoying traveling to places where you're not likely to run into folks just like you, there are still very few Western travelers coming this way. The area is frequented by visitors from other parts of Thailand and Southeast Asia, however, so there are adequate accommodations and other tourism infrastructure.

◖ NAKHON SI THAMMARAT
นครศรีธรรมราช

Nakhon Si Thammarat is one of the oldest cities in the country and has a great collection of interesting historical and cultural sights to visit. If you're looking for an urban break in a small city after soaking up the sun and sea, spend a day visiting the museums and religious buildings. As a whole, the city isn't beautiful. The newer parts suffer from a type of generic urbanization that seems to know no international boundaries. But in the older part of the city you'll find Wat Phra Mahathat, one of the oldest and largest *wats* in the country, and some charming streets to wander around.

Despite the charm and cultural significance, the city is not a typical tourist trap. There are a couple of Tourism Authority of Thailand offices (one in city hall and one near the Ta Chang market), but other than that, the city is pretty much oblivious to travelers. You won't find lots of signs in English or even lots of taxis. To get around, it's best to grab one of the visitor maps from your hotel or the TAT office and set out on foot.

© SUZANNE NAM

mountains in Nakhon Si Thammarat Province

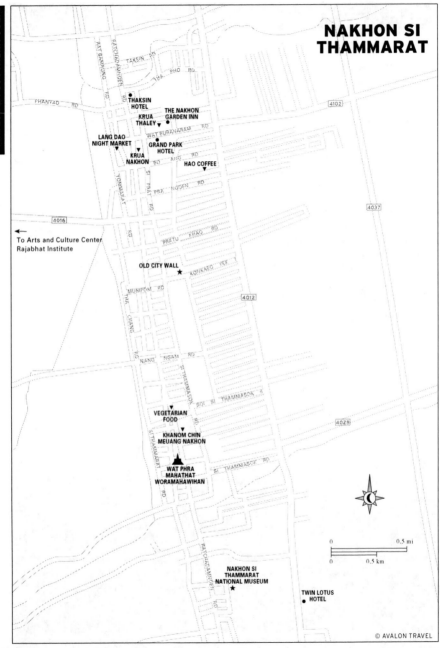

NAKHON SI THAMMARAT

Sights

Nakhon Si Thammarat is one of the oldest cities in the country, and although only fragments of the **Old City Wall** from the 13th century remain, they give a glimpse of what the city must have been like hundreds of years ago. The wall once enclosed the center of the city.

Located in such a historic city, the **Nakhon Si Thammarat National Museum** (Ratchadamnoen Rd., 9 A.M.–4 P.M. Wed.–Sun., 30B) does a nice job of exhibiting artifacts from prehistory through modern times, many relating to Buddhism. You'll find exhibits of local crafts through the ages and also some excellent examples of fine art. The niello ware (engraved metalwork) pieces are worth extra time perusing. There are also some more fun exhibits in the museum's new wing relating to Thai life, marriage rituals, and local food. The museum is 2.4 kilometers out of the center of town, heading south on Ratchadamnoen Road. You can grab a local *song thaew* or public bus from the main road, which will cost about 10B.

Nearly every postcard you see in the city will have an image of the imposing *chedi* at **Wat Phra Mahathat Woramahawihan** (Ratchadamnoen Rd., 8 A.M.–4:30 P.M. daily, 30B, museum 20B extra), which indicates how important the *wat* is to the city and the country. The original structure is believed to have been built between the sixth and eighth centuries, during the Srivijaya period, as a monastery and school. The ornately decorated *ubosot* (coronation hall), from the 18th-century Ayutthaya period, is relatively new, but the foundation of the large Phra Borom That Chedi is believed to have been built when the *wat* itself was founded. There is also a small museum on the premises with Buddhist reliquaries and other objects. While the historical significance may be difficult to grasp for someone unfamiliar with the spread of Buddhism in the region, the grounds themselves are quite stunning, and just wandering around for an hour or two is worth the time. The *wat* is 1.5 kilometers south of the center of town: Grab a local *song thaew* or public bus on Ratchadamnoen Rd. or, if the weather is good, walk.

The Nakhon Si Thammarat **Arts and Culture Center Rajabhat Institute** (Nakhon Si Thammarat–Phrom Khiri Rd., Hwy. 4016, 9 A.M.–4 P.M. daily), 13 kilometers east of the center of town, has numerous archaeological exhibits of artifacts found in the region, including tools and other objects from the Srivijaya Empire. The center, which is unfortunately mostly signed in Thai, also preserves and catalogs local customs, languages, and literature.

Accommodations

Although the city has a lot to offer travelers, the accommodations have yet to catch up (or catch on), and you'll find very limited options in Nakhon Si Thammarat. If you're looking for a place to indulge in a little luxury, or even a charming guesthouse with decent facilities, you're out of luck. If you just want a clean and comfortable place to sleep, there are a few options.

The top-of-the-line hotel in the city is the **Twin Lotus Hotel** (97/8 Pattanakarn-Kukwang Rd., tel. 07/532-3777, www.twinlotushotel.net, 1,500B). The guest rooms are spacious and well equipped, and the property is clean and maintained. Since it's a large city hotel, it's not a particularly interesting place to stay, however. Think beige curtains, Formica, and floral bedspreads. It does have a large pool, a fitness center, and other amenities you won't find anywhere else in the city. The hotel is not quite in the center of all of the action, so if you're looking for a place from which you can easily walk to all the sights, this may be a little far.

The **Thaksin Hotel** (1584/23 Si Prat Rd., tel. 07/534-2790 to 07/534-2794, www.thaksinhotel.com, 600B) and the **Grand Park Hotel** (1204/79 Pak Nakhon Rd., T. Klang, tel. 07/531-7666, www.grandparknakhon.com, 600B) are more central but still suffer from a lack of character that's even more pronounced in a city that's so culturally rich. Thaksin is a large, clean, modern place, just off of the main Ratchadamnoen Road and close to the train station. The guest rooms are well-kept and comfortable, and the price is more than reasonable, but generic decor and a business-conference vibe make it more of a utility choice than anything else. The Grand Park Hotel is similar to the Thaksin—clean, large, comfortable, and generic.

The guest rooms at **The Nakhon Garden Inn** (1/4 Pak Nakhon Rd., tel. 07/534-4831, 700B) are set around a leafy courtyard. This property has perhaps the most character of all the places you'll find in the city, although it's definitely not as modern and tidy as the other options.

Food

Downstairs at the Robinson Ocean Department Store is the highly popular **Hao Coffee** (Robinson Ocean, Pak Panang Kukwang Rd., tel. 07/534-6563, 10:30 A.M.–8:30 P.M. daily, 35–120B), which is actually two restaurants together, and the Ligor Bakery next door, which offers a choice of cakes and pastries. There are plenty of seats, but these restaurants do get busy at lunchtime, especially on the weekend, although chances are you will be able to find a free table among the knickknacks and curios on display and get to try some of their acclaimed food. The English menu has many one-dish choices from just 35B, such as prawns in chili sauce or chicken with holy basil, 10 different types of fried rice, and a wide choice of larger meals featuring curries, tom yam, and the intriguing fried Chinese kale with shellfish sausage. There are 16 coffees and eight types of tea to choose from, along with fresh fruit juices and ice cream or desserts from the Ligor Bakery to finish. The khao gluk gapee (fried rice with shrimp paste) is just right for a light lunch, with a glass of the wonderfully sweet nam makaam (tamarind juice) on the side. There is also a Hao Coffee at Bavorn Bazaar, but they have no English menu. Neither location has English-speaking staff.

Set centrally in a large open-air sala at Bavorn Bazaar is **Krua Nakhon** (Bavorn Bazaar, off Ratchadamnoen Rd. near Thawang Junction, no phone, 6:30 A.M.–2 P.M. daily, 25–100B), well known for the southern specialty kanom chin—a type of thin rice noodle served with dishes of fish curry, kaeng tai pla (fish-stomach curry), and vegetables. This is available in a small size for 1–2 people for 180B, or in a large size for five or more people for 250B. Also available are a selection of premade curries on rice for just 25B, and khao yam—another local dish of fried rice mixed with herbs, lemongrass, and pomelo. There's no menu, and English isn't spoken, so this really is a "choose and point" restaurant. A small shop at the back of the restaurant sells a small selection of local handicrafts and sweets, and the whole place is decorated with old farming and cooking implements, including a rather naughtily shaped coconut grinder.

Out toward Wat Mahathat you can find the spotlessly clean **Vegetarian Food** (496 Ratchadamnoen Rd., on the left about 300 meters before the Provincial Court, 7:30 A.M.–4 P.M. daily, 40–80B) restaurant and store. Each day there are a choice of around 12 premade vegetarian stir-fries and curries, along with a selection of meat-free sausages and cutlets as side dishes. Everything here is free of animal products, so the curries are made with tofu or textured vegetable protein (TVP), and even the fish sauce contains absolutely no fish. Everything used to prepare the food is for sale, and each table has a price list in English of the TVP products for sale including fish balls, sausages, pig intestines, mock duck, and many others. There's no menu, and though the owner speaks English, the staff do not. They will provide a larger helping of food, however, for a few extra baht if you let them know you're hungry.

If you only go to one restaurant in Nakhon Si Thammarat, this is the one. Within walking distance of Wat Mahathat is the specialty **C Khanom Chin Meuang Nakhon** (23 Soi Panyum, left off Ratchadamnoen Rd. about 500 meters before the temple, tel. 07/534-2615, 7:30 A.M.–3:30 P.M. daily, 25B), which serves mountains of freshly made kanom chin every day. There are a few premade curries named in English available, but the kanom chin is a bargain at just 50B for a set meal for two, or 100B for a meal for four. For the money, you'll get a basket of *kanom chin,* light fish curries with and without coconut milk, a sweet curry with tamarind and peanuts, a plate of local herbs with cucumber salad, fried morning glory, and pickled cabbage with bean sprouts on the side. Get a dish of the *kaeng tai pla* (fish-stomach curry) as well and experiment a little—add a little fish curry to your *kanom chin,* maybe a few spoonfuls of *kaeng tai pla,* tear up a few herbs, add some bean sprouts, mix it all up with some cucumber salad, and enjoy. It's the perfect place to come for lunch when visiting Wat Mahathat, especially if you finish with some *kanom jak* (shredded coconut with sugar wrapped in long thin palm leaves and slow grilled until it all caramelizes) from the stalls offering sweets outside.

In the area where most of the places to stay are situated, **Krua Thaley** (1204/29–30 Pak Nakhon Rd., opposite VDO Town video, next to Nakhon Garden Inn, tel. 07/534-6724 or 07/531-7180, 4–10 P.M. daily, 50–250B) is locally recommended for its choice and quality of seafood. The mussels, crabs, prawns, oysters, clams, and fish are all on display, but in the kitchen they're transformed into dishes such as green mussels with hot and fragrant herb salad and steamed butterfish with Chinese plum sauce. The English menu has some cheaper simple Thai food too, but there's a good chance there will be something in the pages of seafood offerings that will appeal. If not, every day there are also 12 specials on the board in Thai, though the owner may need to translate these as the staff do not speak English. The front of the restaurant is decorated with Buddha images, antiques, and collectibles and has a very "old Thai" feel to it, whereas the back room is a little farther from the road, and the trees and plants make for a different atmosphere. Recommendations here are the *tom yam kung* and the southern specialty *kaeng som pla grapong* (orange curry with flakey whitefish).

Around the area in front of the railroad station, the **Lang Dao Night Market** (Yommarat Rd., 4:30–9:30 P.M. daily) has many stalls selling fresh fruit and cheap packet food for a few baht, but this is really the place to come for some proper local food. Pots of steaming curries almost line the road in places, and you can sit and eat a bowlful with rice for just 25B. It's definitely a place to experiment. Noodle stalls and *khao man kai* (chicken and rice) are easy to find, but do look out for the stall selling *hoi thot* (deep-fried shellfish wrapped in egg) for something a bit different. Walking food comes by way of *luk chin* stalls selling skewered fish balls, crab sticks, tofu, quail eggs in batter, and others that are grilled or deep-fried, depending on the stall, then drowned in a bag of spicy chili sauce. For dessert, try the exotic fruit in sickly sweet syrup, or the *bpatong goh* (deep-fried batter), maybe washed down with a bag of sugarcane juice. It's a great place to see what takes your fancy, but if you need to know exactly what you're eating, it's unlikely you'll find many people able to explain in English.

Getting There

The easiest and fastest way to get to the city is to fly from Bangkok, and there are a couple of carriers that have direct flights at least once per day. If you're going by land, the city is about 800 kilometers south of Bangkok, so expect a long ride. By bus, it's about 12 hours from Bangkok, and there are frequent buses, including an overnight bus that leaves from the Southern Bus Terminal in the early evening. Another option is to take the train from Bangkok's Hua Lamphong Station; there are a couple of direct trains that take a little over 14 hours.

◖ KHANOM AND SICHON
ขนอม-สิชล

If you're in the area to enjoy the beaches, these two towns in the northern part of the province are where you want to be. Here you'll find kilometers of beautiful sandy beaches fringed with palm trees and surrounded by mangrove forests and occasional limestone cliffs. If you want to experience the country's physical beauty and feel like you're in a foreign country while you're doing it, this area is unrivaled. In fact, you'll hear from a lot of

river near the coast of Sichon

people that this is one of Thailand's undiscovered gems. The truth is, development is happening, just at a very slow pace. You won't find lots of resorts or tourist diversions compared to Samui, Phuket, or Krabi, but there are a handful of places to stay. You also won't find discos, go-go bars, or much evidence of the sex industry. Although the beaches of Khanom and Sichon are adjacent to each other, for now you cannot go directly from one to the other on a paved path, as there is no road connecting them near the coast. From Khanom to Sichon (or vice versa) you'll have to get out onto the main highway and circle around, which takes about 45 minutes.

Beaches

Starting from Khanom at the northernmost part of the region, the first beach to visit is **Hat Na Dan,** a long stretch of clean, clear beach. Khanom's eastern border is the Gulf of Thailand, and unlike most of the coastline in the region, this beach is undisturbed by many promontories or cliffs. Although the area is referred to as **Khanom Bay,** most of the coastline isn't curved; it's just one long stretch of sea and sand for kilometers. This is the area's most popular beach, and it can get a little busy during weekends or holidays, although the crowds are nothing like you'll see in Samui.

At the bottom of Hat Na Dan is a small bay where you'll find **Hat Nai Pret** and then, separated by a grouping of boulders, **Hat Nai Phlao.** The gently curving coastline is what makes these beaches so attractive. To add to the charm, just around the beach are coconut plantations. The shore is rocky, though, so it's not the greatest place for swimming.

Just south of Hat Nai Phlao are **Ao Thong Yi** and **Ao Thong Yang,** two small secluded bays with excellent beaches for swimming, snorkeling, or just lying around and reading a novel. Ao Thong Yi has some coral just off the coast that's easy to view by swimming out. These beaches are quite isolated and a great place to go if you're looking for a bit of the desert-island feeling without having to trek out for kilometers. You'll be able to reach Ao Thong Yi from

© SUZANNE NAM

a beach in Khanom

Hat Nai Phlao, but because of some mountains in the way, to get to Ao Thong Yang you can either travel by boat from Hat Nai Phlao or by road from Sichon in the south.

In Sichon, a small coastal town on the way to Nakhon Si Thammarat, there are a few beaches worth visiting—**Sichon Beach, Hat Hin Ngam,** and **Hat Piti.** Hat Sichon and Hat Hin Ngam are beautiful and quiet, but there are lots of rocks on the shore, especially in Hat Hin Ngam. Hat Piti (also called Hat Ko Khao) has a smooth, sandy coast and also a few restaurants and resorts. Both Hat Nin Ngam and Hat Piti can be reached easily from Hat Sichon using the small service road that follows the coast.

Accommodations

There's not much in the way of five-star luxury in Sichon and Khanom since the area is still largely unknown by foreign visitors. There are a handful of modest, simple bungalows and small resorts that offer enough amenities and comfort for most travelers.

The basic white wooden bungalows at **Krua Poy Beach Resort** (625 Mu 3, Hin Ngam Beach, Sichon, tel. 07/553-6055, www.kruapoybeachresort.com, 550B) are clean and air-conditioned and even have simple private baths. The small resort fronts a beautiful stretch of beach, and the young manager, Palm, whose family has owned the resort for decades, also gives windsurfing lessons. There is a nice open-air restaurant on the beach and plenty of chairs to lounge on if you're not windsurfing with Palm.

Next door, **Prasarnsook Villas** (Hin Ngam Beach, Sichon, tel. 07/553-6299, www.prasarnsookresort.com, 1,500B) is owned by the grandmother of the family, and the villas, which opened in 2008, are very nicely designed, spacious stand-alone structures with modern baths and small outdoor verandas. Depending on your budget, either choice is a great value for the money. Visitors here are mostly urban Thais on vacation, but staff speak English and are happy to accommodate foreign guests.

© SUZANNE NAM

Krua Poy Beach Resort in Sichon

The **Ekman Garden Resort** (39/2 Mu 5, Tumble Saopao, tel. 07/536-7566, www.ekmangarden.com, 1,200B) is a small family-run resort with clean, basic guest rooms and bungalows, a swimming pool, and a good location on the beach in Sichon. The sunny guest rooms are not luxurious, but they are well-decorated, if simple, and have air-conditioning, comfortable beds, and modern baths. The wooden buildings and thatched roof give the resort a relaxed, unpretentious feeling, and it's family-friendly as well.

Set on a beautiful open stretch of coast is the **Khanom Golden Beach Hotel** (59/3 Mu 4, Nadan Beach, www.khanomgoldenbeach.com, tel. 07/532-6688, 1,200B). This large modern hotel is a great choice if you want hotel amenities (in fact, it's the only hotel in the area), and the guest rooms are clean and well maintained though not particularly interesting. There is also a nice beach bar and a swimming pool. This property tends to attract families, and there are plenty of little kids at the beach and pool.

The **Piti Resort** (Hat Piti, tel. 07/533-5301, 1,500B) is another clean, simple resort right on the beach in Sichon. The guest rooms feel a little more modern and less traditional but still have a basic budget feeling you'd expect for the price and considering the location. The resort also has a small swimming pool and a good inexpensive restaurant with lots of local dishes.

Khanom Hill Resort (60/1 Mu 8, Khanom Beach, tel. 07/552-9403, www.khanom.info, 2,500B) is set on a hill overlooking Khanom Beach, with bungalows and guest rooms dotting the hillside. The guest rooms vary from simple and clean to beautifully decorated with modern Thai touches and nicer-than-usual baths, depending on the rate. The newest guest rooms, which are across the road from the beach, are the nicest, and there's a small swimming pool on that side, but the older guest rooms have a better view of the water. There is direct beach access and a nice restaurant overlooking the water that serves Thai and Western food. Staff and management are friendly and helpful.

Aava Resort & Spa (28/3 Mu 6, Nadan Beach, tel. 07/530-0310, www.aavaresort.com, 2,500B), which opened in 2010, is the area's nicest resort. The minimalist Thai design and massive swimming pool seem almost out of place in otherwise sleepy Khanom, but those who enjoy flashpacking and off-the-beaten-path beaches will love it (as do, it appears, the Finnish, who seem to be most of the guests). The resort is set right on the beach, and there are a couple of high-end restaurants serving Thai and Western food.

Food

There is very limited food in the area, but all of the resorts and bungalows listed above have restaurants serving fresh, well-prepared Thai food, and all also have outdoor areas with beach views to enjoy your meals.

Halfway along the Nadan Beach Road, you will find **Taalkoo Beach Resort and Restaurant** (23/9 Mu 2, Nadan Beach, just south of Golden Beach Resort, tel. 07/552-8218, 7 A.M.–10 P.M., jantima_manajit@yahoo.com, 60–150B) right on the beach surrounded by its 42 bungalows. Sit inside on the heavy gnarled wooden chairs, or head for the veranda in the afternoon after the sun has passed behind the trees and sit with a clear view of the long, empty beach. The English menu is quite small, but the usual Thai stir-fries, *tom yam,* and curries are secondary to the choice of "by-weight" fresh fish and seafood. The fresh fish sold in this restaurant has a good reputation locally; the *yam takrai* (spicy lemongrass salad), *thot man kung* (deep-fried mashed prawns), and *pla lui suan* (fish with cashew nuts and lemongrass) make a great meal for two. The staff generally cannot speak English, but the manager will be able to help.

At the northernmost end of Hat Ko Khao, on the right where the road hits the beach, are 10 **food stalls** (Hat Ko Khao, no phone, 11 A.M.–8 P.M. daily, 50–150B), all serving similar menus based on Isan food and grilled seafood. The food is great with *yam, larb, som tam, tom yam,* and sticky rice, but it's really the low-key atmosphere that appeals here.

Small bamboo-roofed *salas* that look like they should've blown away years ago sit above the beach covering concrete seats or haphazard wooden benches, while a dilapidated jukebox plays Thai music at an unreasonably loud volume just far enough away so you don't really care. Get a bucket of ice and a bottle of something appropriate to pour over it, get a plate of the excellent *namtok mu* (marinated grilled pork salad with ground chilies) to start with, and prepare yourself for a slow afternoon grazing the menus—which will all be in Thai, and it's unlikely anyone will speak much English, but if you're not sure, just point.

Another Thai experience can be had at the Music Kitchen, or **Krua Dondtree** (Talaad Seeyaek, Khanom, tel. 08/6952-7835, 11 A.M.–11 P.M., 40–80B), where Isan food meets with country-and-western and 1970s easy-listening music. It's on the right about one kilometer north out of Khanom Town; look for the green-fronted *sala* 500 meters after the Honda dealer. There may not be many places in Thailand where you can eat your *som tam* accompanied by "Puff the Magic Dragon" or "Tie a Yellow Ribbon," but this is definitely one of them. As well as *som tam, larb mu,* and *larb pla duk,* numerous kinds of *yam, namtok mu, tom yam kung,* and grilled meat and seafood, there is a daily specials board with another five dishes to supplement the small two-page menu. The specials are not in English, however, and the owner does not speak English, so it might be easiest to ask for her most popular meal: *yam pak grut* (spicy local-vegetable salad) with *larb pet* (duck *larb*), another combination you're unlikely to see in many places.

The last restaurant on the beach road before Piti Resort is **Sichon Seafood** (Beach Rd., Hat Sichon, tel. 08/9586-9402, 7:30 A.M.–10 P.M. daily, 80–250B), offering the basic Thai fare of curries, stir-fries, and *yam,* but specializing in seafood dishes such as grilled lobster, crab with plum sauce, and deep-fried sea bass with mango salad, which comes highly recommended. The open-air *sala* has a cozy feel with aged-wood tables, and a veranda projects over the rocky beach while remaining shaded from the afternoon sun. It's a nice place for a long, relaxed evening meal, possibly taking advantage of the wide range of local spirits on offer at the bar. Menus are in English, and a little English is spoken.

Positioned fairly centrally on Hat Hin Ngam is the **Prasarnsook Resort** (625/4 Hin Ngam Beach, tel. 07/553-6299 or 07/533-5601, 6:30 A.M.–9:30 P.M. daily, www.prasarnsookresort.com, 50–250B), a fairly standard resort-based restaurant set in pleasant cultivated gardens and immediately overlooking the sea. The extensive menu runs from breakfasts, with a choice of Thai food, through more Western-oriented Thai food with cream or wine sauces, with fresh seafood being the most expensive of the options. That said, there are lots of choices around 80B. There are also five specials, in Thai only, on the otherwise English menu, but the restaurant manager will be able to explain them to you. The *kung gati jaan rorn* (prawns in coconut milk) is definitely worth a try, especially if you don't like your food too spicy. There's the choice of eating in the large, impressive *sala* or at one of the small tables on the beach itself.

Raan Nong Wee (Hin Ngam Beach, tel. 08/9287-1522, 10 A.M.–7 P.M. daily, 30–100B) is at the southern end of Hat Hin Ngam just before the Isra Beach Resort (turn left at the bottom of the only small *soi* off the Beach Road down to Hat Hin Ngam). It is a place well worth hunting out. You can eat in the small *sala* in front of the owner's house, but it's more enjoyable to sit on a mat on the beach under the trees with a cold beer and a few choice plates of Isan food. There is a only a Thai menu, and don't expect any English to be spoken, but all of the essentials are here— *som tam,* different kinds of *larb,* many different *yam* spicy salads, sticky rice, deep-fried fish cakes, grilled fish and other seafood, fried rice, and simple stir-fries. It's so cheap and delicious that you can get a selection of dishes, and then grab a table and get to chatting with the locals. A good choice for two people would be *som tam pla rah* (papaya salad), *yam wun sen pla muek* (spicy salad of squid and glass noodles),

thot man pla (deep-fried fish cakes) and *pla duk yahng* (grilled catfish). Add a couple of Chang beers to keep the chilies under control.

Back in Sichon Town on the way to the main highway, opposite the police station, the **Kotone Restaurant** (6/1 Talaad Sichon, tel. 07/553-6259 or 07/553-5242, 7 A.M.–9 P.M. daily, 35–150B) comes highly recommended by local people. A 15-page English menu gives ample choice among one-dish Thai food such as curries on rice and stir-fries for just 35B, soups, spicy *yam* salads, and other Isan food, along with southern curries such as *kaeng som pla* (orange curry with fish) and Massaman curry, lots of pork dishes that are the general specialty of this restaurant, and, of course, fresh local fish, crabs, and prawns. The particular specialty here is *khao mu kotone*—leg of pork cooked in the three-flavor "sweet, sour, and salt" style. Well-served tables are available outside on a decked area, inside at street level, or in an air-conditioned room on the upper floor, and the duty manager will help if your waitress doesn't speak English. Not surprisingly, this restaurant is so popular they have opened another one on the main highway, about two kilometers toward Khanom, called **Kotone Restaurant 2.**

Getting There

Sichon and Khanom are between Surat Thani and Nakhon Si Thammarat, and you can take a plane, car, bus, or train to either city and then make your way to your final destination. The cheapest and easiest way is to get to the bus station in Surat Thani or Nakhon Si Thammarat and take a bus for less than 100B. There are frequent buses (at least hourly 8 A.M.–6 P.M. daily) to Sichon and Khanom from both Surat Thani and Nakhon Si Thammarat. If you're driving, Sichon and Khanom are both off Highway 401, which you can access from either Surat Thani or Nakhon Si Thammarat.

KHAO LUANG NATIONAL PARK
อุทยานแห่งชาติเขาหลวง

This national park is named for Khao Luang mountain, at nearly 1,830 meters the highest mountain in southern Thailand. You can hike to the summit and back in two days if you hike 7–8 hours per day. You can also do the hike over three days and include a stay in **Kiriwong Village** (tel. 07/530-9010, 05/394-8286, or 08/1642-0081), which includes basic accommodations in the village and meals, for 1,500B per person. The views from the peak are spectacular—you'll be able to see the tropical cloud forest and the rest of the mountain range from above. The park is also home to more than 300 species of wild orchids, some of which aren't found anywhere else in the world. But this inland park is best known for its waterfalls, and there are 10 major falls in the 570-square-kilometer national park. The Krung Ching waterfall is one of the most spectacular, and there's also a nearby ranger substation and visitors center you can drive to, and then walk to the waterfall, just a few minutes away. To get here, take Route 4016 from Nakhon Si Thammarat until you reach the junction with Route 4140. Turn left onto 4140 until you reach Ban Rong Lek, where you'll turn right onto Route 4186 to Route 4188. Turn left on this road, and you'll find a sign for the visitors center after about six kilometers.

If you're interested in staying in the park, there are bungalows for rent and campgrounds where you can pitch a tent. You must reserve accommodations in advance; check the park's website (www.dnp.go.th) for details.

For a real off-the-beaten-path experience, you can also base yourself in one of the neighboring villages. Kiriwong Village, at the base of Khao Luang in the southern part of the park, is not technically in the park but has become something of an ecotourism destination, and for good reason. The village's primary industry is growing fruit, but instead of clearing forests, the villagers have interspersed their mangosteen, jackfruit, and durian trees within the natural ecosystem. You can tour their organic *suam somron* garden or arrange a homestay with one of the village families. They've been taking in visitors from all over the world for years, so although you won't be in luxurious surroundings, you'll be comfortable, well taken care of, and get a chance to get to know some of the villagers. The **Thailand Community Based Tourism Institute** (tel. 07/530-9010, 05/394-8286, or 08/1642-0081) is a not-for-profit organization that arranges homestays and tours of the area as well as to other places in the region, many of which are once-in-a-lifetime opportunities.

Getting There

If you're driving to the park's main headquarters, take Route 4015 from Nakhon Si Thammarat for about 24 kilometers to Lanksaka. Just past the town, you'll see a turnoff for the park headquarters.

You can also take a *song thaew* from Nakhon Si Thammarat that stops right after the turnoff on Route 4015.

Songkhla Province   จังหวัดสงขลา

Just north of the three southernmost provinces in Thailand, Songkhla Province is bordered on the east by the Gulf of Thailand and on the west by the state of Kedah in Malaysia. It was part of the Srivijaya Empire, then came under the rule of neighboring Nakhon Si Thammarat. It's in this part of the country that you'll feel the dominance of Buddhism give way to Islam, as evidenced in the mosques and attire of many of the people living in the province. Many people in Songkhla Province speak Yawi as their primary language instead of Thai, and although it may be difficult to discern, the Thai speakers here have a markedly different accent from their compatriots up north.

SONGKHLA
สงขลา

Bordered to the west by the large **Tha Le Sap Songkhla** lake and to the east by the Gulf of Thailand, the coastal city of Songkhla is surrounded by magnificent physical scenery.

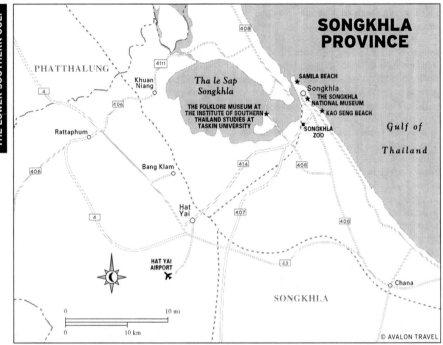

Thanks to its location, it was once a thriving port city attracting merchants from Persia, the Arabian Peninsula, and India. Nowadays it's considerably sleepier, although you'll still find a thriving fishing industry and remnants from its trading past in the city's Sino-Portuguese architecture. This small city offers a great opportunity to observe urban life in Thailand and learn a bit about the culture and history of the southern region as well.

Sights

The city's old quarter, centered around Nang Ngam Road, has a collection of historic buildings and small shops selling everything from snacks to religious wares for monks. Although not vast, it's a nice area to wander around for a while.

The **Songkhla Zoo** (189 Mu 5, tel. 07/433-6268, 8 A.M.–6 P.M. daily, 50B adults, 30B children) covers more than 140 hectares in the

hills just outside of the city limits—it's almost necessary to rent a motorcycle to see the whole thing. Inside the confines you'll find a typical selection of animals that includes tigers, camels, primates, and bird species. This public zoo is also a breeding center for endangered tapirs—large mammals that look like a cross between a rhinoceros and an anteater. In addition to visiting the animals, you'll get a great view of the city from above.

The **Folklore Museum at the Institute of Southern Thailand Studies at Taksin University** (Ko Yo Hill, 9 A.M.–4 P.M. Tues.–Fri., donation) has a wide collection of materials and exhibits on the culture of southern Thais. There are some exhibits on the history of the area in the museum, but the most interesting things to see are the exhibits relating to the everyday life of the people in this part of the country, featuring local art and handicrafts, shadow puppetry, and traditional medicines.

The museum is worth visiting just for its location: It's on the small Yo Island on Songkhla lake, one of the country's largest natural lakes, and the grounds are filled with local plants.

Housed in a sweeping Chinese-style mansion originally built by the deputy governor of Songkhla in 1878, **The Songkhla National Museum** (Vichianchom Rd., Bo Yang, tel. 07/431-1728, 9 A.M.–4 P.M. Wed.–Sun., 30B) now displays a large collection of art and artifacts from the region from prehistoric times to the present. The small collection of prehistoric artifacts includes terra-cotta, pottery, and small beads. The Srivijayan collection has both Buddhist and Hindu art and illustrates the transition the kingdom made from one religion to another. The Dvaravati Buddhist art section has some beautiful examples of 16th–17th-century Buddhist imagery from the Nakhon Si Thammarat School of Art. In addition to the art based on the cultures of the region, the museum also houses a large collection of art from China along with some pieces (mostly ceramics) from Vietnam, Japan, and Europe, illustrating the region's former importance as a trading port.

Accommodations

As in the rest of the region, the accommodations in Songkhla aren't up to international standards. There are some large, generic hotels in the city with basic accommodations but no character, and just a couple of resorts on the water. As the area's charms and attractions become better known, this might change, but for now it's a challenge to find good places to stay in the city and environs.

The **Hat Kaew Resort** (163/1 Km. 5, Ching Ko, Singhanakhon, tel. 07/433-1058-66, 1,200B) on Samila Beach is a large property with clean, comfortable guest rooms, a large swimming pool, and well-maintained grounds. If you're not looking for a five-star experience, this property will be more than adequate. The resort isn't full of local character, however—beige and floral prints seem to dominate the decor. It's also a popular place for conventions, thanks to the large banquet hall and meeting areas.

The **Pavilion Songkhla Hotel** (17 Palatha Rd., tel. 07/444-1850, www.pavilionhotels.com, 1,200B) is another large, generic hotel in the city. It's often bustling with organized tours, and the tour buses can be a little off-putting. But it is inexpensive and right in the city if you're looking for a place to stay while you set out to explore Songkhla.

Food

Coffee Peak (95/5 Somrong Junction, Songkhla–Natave Rd., tel. 07/431-4682, 11 A.M.–9 P.M. daily, 100B) is a casual restaurant with a small outdoor seating area in town. In addition to coffee, the menu also offers a nice combination of Thai food and international dishes. This is not a restaurant that tries to please Western palates: International dishes are geared toward Thai tastes, so some items may not taste as you would expect them to, so it's best to stick with the Thai dishes and the delicious desserts.

Another great place for Thai food and coffee is **Crown Bakery** (38/1 Tai Ngam Rd., tel. 07/444-1305, 11 A.M.–8 P.M. daily, 100B). The atmosphere is casual but is much more upscale than your typical noodle shop or shophouse eatery. The menu has typical Thai and Chinese-Thai dishes—there's no standout here, but everything is well prepared, and the atmosphere is nice.

If you don't mind trading atmosphere for taste, **Pajit Restaurant** (1/25 Saiburi Rd., tel. 07/432-1710, 11 A.M.–8 P.M. daily, 40B) has excellent *guay teow* (traditional noodle soup). This is a typical shophouse with outdoor seating, mismatched dishes, and toilet-paper rolls for napkins—a very casual, inexpensive place for a quick meal.

For some Isan fare, stop at **Deeplee's** (211 Nakornnai Rd., tel. 08/9463-3874, 11 A.M.–10 P.M. daily, 80B). You'll find *som tam, kai yang* (grilled chicken with smoky, spicy sauce), and sticky rice. The atmosphere is very local and casual, making it another great place for a quick, inexpensive meal. Another Isan restaurant, **Rotsab** (39/11 Mu 1, Pawong, tel. 07/433-4602, 11 A.M.–9 P.M. daily, 100B), offers similar dishes but is a little larger and fancier. This spot is very popular with families and large groups in the evening.

Getting There

To get to Songkhla by rail or air, you'll have to arrive in neighboring Hat Yai and make your way the 30-something kilometers to Songkhla either by bus (there are numerous daily buses between the cities) or by car. If you're taking the bus from Hat Yai, make your way to the city's main bus terminal to get to Songkhla.

HAT YAI
หาดใหญ่

Until the construction of a railroad line linking Thailand with Malaysia in the 20th century, Hat Yai was just a small village with nothing particularly special going on. When the railroad station came, the city seemed to develop around it, and while Songkhla is the provincial capital, neighboring Hat Yai has become the economic hub of the area and is a much more bustling, urban, industrialized city. If you spend time in Hat Yai, you might thing that Songkhla got the better end of the deal, and that's probably an accurate assessment. Some southern Thais half-jokingly refer to Hat Yai as the ugliest city in Thailand. It's not so much the concrete buildings, traffic, and generic urban feeling in Hat Yai that makes it unappealing, but the seedy feeling the city seems to have. There's a lot of neon and plenty of nightclubs, and it's a big spot for visitors from neighboring countries. Unfortunately, it seems like most people are visiting the city as sex tourists. In Hat Yai there's no ambiguity about what's going on—you'll see plenty of massage parlors, strip clubs, and bordellos, and also plenty of people frequenting them. Use Hat Yai as a transit hub (since it's the southernmost airport currently connected to Bangkok) and spend your time in the regions outside of the city.

Sights

Just on the edge of Hat Yai is **Samila Beach,** a surprisingly quiet and uncrowded stretch of coast given its proximity to the center of the city (you can easily walk there from the main market in about 20 minutes). The water is shallow and fine for swimming, although you won't see many people swimming here, and it's not as beautiful as some of the beaches you'll find in Sichon and Khanom to the north. You'll also find Hat Yai's unofficial symbol on Samila Beach—a large sculpture of the Hindu goddess Mae Thorani as a mermaid.

About three kilometers south of Samila Beach is **Khao Seng Beach.** Like its neighbor, Khao Seng is relaxed and uncrowded. The shoreline has some very large rocks, one of which is said to have treasure buried beneath it. As the legend goes, a wealthy merchant was bringing some treasure to a *wat* in Nakhon Si Thammarat but had to stop on Khao Seng Beach. He left the treasure here under a large rock and promised that anyone who could move the rock would get the treasure. The Muslim fisherfolk at Kao Seng village ply the waters with colorfully painted Kolae boats, which you'll be able to see if you're at the beach.

Accommodations and Food

Selection is bleak in Hat Yai. If you've arrived late and need to spend the night before heading out, you'll have to choose among sometimes dicey-looking small hotels, guesthouses, and mediocre large hotels.

Laem Thong Hotel (46 Thamnoonvitti Rd., tel. 07/435-2301, 500B) isn't really stylish or modern, but it's well located in the city and doesn't seem to have too much brothel activity going on in the area. Guest rooms look like they haven't been updated in decades (nor has the lobby), but they do look like they were cleaned this morning. Another inexpensive guesthouse is **Cathay Guesthouse** (93/1 Niphat U-Thit 2 Rd., tel. 07/424-3815, 300B). Cathay is a longtime favorite of backpackers, so if you're craving some conversation in a language you're fluent in, you'll definitely find it at the hotel's downstairs café-restaurant.

There's also plenty of tourist information available here. Guest rooms are pretty shabby, but you can't really complain for the price. The only drawback, which may be a showstopper for some, is the squat toilets.

The most reliable and nicest hotel in the city is the **Hotel Novotel Hat Yai Centara** (3 Sanehanusorn Rd., tel. 07/435-2222, 2,000B). You'll welcome the slightly generic, very clean guest rooms with crisp sheets and modern baths compared to the musty digs in the other large hotels in this area. The hotel also has a pool, a fitness center, and a good restaurant.

Getting There

Hat Yai is well served by an international airport with flights from Malaysia and Singapore as well as Bangkok, a large train station, and buses from Bangkok's Southern Bus Terminal as well as surrounding localities. If you're planning to fly from Bangkok, Air Asia, Nok Air, and Thai Airways all have direct flights to Hat Yai. The train station is one of the largest in the region, and there are five daily trains from Bangkok as well as daily trains from Butterworth in Malaysia if you happen to be coming from the south.

THE ANDAMAN COAST

If paradise were a place on earth, it would be somewhere on the Andaman coast of Thailand. The region is astoundingly beautiful—bright, clear, warm water teeming with wildlife from tropical fish to magnificent coral, even occasional sea cows and reef sharks (the kind that don't eat people). The coast and islands have sandy beaches, and there are hundreds of small islands and limestone rock formations rising up out of the ocean to stay on, dive around, or just gaze out to at sunset. Inland, there are tropical rainforests, mangrove swamps, mountains, and waterfalls. If it's an active vacation you're looking for, there are abundant opportunities to snorkel, dive, sea kayak, or hike, especially in the numerous national parks.

But it's not just the physical beauty and activities that make the area such a great traveling experience. The region still offers a chance to glimpse rural and small-city life in Thailand. While Phuket has attracted residents from all over the world as well as transplants from Bangkok and other parts of the country, and largely feels like a commercialized tourist destination, if you travel north to Phang Nga Province, you'll find small fishing villages along the coast where fishing families can often be found clearing nets at the end of the day or setting out squid to dry in the sun. To the south, in Satun, you'll find a largely Muslim population and a fascinating blend of Islam and Buddhism evidenced in the houses of worship and the dress of the local people.

In the past few decades, Phuket has really blossomed into a world-class destination for

© MING THIEN

HIGHLIGHTS

Surin Beach: This beautiful beach on the northwest coast of Phuket is quiet and relaxed but still offers plenty to do and great accommodations options (page 69).

Kata Yai and Kata Noi Beaches: These two beaches on the southwest coast of Phuket have clean, white sand and beautiful views, without the big crowds (page 71).

Rai Le Beach: Dramatic limestone cliffs along with warm, clear, emerald-colored water and plenty of outdoor activities make the beach on the west side of Rai Le in Krabi perhaps Thailand's best beach destination (page 103).

Ton Sai Bay: This is the most popular area of Ko Phi Phi, and even with the crowds of day-trippers, the scenery of the little island is amazing, as are the diving and snorkeling options surrounding it (page 110).

Khlong Dao Beach, Ko Lanta: This beach is beautiful and quiet, and it has just enough amenities and accommodations choices, with none of the overcrowding found at some of the more popular island destinations (page 118).

Ko Kradan: Arguably the prettiest island in Trang, Ko Kradan offers amazing views of neighboring islands and accessible reefs for snorkelers (page 125).

LOOK FOR **(** TO FIND RECOMMENDED SIGHTS, ACTIVITIES, DINING, AND LODGING.

vacationers from all over the world, with all of the pros and cons that go with it. But traveling either north to Phang Nga or south to Krabi and Trang, things slow down again, although even in Trang there are more and more bungalows, resorts, and hotels for visitors being built every year. Though many travelers go to one spot on the Andaman and plant themselves there for the duration, if you want to both indulge and explore, it's an easy place to be a little more adventurous. Public and private buses can take you from Phuket or Krabi either north or south along the coast, and if you rent a car, you'll find the highway system exceptionally

well maintained and generally navigable, even if you can't read a word of Thai.

The Andaman coast is also perfect for island-hopping, and the best way to do that is by boat. There are plenty of ferries, speedboats, and longtails to take you from island to island and beach to beach. You can fly into Phuket, spend a few days on one of the nearby beaches, then take a boat to Phi Phi, Ko Lanta, or one of the other numerous islands in Phang Nga Bay, or hit 3–4 islands in one trip; there are hundreds of islands in the region to choose from. Some, such as Phi Phi, are arguably overpopulated with travelers and resorts. But there are

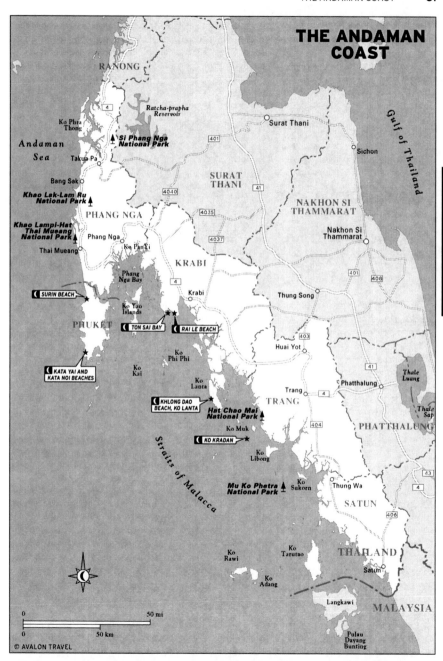

THE ANDAMAN COAST

RANONG

Ratcha-prapha Reservoir

Ko Phra Thong

▲ Si Phang Nga National Park

Andaman Sea

Takua Pa

Surat Thani

Sichon

Bang Sak

SURAT THANI

Khao Lak-Lam Ru National Park ▲

PHANG NGA

NAKHON SI THAMMARAT

Khao Lampi-Hat Thai Mueang National Park ▲

Phang Nga

Ko Pan Yi

Nakhon Si Thammarat

Thai Mueang

Phang Nga Bay

KRABI

Krabi

Thung Song

◖ SURIN BEACH ★

Ko Tao Islands

PHUKET

◖ TON SAI BAY ★★ ◖ RAI LE BEACH

Huai Yot

Thale Luang

◖ KATA YAI AND KATA NOI BEACHES ★

Ko Phi Phi

Ko Kai

Phatthalung

Thale Sap

Ko Lanta

◖ KHLONG DAO BEACH, KO LANTA

Hat Chao Mai National Park ▲

Trang

TRANG

PHATTHALUNG

Ko Muk

◖ KO KRADAN ★

Ko Kradan

Ko Libong

Mu Ko Phetra National Park ▲

Ko Sukorn

Thung Wa

SATUN

Straits of Malacca

Ko Rawi

Ko Tarutao

THAILAND

Satun

Ko Adang

MALAYSIA

Langkawi

0   50 mi

0   50 km

Pulau Dayang Bunting

© AVALON TRAVEL

Gulf of Thailand

(route numbers) 4, 401, 41, 4040, 4035, 4037, 403, 404, 406, 43

still some beautiful islands you can stay on that feel less exploited by tourism and kinder to the natural surroundings.

Prices are still amazingly reasonable considering the physical landscape. Even in the most coveted areas, you'll be able to find simple accommodations, sometimes right on the beach, for less than US$40 per night, even cheaper the farther away from Phuket you are. Of course, if you're looking for five-star luxury, you'll be able to find that too. Some of the best resorts in the world have Andaman coast addresses.

PLANNING YOUR TIME

The region is not so much filled with must-sees and must-dos as it is an opportunity to relax on beautiful beaches, explore the stunning physical landscape, enjoy local foods, and pamper yourself in a bit of luxury. You can spend three weeks island-hopping, diving, hiking, and playing golf, or spend just a few days lying on the beach without even touring the neighboring areas, and you'll still have something of value from the region. While it may be tempting to idle your days away in the immediate vicinity of your hotel, if you are on Phuket, make sure to set aside at least one day to explore the surrounding islands by boat. The small islands you'll pass on the way create scenery that's enchanting and like nothing in North America. Off the smaller islands is some of the best scuba and snorkeling in the world. If you've never dived before, Phuket is the place to start. There are numerous dive schools that offer PADI certification, and the courses are inexpensive and a lot of fun. Even if you're not interested in diving, set aside a couple of hours to snorkel above some of the shallow coral reefs.

Phuket is open year-round for visitors, but the best time to go is November–March, when the weather cools off a little and the Andaman Sea is at its calmest. This is peak tourist season, though, so expect lots of other international tourists sharing your beach space with you and enjoying the 30°C temperatures. Also, expect to pay more for accommodations. All prices listed in this chapter are based on peak

season, but in the two-week period starting before Christmas and ending after the first of the year, most hotels and guesthouses will tack on an additional 20 percent or more above peak prices. Even with the higher prices, the choicest places will often be booked full months in advance of this season. If you are in the area during Christmas or New Year, many resorts will also require that you pay for a compulsory holiday dinner.

May–October is the rainy season, and while it rains often, the showers generally end quickly. If you can tolerate getting a little wet, it can be pleasantly cool, the island is a little quieter, and prices can be half of peak-season prices. If you like to surf, it's the best time to go, as the waves can be quite dramatic. If you are there primarily to dive and snorkel, however, stick with the high season, when visibility is at its best.

If you choose to explore some of Phuket's surrounding islands, remember that getting from one place to another can often take a few hours and involve taking land transportation to a pier and then a sometimes-long boat ride, especially if you are relying on public transportation. Many tour operators offer day trips to surrounding islands, and these can be an excellent way to see many different places at once, although you won't have any control over the schedule or itinerary. If you really want to explore each island (or stay overnight), your best bet is to take one of the large ferry boats from Phuket to Ko Phi Phi, Ko Lanta, or Krabi and then use the smaller longtail boats to take you to other islands in the vicinity. Some people prefer to base themselves on one of the more built-up islands (Ko Lanta or Ko Phi Phi) and explore the surrounding islands on day trips, but it's just as easy to sleep on different islands or even camp at one of the island national parks. If you plan on island-hopping, make sure to pack light. Longtail boats, which are colorful wooden boats used for short trips, are small, usually not covered, and sometimes a little leaky. There's no room for a large suitcase or even a very large backpack. It is also possible to charter a sailboat or speedboat to island-hop, but the cost is in the thousands of dollars for a multiday trip.

If you've come to the region primarily to dive, you'll actually find it much easier to get around, as there are numerous large dive boats offering live-aboard, multiday dive trips that will take you to some of the best diving sites in the country. Trips generally depart from Phuket, Krabi, and Khao Lak.

HISTORY

During prehistoric times, Phuket was inhabited by indigenous people sometimes referred to as Negritos, a group of hunter-gatherer pygmies who were, like many indigenous Southeast Asians, displaced and assimilated during waves of successive migration. Although no clear records exist, the last of the pygmy tribes was probably wiped out in the 19th century.

Although Phuket, then called Jang Si Lang or Junk Ceylon, shows up in some of Ptolemy's maps and writings, the island's history is largely unknown until about 800 years ago. Phuket's main natural resource, tin, was mined by prehistoric inhabitants, but what is now known as Phuket didn't come to the attention of the Thai people until the 13th century, when they arrived for trading and tin mining.

rubber tapping

Word spread of the abundant natural resources, which included not only tin but also pearls, and by the 15th–16th centuries Talang, as the island was then known, became a popular trading center, attracting the Dutch, Portuguese, and French. While Thailand has never technically been colonized, the Dutch set up trading posts in the region in the 16th century and parts of the island were governed by tin traders under a concession. Phuket was even under the administration of the French between 1681 and 1685.

At the end of the Ayutthaya period, after the Burmese had sacked the capital city and were pushed back by General Taksin, they set their sights on Phuket and the surrounding region, invading the island and trying to take it over in 1785. The island's governor was killed by the intruders, but Phuket did not fall, according to the story told by nearly every islander. The

governor's widow and her sister, both disguised as men, led a force against the siege and succeeded in repelling the Burmese after weeks of fighting. In recognition of their heroism, the two women were granted noble titles by King Rama I, and today there is a statue dedicated to them in the middle of the island.

After that dramatic high point in Phuket's history, the island continued to be used primarily as a tin-mining area, and later for rubber plantations, attracting thousands of Chinese immigrants in the 19th century, many of whom remained and, with the Muslim fisherfolk who immigrated from what is now Malaysia, constitute much of the modern indigenous population.

It wasn't until the 1970s that intrepid foreign travelers "discovered" Phuket's beauty and began to visit the island to enjoy the mountainous rainforests and pristine beaches. Starting with some small bungalow developments on Patong Beach, the island has boomed into a world-class tourist destination over the past three decades. Urban Thais in their 50s and

60s will often laugh and reminisce about what the Andaman coast used to be like before travelers and developers realized it was a natural tourist destination, when they'd head down on motorcycles to the largely untouched island for some adventure. Fast-forward 30 years, and the dirt roads and simple local folks have since been replaced by an exceptionally sophisticated infrastructure with easily navigable roads, hospitals, shopping malls, and an international airport.

Nowadays Phuket's "local" population is not just the Chinese immigrants and Muslim fisherfolk but thousands of Thais who've moved here to open hotels, restaurants, and other tourism-related businesses. The mining industry is virtually gone, but rubber tapping remains one of the island's income generators. The island's identity is tourism, attracting millions of visitors each year and accounting for the majority of the island's revenues.

Phuket   ภูเก็ต

It's no wonder millions of people visit Phuket each year. If you're in the market for the perfect beach vacation and don't mind sharing your space with others, nothing can beat it. The landscape, with its hilly, green, forested interior and clean sandy beaches, is awe-inspiring. The vibes of the beaches and their surrounding areas vary from spring break fun to secluded romantic getaway to family-friendly. The accommodations range from unbelievably cheap to unbelievably luxurious. The tourism infrastructure is solid, and anything you want—perhaps a spur-of-the-moment diving trip, a midday massage on the beach, or a bespoke suit made in 24 hours—is available with no hassle. As if that weren't enough, nearly all of the clean, inviting beaches face west, so picture-perfect sunsets are a given. On an island this popular and this built-up, there are no more absolutely deserted places, but the northern and southern parts of the west coast offer some surprisingly quiet, quaint, and relaxed places to pull up a beach chair and chill out.

Phuket, Thailand's largest island, is about 48 kilometers long and 16 kilometers across. Imagine an elongated star with extra points and you'll have a rough idea of what Phuket looks like from above. The points are promontories, rock formations jutting out into the ocean and separating the island into numerous individual beaches with curving coasts. The road system on the island is very well maintained, and there is both a coastal road that encircles nearly the whole island and large multilane inland roads as well. Off the main island, the Andaman Sea is littered with small islands and elegant rock formations jutting out from the sea. Many of the surrounding islands could be destinations in their own right, if not overshadowed by the main island.

Phuket and the surrounding areas rebuilt quickly after the 2004 tsunami, but the momentum from the redevelopment seems not to have slowed once all of the damage was repaired. There are new resorts and villas popping up in every corner, and more visitors coming every year to stay in those new places. If you want to experience some of what Phuket became famous for, hurry up and come now: Even the most remote beaches and islands will surely become developed in the next few years.

SIGHTS
If you can drag yourself away from the beautiful beaches, the island is actually full of interesting places to see. Aside from sights geared for visiting tourists, Phuket and the surrounding islands are home to some amazing natural sights, including rainforests, mangrove swamps, karst rock formations rising out of the ocean, and marine areas with colorful fish and coral. Since it is a vacation town, there are tons of fun or silly ways to spend your afternoons,

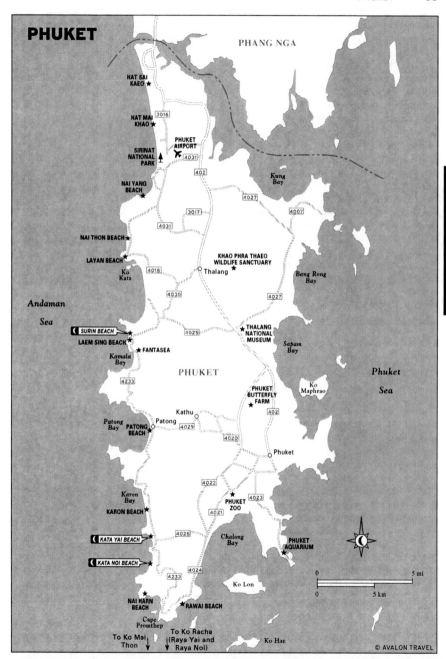

THE ANDAMAN COAST

PHUKET

PHANG NGA

HAT SAI KAEO ★

HAT MAI KHAO ★

3016

PHUKET AIRPORT ✈

SIRINAT NATIONAL PARK

4031

402

Kung Bay

NAI YANG BEACH ★

4027

3017

4007

4031

NAI THON BEACH ★

LAYAN BEACH ★

4018

KHAO PHRA THAEO WILDLIFE SANCTUARY ★

Ko Kata

Thalang

Bang Rong Bay

4030

4027

Andaman

Sea

☾ SURIN BEACH ★

LAEM SING BEACH ★

4025

THALANG NATIONAL MUSEUM ★

Sapam Bay

Phuket

Sea

★ FANTASEA

Kamala Bay

PHUKET

Ko Maphrao

4233

PHUKET BUTTERFLY FARM ★

Kathu

402

Patong Bay

PATONG BEACH ●

Patong

4029

4020

Phuket

4022

Karon Bay

KARON BEACH ★

PHUKET ZOO ★

4023

4021

☾ KATA YAI BEACH ★

4028

Chalong Bay

PHUKET AQUARIUM ★

☾ KATA NOI BEACH ★

4233

4024

Ko Lon

0   5 mi

0   5 km

NAI HARN BEACH ★

★ RAWAI BEACH

Cape Promthep

To Ko Mai Thon ↓

To Ko Racha (Raya Yai and Raya Noi) ↓

Ko Hae

© AVALON TRAVEL

whether taking in a cabaret show or seeing captive butterflies. They may not be all that culturally significant, but they'll certainly keep you distracted on a rainy day.

Inland Phuket
THALANG NATIONAL MUSEUM
พิพิธภัณฑสถานแห่งชาติถลาง

The Thalang National Museum (Mu 3, Si Sumthon, Thalang, tel. 07/631-1426, 8:30 A.M.–4:30 P.M. daily except national holidays, 30B, free under age 7), eponymous with one of Phuket's historical names, houses a number of exhibitions demonstrating Phuket's history and includes some prehistoric artifacts such as stone tools as well as religious items. The museum isn't vast or particularly comprehensive, but there are some entertaining displays reenacting life on the island throughout the ages, including a reenactment of the famous Battle of Thalang, involving the two sister-heroines. The highlight of the museum might be a ninth-century statue of the Hindu god Vishnu, discovered in the forests of Phang Nga about 200 years ago.

KHAO PHRA THAEO WILDLIFE SANCTUARY
อุทยานสัตว์ป่าเขาพระแทว

Instead of taking the kids to the zoo, where they'll see animals in captivity, or to monkey, elephant, and crocodile shows bordering on exploitation, bring them to the wildlife sanctuary (Bang Pae Waterfall, Pa Khao, tel. 02/896-2672, 9 A.M.–4 P.M. daily). Covering the only remaining virgin rainforest on the island, the sanctuary is home to barking deer, wild boars, monkeys, lizards, and a host of other creatures as well as some lovely waterfalls such as **Namtok Ton Sai** and **Namtok Bang Pae.** The sanctuary is also home to the **Gibbon Rehabilitation Project,** an organization that takes in formerly captive gibbons and rehabilitates them for return to the wild. Gibbons have been poached to extinction in Phuket but are now kept in captivity on the island, often to lure visitors into bars. The project has been working to reintroduce gibbons

to Phuket and has set up a facility at the wildlife sanctuary staffed by volunteers from all over the world who come to feed, care for, and train the animals. The project is open for visitors during the day and also accepts volunteers year-round. There's no admission fee, but they do accept donations.

Phuket Town and the East Coast
PHUKET AQUARIUM
สถานแสดงพันธุ์สัตว์น้ำภูเก็ต

This aquarium (Cape Panawa, 51 Sakdi Det Rd., Phuket Town, tel. 07/639-1126, 9 A.M.–5 P.M. daily, 100B adults, 50B children), a part of the Phuket Marine Biological Center, has a collection of ocean and saltwater fish as well as sharks, rays, and sea turtles housed in over 30 tanks. It's a great opportunity to see some of the exotic tropical fish that might have swum by you in the ocean (except for the gigantic cod, which you'll be hoping aren't swimming anywhere near you). The coolest part of the aquarium is a clear tunnel through one of the large tanks, which you can walk through to see the sharks, fish, and rays. For kids, there's a touch pool where they can experience firsthand what a sea cucumber feels like. The center, located at Cape Panawa on the southeast part of the island, also has a research vessel you can visit when it's not out at sea.

PHUKET BUTTERFLY FARM
สวนผีเสื้อและโลกแมลงภูเก็ต

If you can't get enough of flying insects during your tropical vacation, check out the butterfly farm (71/6 Samkong, Phuket Town, tel. 07/621-5616, www.phuketbutterfly.com, 9 A.M.–5:30 P.M. daily, 300B adults, 150B under age 10), which is home to tens of thousands of butterflies fluttering around its outdoor garden. There's also an insectarium, with bugs of all types to see, including giant grasshoppers, bugs that look like leaves and sticks, and even tarantulas. The farm is also home to a domesticated otter the staff adopted from its former owner and keeps on the grounds to protect it from the wild. The butterfly farm

© SUZANNE NAM

Phuket Town

can arrange to pick you up from your hotel for a small fee.

PHUKET ZOO
สวนสัตว์ภูเก็ต
This private for-profit zoo (23/2 Mu 3, Soi Palai, Chaofah Rd., Phuket Town, tel. 07/638-1227, www.phuketzoo.com, 8:30 A.M.–6 P.M. daily, 400B adults, 200B children) is not the greatest in the world, but it's a decent place to take children if they want to see tigers, rare birds, camels, and other animals while on vacation. There are also daily monkey shows (9 A.M., noon, 2:30 P.M., and 4:45 P.M.), crocodile shows (9:40 A.M., 12:45 P.M., 3:15 P.M., and 5:30 P.M.), and elephant shows (10:30 A.M., 1:35 P.M., and 4 P.M.).

BEACHES AND ISLANDS
While there are plenty of other sights that can fill your day, Phuket really is all about hanging out on the beaches and exploring the surrounding islands. Phuket is ringed with beaches, each with its own distinct personality. If you don't

like one, go up a kilometer or two to the next one to find your perfect spot. Almost all of the sandy beaches on the island face west and look out onto the clear blue Andaman Sea, they are all clean, and they all offer at least minimum amenities (restrooms and small shops or food vendors for drinks and snacks) close by. Due to the island's topography, most of the beaches are separated from each other by rocky outcroppings, creating a natural curving bay at each. What really sets the beaches apart aside from size is what's going on behind them. A cozy beach chair with a great view will feel a lot different depending on whether there are copses of pine and palm trees behind you or a big street lined with shops, cafés, and restaurants. Luckily, whether you're looking for some action or just want peace and quiet, Phuket has both.

For most people, it's a good idea to pick the beach first, then the accommodations. Phuket has a main road running down the west coast, making all beaches easily accessible by car or scooter. On the island, the *sabai sabai* attitude

DROWNING HAZARDS

During high season, the Andaman Sea is often calm and clear, with few waves and no dangerous tides. But during the April-October monsoon season in the low season, the sea can become deadly, especially if there is a storm in the surrounding area. Dozens of people drown in Phuket every year, both locals and visitors.

Phuket has a flag system on all of its beaches, and anytime you see a red flag, it means authorities have decided that the waves and undercurrent are too dangerous. Swimming is not advised at these times, although during low season there are generally no lifeguards around to enforce this rule on even the most popular beaches.

For surfers, this is the best time of year to be in Phuket, as the waves are great, particularly on Nai Harn and Kata Beaches. It's also a great time to learn how to surf, as you can rent a board for a few hundred baht at Kata

Swimmers are warned of rough seas during the rainy season on Kata Beach in Phuket.

and even take some lessons at one of the many casual surf schools that set up shop on the south end of the beach. But if you are not a strong swimmer, stay out of the water or remain very close to shore.

tends to take hold quickly, and although all of the beaches are easy to access, it's a lot nicer to be able to walk to your favorite spot in a few minutes instead of taking a taxi or driving.

Patong and Vicinity
ป่าตองและบริเวณใกล้เคียง
PATONG BEACH
หาดป่าตอง
Not quite the desert-island paradise you may have imagined, Patong is a built-up, bustling beach community filled with Starbucks, McDonald's, scores of hotels and restaurants, a full-fledged shopping mall within walking distance of the beach, and a vibrant nightlife scene. For some, Patong is the only place to go in Phuket; for others, it's the worst-case scenario for a tropical vacation. If going out till the wee hours of the morning then rolling onto the beach to sleep it off with your fellow revelers is your thing, pick Patong. If you're looking for a quiet place to relax away from the hustle and bustle of urban life, stay away. The white-sand beach is generally covered with beach chairs and umbrellas by day but, despite being crowded, is a wide, clean beach with soft sand and clear water. It is one of the island's nicest beaches, if you don't mind lots of people or Jet Skis. The beach is one of the largest in the area, and the wide sidewalk has some small playgrounds and some interesting sculptures too, if you get bored of the natural scenery.

LAEM SING BEACH
หาดแหลมสิงห์
Just 20 minutes north of Patong is Laem Sing Beach, which feels worlds away from the crowds and development. To access the small, curved beach, you'll have to walk down a steep path, and the shore is hidden from the main road. There are still some vendors selling fruit, snacks, and random souvenirs at Laem Sing, places to rent chairs, and even a few casual shops to grab lunch, so don't worry about amenities. Laem Sing also has some granite rock formations along the shore, making it a nice place to do a little casual snorkeling.

Northern West Coast

Aside from the more popular Kamala Bay, this part of the island is home to some of the more serene and secluded beaches, for now at least. The beaches of Kamala, Surin, and Pansea along the curving Kamala Bay are a nice compromise between secluded and overcrowded. A little farther north, private villas for wealthy expatriates and high-end hotels seem to be coming up in nearly every village.

KAMALA BAY
อ่าวกมลา

Not quite like Patong, but with a little more going on than Laem Sing, The relatively undeveloped stretch of wide beach, shaded by trees, is large compared to other beaches. In the hills above the bay are a handful of small upscale hotels, and part of the beach is bordered by protected lands. Kamala Bay also houses Kamala village, a former fishing village with some residents still plying the ocean in their colorful longtail boats. Kamala village has a number of inexpensive guesthouses and places to get fresh seafood meals.

◀ SURIN BEACH
หาดสุรินทร์

The perfect balance of secluded and interesting, at Surin Beach there's plenty to do, if you want, but none of the fast-paced activity you'll find on other popular beaches. The small, clean beach is backed by large green lawns and tall trees with only a small road behind it. Although there's no boardwalk, a pedestrian lane between the palms and pine trees is lined with small shops and restaurants, many of which set up dining areas right at the edge of the sand. Surrounding the beach area are some nice modern luxury resorts and some excellent dining options. But what really makes Surin special is that it still feels like a local family beach, and it still feels like Thailand. There's a sort of small town–meets–Miami Beach vibe here—local school kids playing volleyball on the lawn behind you while you sip a glass of wine on a comfy beach chair and watch the sun set. If you want modern luxury without the feeling of a sterile, generic resort town, Surin is the place.

© SUZANNE NAM

sunset on Phuket's west coast

SIRINAT NATIONAL PARK
อุทยานแห่งชาติสิรินาถ

This small national park (89/1 Mu 1, Ban Nai Yang, Amphoe Thalang, tel. 07/632-8226 or 07/632-7152, 8 A.M.–6 P.M. daily, 50B) is actually located right on the coast of the Andaman Sea, near the Phuket International Airport, and covers **Hat Mai Khao, Hat Nai Thon, Hat Sai Kaeo, Ko Kata,** and **Hat Nai Yang.** Aside from the little islands, the park comprises white sandy beaches shaded by casuarina pine trees; thin forest full of birds, including magpie robins, spotted doves, and Asian fairy bluebirds; and a small mangrove forest. Although it is just a few kilometers from the airport, the park is tranquil and quiet, except for the sounds of the birds and the waves. The beach is a small curving coast, and because there are no big developments around, it feels more secluded. The park is a great destination to bring a picnic or to hang out for the day on the beach. Off the coast, and technically part of the park, are a collection of coral reefs just under one kilometer out, if you're up for some snorkeling (and

are a strong swimmer, since the coral is out quite far).

If you're really looking to check out and unplug for a while, you can also camp on **Mai Khao** and **Nai Yang** Beaches in designated areas. There is a visitors center in the middle of the park along the main lane where you can rent a tent and some supplies or, better yet, one of the park's very rustic bungalows. You'll be sleeping closer to the beach than at most of the high-end luxury resorts on the island for just a couple of hundred baht per night. If you choose that path, bear in mind that the bungalows sell out very quickly, and you have to reserve and pay in advance. The parks department has an impressively sophisticated system that allows you to transfer funds either from a local ATM or via wire transfer. Call 02/562-0760 to make reservations; you can also email reserve@dnp.go.th but you may not get a response. There are clean, basic showers and bath facilities and a few very casual canteens open 8 A.M.–9 P.M. as well as a couple of vendors who set up small stalls and sell water, soft drinks,

the coast at Sirinat National Park, Phuket

© SUZANNE NAM

beer, and even *som tam.* If you're looking for something a little more substantial, just outside the park there are plenty of shops selling whatever you might need.

NAI THON BEACH
หาดในทอน

Another small, simple, quiet beach heading toward the airport is Nai Thon Beach. The golden sand beach is quite deep, so there's plenty of room to lay out a towel (it's one of the few beaches where there are no beach chairs for rent, very few vendors, and no restroom facilities). The area surrounding the southern part of the beach has just a couple of hotels and restaurants, but to the north, Nai Thon is part of Sirinat National Park, so the area behind it remains in its natural state.

NAI YANG BEACH AND
MAI KHAO BEACH
หาดในยางและหาดไม้ขาว

Just below Nai Thon are Nai Yang and Mai Khao Beaches, separated by a small outcropping of trees. The beach is home to endangered giant leatherback turtles who lay their eggs in the sand during the cool season. When they hatch a few months later, usually in April, the babies make their way to the ocean en masse, a fascinating spectacle if you happen to be around when it happens. In recent years, community groups have beefed up protection of the turtles, restricting access to the beach during nesting and hatching periods. Although much of it is still a part of the national park and therefore undeveloped, not all is protected. There's a large resort on the southern part of Nai Yang, but otherwise accommodations options are limited in this area. There are two coral reefs 1.5 kilometers out that can easily be seen with just a snorkel.

LAYAN BEACH
หาดลายัน

During the April–October low season, this pristine beach is nearly deserted, and it may be as close to the desert-island experience as you'll find on Phuket. There's really nothing

in the area aside from a couple of simple beachfront restaurants serving local food. Behind the beach is a more residential area, although there are numerous villas being built in the vicinity.

Southern West Coast

South of Patong Beach are a group of picturesque beaches that aren't as crowded as neighboring beaches but still have plenty of accommodations, food, and activities.

KARON BEACH
หาดกะรน

Karon is a big, wide beach, another popular spot for visitors but much less built up than Patong. For some it's a perfect balance between amenities and quiet. Karon is one of the largest beaches on the island, and instead of being bordered by trees or a quiet street, there is a fairly main road adjacent and numerous shops across the street. There will still be some loud water sports such as Jet Skis, but the beach is large enough that noisy activities are confined to the southern end.

◖ KATA YAI AND KATA NOI BEACHES
หาดกะตะใหญ่และกะตะน้อย

What's so great about Kata Beach is what it's missing. Most of the land directly in front of Kata Yai, separated by a narrow lane, is used by an enormous but discreet Club Med, virtually ensuring that there will be no highrise hotels or other development on the spot for years to come. Kata Yai's beach is used by another high-end hotel (the beach is not private, but some access points are only for hotel guests). As a result, Kata, just south of Karon Beach, is one of the few large beaches on the island without a built-up boardwalk of sorts. That doesn't mean there are no amenities, however. *Som tam,* pad thai, and roti vendors set up stalls in the parking lot every day, there are public showers and restrooms across the lane, and some of the nicest waterfront restaurants on the island are right on the beach. In the low season, the beach attracts surfers looking to take advantage of

© SUZANNE NAM

view of Karon and Kata Beaches

the waves as well as surf instructors and board-rental stands. The Kata and Karon area also has some great relaxed nightlife if you're looking for a place to have a drink and listen to live music. Behind the beach area is a small hilly village filled with everything you would expect from a beach town—restaurants, cafés, small shops selling local products, and many tailors trying to lure in passing travelers.

NAI HARN BEACH
หาดในหาน

Nearly at the southern tip of the island is the secluded Nai Harn Beach, with a small coastline set off by long strips of land on either side. The area right behind the beach is a patch of casuarina pine trees, offering shade and further enhancing the feeling of seclusion. In front, there's a beautiful view of some of the rock formations just off the coast. Compared with some of the other beaches in the center of the island's west coast, Nai Harn is a little more difficult to access, but the drive, through winding country roads and past rubber plantations, is worth the

extra time involved (there's also a bus that goes directly from Phuket Town for 100B). Perhaps because it's at the end of the island, the beach is less crowded, even during high season. During the monsoon season, Nai Harn often has the biggest waves on the island, thanks to a quick drop from shallow to deep water. It's a popular spot for surfing, but the waves can be treacherous during parts of the year for inexperienced swimmers. The area right behind Nai Harn is steep, stony cliffs, and there are no big roads or built-up areas in the immediate vicinity, just a couple of resorts and a Buddhist monastery. Although there's no boardwalk and no nightlife to speak of, there are still a handful of small shops right next to the beach and even a couple of little restaurants.

CAPE PHROMTHEP
แหลมพรหมเทพ

The southernmost point of the island is a small headland jutting out into the sea like the point of a star. It's not a place to go and swim for the day, rather a place to take in the view. This is a popular place for enjoying the sunset.

© SUZANNE NAM

fishing boats on Rawai Beach

RAWAI BEACH
หาดราไวย์

It's tough to lay out a towel or beach chair and spend the day at this beach, as many longtail fishing boats are moored here during the day, and the coral fragments on the coast make it really uncomfortable on bare feet for wading in the water. But the area surrounding it is a small fishing village with a wet market selling lots of fresh seafood as well as some touristy souvenirs made from shells, making it a pleasant little excursion if you happen to be in the neighborhood. This is one of the few beaches not facing west, something to keep in mind if you're looking for a sunset view.

KO RACHA (RACHA YAI AND RACHA NOI)
เกาะราชา (รายาใหญ่ และ รายาน้อย)

Made up of two islands, **Racha Yai** and **Racha Noi,** about 13 kilometers off the southern coast of Phuket, Ko Racha is generally visited on diving and snorkeling trips. There are no accommodations on Racha Noi, but now

a handful of little bungalows and resorts dot Racha Yai. On Racha Yai the most popular spot to go is Tawan Tok Bay, sometimes called **Ao Bungalow.** The sand here is very fine and soft. When the seas are calm and the water is clear, this is a great place for snorkeling, especially as it's so close to the mainland. Racha Noi, which can only be visited on day trips, has some excellent diving at the hard coral reefs off the northern and southern coasts of the island, and it is not uncommon for divers to see manta rays and even occasional whales. There's also a relatively new shipwreck off the southwest coast. Not yet overgrown with sealife, it nonetheless attracts lots of fish and is a fun thing to do if you've never wreck-dived before. Diving off of Racha Noi, however, is not for beginners because of the depths and strong currents. Newbies should stick with Racha Yai, which has some great coral reefs of its own and can easily be viewed by novice divers and even snorkelers. Many dive, snorkel, and touring companies offer day trips to the islands; otherwise you can get a longtail boat from Chalong Bay if you're interested in going there on your own.

Phuket Town and the East Coast

Less visitor-oriented, Phuket Town offers a quick glimpse into the region's history and a bit of normal city life in Thailand. Although most of the small city is not particularly interesting for visitors, Phuket Town has some excellent examples of Sino-Portuguese architecture, a reminder that although Thailand was never colonized, European influences nevertheless have seeped into the country. The turn-of-the-20th-century buildings, many with porticoes on the street, were actually built by wealthy Chinese merchants who took their design cues from places such as Penang in Malaysia and Singapore, where the Portuguese did have a presence. A handful of those mansions have been converted into inexpensive guesthouses, which, though not full of amenities, are quite charming places.

KO LON
เกาะโหลน

Just a few minutes by boat from the mainland is the chilled-out Ko Lon. There's not a ton to do here, but if you're looking for a bit of that desert-island feeling that's easy to get to, it is a good option. There's just one resort on the island, although you can take day trips if you're just interested in hanging out on their sandy beach.

CHALONG BAY
อ่าวฉลอง

The bay is not suitable for swimming, but it serves as the launching point for a number of charter and tour boats heading to different islands off the coast. In the morning the pier is filled with visitors getting ready for excursions, and in the afternoon you'll see the same folks heading back. The little streets surrounding the bay have a relaxed atmosphere and some inexpensive guesthouses, as well as diving and other marine-activity supply shops. In the afternoon and at night, there are a couple of modern restaurants with outdoor seating and

great views, perfect if you've just returned from an excursion and are looking for a place to unwind and watch the sunset.

KO MAI THON
เกาะไม้ทอน

Ko Mai Thon is known for some excellent coral formations within snorkeling distance of the shore and can be reached from the mainland in less than an hour. This small island is home to a private resort, so any visits have to be arranged through them.

ENTERTAINMENT AND EVENTS

Fantasea
ภูเก็ตแฟนตาซี

More a Las Vegas spectacle than a mellow evening, Fantasea can put on a show (99 Mu 3, Kamala Beach, tel. 07/638-5000, www.phuket-fantasea.com, 5:30–11:30 P.M. Fri.–Wed., dinner 6–8:30 P.M., show begins 9 P.M., show and dinner 1,200B): Special effects, scores of acrobats and other performers in costume, and even dancing elephants make for quite an event at this nightly performance. There's also a buffet dinner, carnival games, and shopping to keep you busy after the program. It's not quite a romantic night out, but great for families with children.

Nightlife

Much of the island's nightlife is centered around Patong Beach, which becomes a sort of red-light district meets frat party come nightfall. There are scores of bars and discos packing in the travelers, and music and people seem to pour out of every doorway into the streets surrounding Bangla Road. The music is almost always pop, Top 40, or techno. If that's not your scene, it can be tough to find live music venues or sophisticated places to hang your hat, get your drink on, or do a little dancing. Although there are plenty of high-end accommodations, this trend historically has not spilled over into the nightlife choices, and many visitors not interested in extreme partying tend to spend their nights hanging out at the bars in their hotel or resort. That may be changing, as small bars sans working women or eardrum-bursting music are beginning to appear in small numbers.

The nightlife scene in Phuket is very fluid, and bars and clubs that were popular a year ago may already be closed down, or reincarnated with a different name, by the time you visit. Bars generally close at 1 A.M., nightclubs at 2 A.M., although those rules are sometimes less strictly enforced in Phuket.

PATONG BEACH

It's hard to understand why **Tiger Entertainment** (Bangla Rd., tel. 07/629-2771, 7 P.M.–2 A.M. daily) is always so crowded. Imagine about a dozen small bars and discos bunched together in an area that looks like a large fake cave, then add go-go dancers, throngs of people, and strange animal figures, and you'll have a good idea what the place looks like. Perhaps it's the beer goggles or the fact that most who visit just won't remember in the morning, but everyone always seems to think they had a good time at Tiger. Music tends to be very pop-oriented.

Banana Disco (96 Thawiwong Rd., tel. 08/1271-2469, 7 P.M.–2 A.M. daily, cover 200B) is one of the area's most popular nightclubs. Despite (or maybe because of) the name, it seems to attract lots of young, single local women. Though it is known as a pickup joint, it doesn't feel too sleazy, especially compared to the choices on Bangla Road. The music selection is techno and pop, and the cover charge includes one drink.

There are plenty of gay nightclubs in the Bangla area, but for something a little more interesting, check out **Paradise Kiss Club** (123/809 Paradise Complex, Rat-U-Thit 200 Pee Rd., tel. 08/6944-2423, 6 P.M.–2 A.M. daily, no cover). This house-music venue also has live dancing and singing cabaret performances every night.

If you're looking to party on Patong Beach but want something a little more . . . decent, **Club Lime** (Patong Beach Rd. at the corner of Soi Namyen, tel. 08/5798-1850, www.clublime.

info, 9 P.M.–2 A.M. daily, no cover) is a relatively new nightclub that's about as urban and hip as one can be on an island. Local and international guest DJs are usually playing house and techno mixes to the young and beautiful. It may not be the smartest way to spend an evening, but Monday and Thursday, pay 900B to drink all you can 8–11 P.M. There's also a free buffet on those nights to help keep all the booze down.

SOUTHERN WEST COAST

Perched in the rocks at the far southern end of Kata Beach is **Ska Bar** (no address, tel. 07/893-4831, 4 P.M.–1 A.M. daily). Stop in for a drink and you may think you're vacationing in Jamaica instead of Thailand. The DJ at this casual outdoor bar is always spinning reggae music, and there's plenty of Bob Marley paraphernalia around; no surprise that the vibe here is always relaxed and friendly. There is no dancing, but later in the evening the staff put on a fire show. It's either totally trippy or just really cool, depending on your state of mind.

Decked out with photos of Peter Fonda and old motorcycles, **Easy Rider** (87/4 Taina Rd., Kata Town, no phone, 8 P.M.–1 A.M. daily) looks a little scary from the outside, but once you enter, it is a fun and laid-back live-music venue. The local cover band is usually playing soft-rock covers (lots of Guns N' Roses and Aerosmith) to a slightly older crowd.

Karon's nightlife ambience is somewhere between that of Patong Beach and Kata. You'll find some rowdy bars filled with working women, especially on Luang Poh Chuan Road, but it doesn't dominate the area, so if you just want to go for an evening stroll, you won't feel bombarded by loud music. One spot worth grabbing a drink in is **Bang Bar II** (Patak East Rd., no phone, noon–1 A.M. daily). Similar to Ska Bar in its reggae-oriented music and decor, the inland bar is relaxed and comfortable.

SHOPPING

If you're just looking for small souvenirs to take home, every village near every beach has small items such as seashells or Thai-styled handicrafts, although after you've seen the same products over and over again, they start to look less appealing. There are some small shops throughout the island selling items that are a little more authentic, as well as some high-end antiques stores, some gem stores, and even full-fledged shopping malls.

If you're shopping for gems or antiques on the island, it's difficult to ensure you are getting a good deal unless you have some amount of expertise to evaluate the merchandise. Although there are some good deals to be had, there is no redress should you get home and realize you are unhappy with your purchase.

There are a couple of large shopping malls on the island, serving both visitors and the year-round folks—a real convenience if you find you've forgotten something from home.

Patong and Vicinity
Jungceylon (181 Rat-U-Thit 200 Pee Rd., Patong, tel. 07/660-0111, 11 A.M.–midnight daily) is about a 10-minute walk from Patong Beach up Soi Bangla. The mall, which opened in 2007, is a considerable step up from the shopping that was previously available in the area. There's a full-sized **Robinson Department Store,** a **Carrefour** hypermarket stocked with food, appliances, electronics, and everything in between, and many other stores to fulfill your shopping needs. The mall also has a nice little food court in the basement, serving up noodle and rice dishes, smoothies, and even fresh seafood. Aside from the food court, the bottom level also houses That's Siam. This shop, really a group of small shops, carries scores of Thai handicrafts and other decorative items, including home textiles, silk products, and delicious-smelling bath and body goodies.

Northern West Coast
This area is where you'll find lots of antiques shops and galleries, catering mainly to people who are furnishing villas they've purchased on the island.

Oriental Fine Art (106/19-20 Bangtao Rd., Thalang, tel. 07/632-5141, 9 A.M.–8 P.M. daily)

is a large multistory shop that feels more like a gallery for Asian sculpture, except that you can buy everything on display. They also carry furniture, mainly with classic Chinese styling, and will arrange worldwide shipping.

Songtique (8/48-49 Srisoontorn Rd., Cherngtalay, tel. 08/1668-2555, 9 A.M.–6 P.M. Mon.–Sat.) carries mostly original-period Buddha images and reproductions. Some of the pieces are stunningly larger than life, although the owner also stocks images small enough to take home with you. There is also a selection of antique Chinese furniture. This store is worth dropping by just to see the beautiful Buddhas.

On the road to Laguna Phuket, there are a handful of furniture and antiques stores. **Heritage Collection** (60 Phuket Laguna Rd., tel. 07/632-5818, 9 A.M.–8 P.M. daily) has an inventory of beautiful antiques from China and Southeast Asia. There are Chinese chests, paintings, sculptures, and plenty of Buddhist objects in this large shop.

For more contemporary items, **Ceramics of Phuket** (185/6 Mu 7 Srisoontorn Rd., Talang, tel. 07/627-2151, 8 A.M.–5 P.M. Mon.–Sat.) carries vases, display bowls, and decorative figures, all from a local designer.

Located in the swanky Plaza Surin, **Ginger Shop** (Plaza Surin, 5/50 Mu 3, Cherngtalay, Thalang, tel. 07/627-1616, 10 A.M.–8 P.M. daily) is a fun shop carrying everything from cushions to glassware and even spa products. What really sets the shop apart, though, is the clothing and women's accessories. There's a lot of beading going on in their collection of tops, dresses, bags, and scarves, but since they design their clothes with contemporary lines, the result looks modern and just a little funky.

Phuket Town
Just outside of the center of Phuket town is the large, convenient **Central Festival Mall** (74/75 Mu 5, 5 Vichitsongkram Rd., tel. 07/629-1111, 10:30 A.M.–11 P.M. daily), which has a large high-end department store, a sports store, a bookstore, and plenty of other shops carrying both local and international products. The

mall also has a large movie theater, multiple restaurants, and a food court.

Ban Boran Textiles (51 Yaworat Rd., tel. 07/621-1563, 10:30 A.M.–6:30 P.M. Mon.–Sat.), a funky little shop in Phuket Town, sells a nice selection of mostly handwoven textiles from Thailand and other countries in the region. Offerings include wall hangings as well as clothing, and prices are quite reasonable. There are also some small curios and decorative jewelry.

Rasada Handmade (29 Rasada Rd., tel. 07/635-5439, 9:30 A.M.–7 P.M. Mon.–Sat.) is another little shop specializing in textiles and small objects for the home that stocks items such as bed covers, tablecloths, and Buddhist figures.

For more upscale decorator objects, stop in at **Fine Orient** (51/20 Chaofa West Rd., tel. 07/622-3686). The shop specializes in reproduction and antique furniture from China but also carries furniture and other items from neighboring countries. Many of the things sold here are beautiful, expensive, and too big to fit in a suitcase. The shop will arrange shipping for anything you buy there.

Kai Tak Interior Designs (Royal Phuket Marina, 63/202 Thep Kasattri Rd., tel. 07/636-0891, 9 A.M.–7 P.M. Mon.–Sat.) carries some beautiful furniture and decorator items from all over the region. The prices here are on the high to very high end, but the shop is worth visiting if only to look at what they've got.

Fortune Shop (12–16 Rasada Rd., tel. 07/621-6238, 9:30 A.M.–7 P.M. Mon.–Sat., 10 A.M.–3 P.M. Sun.) has lots of small Thai souvenir items, including Thai silk decorative pillows and wall hangings, pottery, jewelry, and spa products. This is a great one-stop shop if you're looking to pick up some nice gifts to bring home.

SPORTS AND RECREATION
Snorkeling
If you're not a diver, there is still a lot to see in relatively shallow waters if you're armed with a snorkel and a mask. The **north end of Patong, the north end of Kata, the south end of Karon,** and the **north end of Kamala** beaches

have lovely coral or rocks just off the coast, and you'll definitely see some tropical fish around most of the beaches even if the bottom of the sea is sandy. Otherwise, you can arrange a day trip to tour some of the islands in **Phang Nga Bay,** which will include some snorkeling time. Most tour providers will rent snorkels and fins too. These tours are almost exclusively sold through travel agents, and there are scores of them in Phuket. If you're buying a snorkeling trip, make sure to ask how much time you'll spend on the boat versus in the water, the type of boat you'll be traveling on, and the islands you will visit.

Sailing and Speedboat Charters
There are a number of sailing companies that offer everything from just the sailboat to a whole crew. If you have the time and money, spending a week sailing around the Andaman coast is a luxury adventure you'll never forget. For large groups, the cost of chartering a sailboat and doing some private island-hopping can be even cheaper than staying on a resort, and all the charter companies will take care of food, supplies, and fuel. Chartering a sailboat or speedboat will cost 15,000–100,000B per day, depending on the type of vessel and whether it has a crew. **Phuket Sailing** (20/28 Soi Suksan 2, Mu 4, Tambon Rawai, Amphoe Muang, tel. 07/628-9656 or 08/1895-1826, www.phuket-sailing.com) offers both crewed and noncrewed boats and will help you design an itinerary. **Yacht Pro** (adjacent to Yacht Haven Marina, tel. 07/634-8117 to 07/634-8119, www.sailing-thailand.com) has day sailing trips and also offers lessons.

If you're interested in sailing in the area around Phuket and you have your own boat, there are three separate marinas, the **Phuket Boat Lagoon, Royal Phuket Marina,** and **Yacht Haven Phuket Marina,** with year-round anchorage.

Golf
Phuket boasts a handful of well-maintained golf courses open to visitors. Playing on courses surrounded by palm trees and overlooking the

ocean is a real treat. Although you can walk on during the low season, it is essential to make reservations as far in advance as possible during the high season, when the cooler weather makes a day on the greens that much more enjoyable. Caddies are obligatory at all of the clubs.

Located closer to the east coast near Phuket Town, the **Phuket Country Club** (80/1 Mu 7, Vichitsongkram Rd., Kathu, tel. 07/631-9200, www.phuketcountryclub.com, 3,000B) has an 18-hole par-72 course over a former tin mine. The course is great for less-experienced players, although it's not as challenging for low-handicappers.

Set between Phuket Town and Patong Beach in the middle of the island, the **Loch Palm Golf Club** (38 Mu 5 Vichitsongkram Rd., Kathu, tel. 07/632-1929, www.lochpalm.com, 3,000B) is a hilly course but otherwise good for beginner golfers.

One of the island's newest courses, **Red Mountain Golf Course** (38 Mu 5 Vichitsongkram Rd., Kathu, tel. 07/632-1929, 4,500B), in the middle of the island, opened in 2007 on another former tin mine. This course is well designed for shorter hitters, and there are lots of slopes and water to contend with.

Located at the Laguna Phuket, home to a handful of luxury resorts, the **Laguna Phuket Golf Club** (34 Mu 4, Srisoonthorn Rd., Cherngtalay, tel. 07/627-0991, www.lagunaphuket.com/golfclub, 3,400B) has an 18-hole par-71 course with great views of the Andaman Sea.

Although **Thai Muang Golf** (157/12 Mu 9, Limdul Rd., Thai Muang, Phang Nga, tel. 07/657-1533, www.thaimuanggolfcourse.com, 2,200B) isn't the fanciest course in the area, it does have the only course set right next to the beach. But for the view, you'll have to travel a bit, as the course is actually about an hour's drive off the island in Phang Nga.

Blue Canyon (165 Mu 1, Thep Kasattri Rd., Talang, tel. 07/632-8088, www.bluecanyonclub.com, canyon course 5,600B, lakes course 4,000B) has two separate 18-hole courses. The lakes course, as the name implies, is surrounded by small water hazards on 17 of the 18 holes. The canyon course, home to the Johnnie

Walker Classic, is the nicest in Phuket and has been played by the likes of Tiger Woods and Ernie Els.

The Nicklaus Design **Mission Hills Phuket Golf Club** (195 Mu 4, Pla Khlock, Talang, tel. 07/631-0888, www.missionhillsphuket.com, 3,800B) has both an 18-hole and a separate nine-hole course and is located in the northeast part of the island. This is a favorite course among regular golfers on the island, with not only great views of the ocean but challenging sea breezes to contend with.

Go-Karts

If you get really bored staring at the beautiful views or island-hopping and want to try something a little more adventurous on land, check out the **Patong Go Kart Speedway** (118/5 Vichitsongkram Rd., Mu 7, Kathu, tel. 07/632-1949, 10 A.M.–7 P.M. daily Nov.–May, from 1,000B). You can spend your time circling the course or practice a few times before you compete in a Grand Prix race with other participants. Kids have to be at least age 16 unless they're participating in one of the kids-only races. Make sure to book ahead, as the course is very popular.

Cycling

If you're interested in touring the island on two wheels, **Action Holidays Phuket** (10/195 Jomthong Thani 5/4 Kwang Rd., Phuket Town, tel. 07/626-3575, www.biketourstailand.com) offers full-day (2,400B) and half-day (1,400B) bike tours around the island. Most of the tours will keep you in the less-touristed eastern part of the island and are a great way to see some smaller villages and rubber plantations. They also offer tours of a neighboring island, Ko Yao Noi, that start in Phuket and involve a short boat ride.

Sea Kayaking

Most of the sea kayaking and sea canoeing trips that originate in Phuket will involve taking a motorboat to **Phang Nga Bay,** where you'll explore the smaller islands, lagoons, and caves for the day before being shuttled back to the big island. Paddling around Phang Nga Bay is a spectacular way to see the area. You can get up close to many of the smaller islands with no beaches to land on, and as opposed to a speed-boat tour, you'll be traveling slowly enough to look closely at the nature around you. Most guides will require only that you are in reasonably good shape to participate. Some will also even paddle for you, should you wish to just sit back and enjoy the scenery. If you're already an experienced paddler, these group tours may feel a little slow, but all of the tour guides can arrange personalized itineraries if you give them enough notice. **Sea Canoe** (367/4 Yaowarat Rd., Phuket Town, tel. 07/621-2172, www.sea-canoe.net) has trips that run from one day to one week and has been running trips in the Andaman every day for nearly 20 years.

Andaman Sea Kayak (tel. 07/623-5353, www.andamanseakayak.com) also has one-day and multiple-day trips from Phuket, which they combine with camping in a national park. Day trips start around 3,200B pp.

Experienced paddlers may want to rent their own kayaks to explore the islands. **Paddle Asia** (tel. 07/624-0952, www.paddleasia.com) rents well-maintained, high-quality kayaks, although they will only rent to experienced kayakers. If you are not experienced or familiar with the area, unguided kayaking is not recommended unless you're paddling around close to the shore. Many area beaches are filled with Jet Skis and speedboats, and fishing boats travel frequently between beaches and islands.

ACCOMMODATIONS

Phuket already has hundreds of accommodations options along the coast, and new ones are being built every year. While it may be hard to find that secluded beach feeling when all you can see around you are hotels, guesthouses, and cranes building them, the competition keeps costs very competitive, especially during the low season. If you're willing to pay for it, there are still quiet places on the island, and some of the high-end resorts even have small private or semiprivate beaches. And if you stay in the northern part of the island, around the airport,

you'll find the beaches much less crowded. If you're traveling with children, bear in mind that Patong Beach can get pretty seedy at night. There are plenty of discos and clubs catering to both gay and straight clientele, and passing through the nightlife neighborhood at night is difficult to avoid if you're staying here.

While you'll still be able to find a few inexpensive bungalows on the beaches in the northern part of the island, if you're basing yourself in the southern part of Phuket or anywhere around Patong Beach, inexpensive accommodations are almost exclusively guesthouses set inland from the beach, and you'll need to walk at least a few minutes to get to the water. In those areas, waterfront rooms are only available at mid-range and high-end resorts.

Patong and Vicinity
UNDER 1,500B

A great option in Patong if you don't want to stay in the thick of it all and don't want to sleep in a generic or messy guesthouse is the **Little Buddha Guest House** (74/31 Nanai Rd., Patong Beach, tel. 07/629-6148, www. littlebuddhaphuket.com, 500B). Rates are an exceptionally good value considering the very clean guest rooms, nice baths, and tasteful furnishings. There's even a small lobby done in muted colors and natural materials. Located behind the Jungceylon Mall, it is about a 10-minute walk to the beach. The economy guest rooms are small but inviting. For two people, upgrade to a standard guest room.

Set right against the hills in Patong, **Jinny** (87–89 Phisitkoranee Rd., Patong Beach, tel. 07/634-2457, www.jinnyphuket.com, 1,000B) is a small, simple hotel with comfortable, airy guest rooms, all with balconies and a small common swimming pool. Baths are just a bit more than basic, but certainly a step above what you can usually get in this price range. It's a short walk to the beach and the middle of all the action.

The small, cheap, pleasant **FunDee Boutique Hotel** (232/3 Phung Muang Sai Gor Rd., Patong Beach, tel. 07/636-6780, www.fundee.co.th, 1,200B) is a few blocks from Patong Beach but worth the walk if you're looking for something a little nicer than the average guesthouse. The property is only a few years old, spotlessly clean, and somewhat stylishly decorated with modern Thai furnishings and textiles. It's not really a boutique hotel and doesn't have a pool, but there is a very small bar and café as well as plenty of food and drink options just outside the door.

Cheap and chic **SleepWithMe** (39/119 Prabaramee Rd., Patong Beach, tel. 07/634-3044, www.sleepwithme.co.th, 1,200B), has small, stylish guest rooms and very cheap prices. Beds are decked out with crisp white sheets and duvets, and the modern baths are equally minimalist and stylish. The lobby area is very small but so well-decorated it looks totally out of place in the neighborhood. The downside is that you'll have to walk about 20 minutes to the beach (or take a taxi or *tuk tuk*), but for those who would rather save their money for martinis, it's not such a bad trade-off.

1,500-3,000B

The slightly more grown-up cousin of Little Buddha (they're owned by the same people) is **Nirvana Hotel** (241/17–18 Rat-U-Thit 200 Pee Rd., Patong Beach, tel. 01/080-1365, www.nirvanaphuket.com, 1,850B). Although not quite expensive enough to qualify as a boutique hotel, it's certainly a great, cheap urban property in the middle of the tropics. Nirvana has modern guest rooms more spacious than a typical guesthouse and a small restaurant with Italian and Thai food. They'll also set up very reasonably priced spa treatments in your room if you'd like.

3,000-4,500B

If you get a guest room in the newer, low-rise wing, **Royal Paradise** (135/23 Rat-U-Thit 200 Pee Rd., Patong Beach, tel. 07/634-0666, www.royalparadise.com, 3,300B) is a great value since the simple but modernly decorated guest rooms are only a few years old; the tower rooms definitely feel like a generic high-rise hotel. It's right in the middle of everything going on in Phuket, and for some it is a perfect place to relax after partying. For others, being right next to some of the nightclubs might feel a little uncomfortable.

Closer to the center of the action is **Thara Patong Beach Resort and Spa** (170, 170/1 Thaweewong Rd., Patong Beach, tel. 07/634-0135, www.tharapatong.com, 3,200B), another good choice if you're looking to stay on a larger property near the beach but not pay international-resort prices. The guest rooms are nicely decorated with Thai-style furnishings, and the swimming pool in the center of the property is large and nicely maintained. The resort is also very kid-friendly, with a couple of large restaurants on the property and a separate children's swimming pool.

The hip, retro **Album Hotel Patong** (29 Sawatdirak Rd., Patong Beach, tel. 07/629-7023, www.thealbumhotel.com, 3,500B) fills its spotlessly clean guest rooms with crisp white sheets and creative but understated art. Although this isn't a luxury property, there is breakfast service in the morning and even a small rooftop swimming pool. The location, just two blocks in from the beach, is idea for some because it's so convenient to everything, but it can get a little noisy at night. Published rates are significantly discounted, so if you are booking here, make sure to check other booking websites.

The large **Phuket Graceland** (190 Thaweewong Rd., Patong Beach, tel. 07/637-0555 or 02/655-1736, www.phuketgraceland. com, 3,800B) is more of a hotel than a resort. Although there are some nice grounds, a spa, and a restaurant, the ratio of guests to common space is high, and it can feel a little crowded during the high season. Graceland is still a great value for the price if you're looking for amenities and comfort a step above the guesthouse offerings. And the guest rooms are well furnished, albeit in a more generic modern style than Thai style. It's located just north of the center of Patong but right across the street from the beach, and the guest rooms are spacious and well maintained.

OVER 4,500B

The lovely 🅒 **Baan Yin Dee** (7/5 Muean Ngen Rd., Patong Beach, tel. 07/629-4104, www.baanyindee.com, 4,500B) resort has only 21 guest rooms, so it feels less like a generic resort and more like a boutique hotel, but it has many of the amenities, such as a large pool and restaurant, that you'd find in bigger properties. Set in the hills behind Patong, the hotel is designed like a Thai wooden house on the outside, and the guest rooms themselves are furnished with modern Thai-style furnishings and decorations. The only downside is that it's located right on a main road, but if you're looking to stay in the Patong area, it's much quieter than anything you'll find in the main center.

Northern West Coast
UNDER 1,500B
With all of the development going on, it's surprising that simple beach bungalows such as **Mai Khao Beach Bungalows** (Mai Khao Beach, tel. 08/1895-1233, www.mai-khao-beach.com, 800B) still exist. The very basic thatched-roof huts don't have air-conditioning—only fans—but do have their own very basic baths with coldwater showers. Mai Khao Beach is a very quiet spot with limited amenities, but there is a beachfront restaurant on the premises serving good inexpensive Thai food. There's also camping available, and the bungalows close during low season (May–Nov.).

Though it's a bit of a walk to the beach, **Wong Lee House** (65/15 Mu 5, Nai Yang Beach, tel. 08/6276-1908, 800B) is an excellent budget option. Most of the guest rooms in this house have air-conditioning and are clean, although the furnishings are simple. Guest rooms are reasonably sized and baths are basic but functional and maintained. This is a small family-run operation and not the place to go if you are looking for an anonymous hotel experience.

1,500-3,000B
Near a quiet, pretty beach is the comfy **Golddigger's Resort** (74/12 Surin Rd., Nai Yang Beach, tel. 07/632-8424, www.golddigger-resort.com, 2,100B). This very small resort has clean, basically furnished guest rooms and some larger family accommodations that can

sleep four people. There's also a nice swimming pool on the grounds, but if you want to go to the beach, it's only a five-minute walk. The decor leaves a lot to be desired, but this is an excellent deal in the off-season, when rates are just over half price.

Kamala Beach Resort (96/42–3 Mu 3, Kamala Beach, tel. 07/627-9580, www.kamalabeach.com, 2,000B) is a large mid-range resort right on Kamala Beach. Guest rooms are clean and modern and share the same subtle Thai style seen in most hotels in this price range. The decor isn't particularly charming, but it is inoffensive and practical. This is not a five-star luxury resort but has most high-end amenities, including minibars, satellite TV, and high-speed Internet in the guest rooms. The common grounds have multiple swimming pools, bars, and restaurants. Overall, Kamala Beach Resort is a very convenient and easy place to stay, especially for those traveling with children or large groups.

Courtyard Marriott Kamala Beach (100/10 Mu 3, Kamala Beach, tel. 07/630-3000, www.marriott.com, 2,800B), an all-suites resort about 10 minutes on foot from Kamala Beach, offers clean guest rooms and grounds as well as consistent, friendly service. Suites are comfortably furnished with modern, generic furniture, and some have nice views of the surrounding gardens. The property's main pool is kid-friendly, and there is a kid's club with activities and babysitting services. There is also a large restaurant for those who do not want to venture out. The oversized suites tend to attract mostly families and groups.

OVER 4,500B
Laguna Phuket (390/1 Mu 1, Srisoonthorn Rd., tel. 07/636-2300, www.lagunaphuket.com, 4,000B) is an expansive compound with six separate world-class resorts set around a small lagoon just off the coast. With about 240 hectares of shared space along with private beaches, the resort feels like a large village of its own instead of part of the rest of the island. The land it sits on, now prime property on Bang Tao Bay, was once a tin mine that

had been abandoned, the land left fallow for years. In the 1980s the land was reclaimed at a cost of US$200 million. There's also an 18-hole golf course, tennis courts, activities for children, and even a wedding chapel, should you choose to tie the knot on a romantic vacation. The upside of Laguna Phuket is that it's completely enclosed and has everything you'll need for a relaxing vacation. But that can be a downside too, as there's little chance to experience Thailand when you're there unless you venture off the compound.

The Bill Bensley–designed **Indigo Pearl** (Nai Yang Beach, tel. 07/632-7006, www.indigo-pearl.com, 5,500B) is a standout in the luxury-resort category. Designed to convey Phuket's mining history, the property has cement flooring, exposed beams, and thatched roofs juxtaposed against colorful, modern design elements in addition to verdant landscaping throughout. The guest rooms are as funky as the common space. Expect modern modular furniture and color combinations not often seen in generic hotel rooms. There are also tennis courts, a library, and activities for children.

The swankiest, and most expensive, of the resorts is **Banyan Tree Laguna** (33, 33/27 Mu 4, Srisoonthorn Rd., Nai Yang Beach, tel. 07/632-4374, www.banyantree.com, 14,000B), filled with large luxury villas with small private pools and beautifully manicured grounds. Individual Thai-style villas are decorated with modern furnishings and have separate sitting and sleeping areas. The villas are exceptionally well maintained and feel more like five-star hotel rooms than beach bungalows.

Situated in Surin, just across the main road from the beach, ◖ **Twin Palms** (106/46 Mu 3, Srisoonthorn Rd., Surin Beach, tel. 07/631-6500, www.twinpalms-phuket.com, 5,000B) is the perfect blend of urban chic and tropical resort. The guest rooms look out onto two big, beautiful pools and perfectly landscaped grounds, and inside is a blend of dark woods and clean whites—it's definitely designed for the jet-set crowd. What really makes the property stand out is the location. Though you could spend all your time lazing around the pool and

eating at their restaurants, it's two minutes to the shore, and the resort has a small area reserved for guests, so you can enjoy comfortable chairs and great service on the beach too.

Right next door to the Twin Palms is the **Manathai** (121 Srisoonthorn Rd., Surin Beach, tel. 07/627-0900, www.manathai.com, 4,000B). Not quite as swanky or expansive, the Manathai still has pleasant, well-designed, modern guest rooms and excellent friendly service. Neither of the two pools is large, but they are beautifully laid out with indigo-blue tiles. The common lobby and bar area, which has soaring ceilings and plenty of plush and comfortable sitting areas, almost makes up for the fact that the pools and other common areas are just too small for the number of guest rooms.

The **Allamanda Laguna** (29 Mu 4, Srisoonthorn Rd., tel. 07/632-4359, www.allamanda.com, 3,000B) is a more down-to-earth property and has very spacious suites that are perfect for families or larger groups traveling together. There are three large pools on the property and three separate pools for children; it's hard to get bored hanging out on the property. Although the Allamanda is not directly on the beach, it offers a shuttle to its own beach area with sun chairs and changing rooms.

Dewa Phuket (Nai Yang Beach, tel. 07/637-2300, www.dewaphuket.com, 5,000B), a pretty, pleasant hotel resort just south of the airport, has spacious suites and villas—essentially luxury serviced apartments with living rooms and small kitchens. The property is right across the street from the beach, and there is also a very large swimming pool on the premises. This is a great place for families. Though Dewa Phuket is right near the airport and guests can sometimes hear airplane activity, it feels much quieter and more secluded than most other places on the island.

The **Anantara Phuket Villas** (888 Mu 3, Mai Khao Beach, tel. 07/633-6100, www.phuket.anantara.com, 15,000B), on the relatively quiet and peaceful Mai Khao Beach, has luxurious large villas with private pools. The lush property is unmistakably Thai; all the villas are filled with traditional Thai furnishings but are still modern and stylish. The Anantara spa is likewise luxurious and traditional, and though treatments can be pricey, the surroundings make it worth the cost. Service is discreet, but staffers are very focused on making sure guests are well taken care of. For an indulgent, romantic vacation in a secluded spot on a beautiful beach, the Anantara will not disappoint.

A world-class resort with just about every luxury you could ask for, the **J. W. Marriott** (231 Mu 3, Mai Khao Beach, tel. 07/633-8000, www.marriott.com, 9,000B) is on the northwest coast of Phuket. There are large, modern guest rooms, a gigantic swimming pool and two other pools, a spa, 10 restaurants, and plenty of activities to fill the day. All of the guest rooms face the ocean, and the property is set on its own private beach. It's a great property if you want to spend most of your time on the grounds; otherwise you'll have to rely on the hotel's shuttles or rented transportation to explore the rest of the island. The property is also very family-friendly and attracts parents with young kids.

Set in the hills above Kamala Beach, the **Paresa** (49 Mu 6, Layi-Nakalay Rd., Kamala Beach, tel. 07/630-2000, www.paresaresorts.com, 20,000B), offers guests high-end, jet-set luxury in a convenient central location. The property's style—modern and minimalist—isn't oozing Thai character, but since the views of the island and the ocean are so stunning, guests won't be able to forget they are on Phuket. The large main infinity pool is set right in the cliffs over Kamala Beach. Villas and suites are spacious, and many have private pools and indoor and outdoor areas for entertaining.

Perhaps the most beautiful and luxurious resort on the island is **Trisara** (60/1 Mu 6, Srisoonthorn Rd., Nai Thon Beach, tel. 07/631-0100, www.trisara.com, 22,500B). The guest rooms are larger than most city apartments and furnished with impressive teakwood pieces. The multibedroom villas are pricey but come with their own waitstaff, private pools, and amazing views of the ocean. There is also a larger pool at the resort right on the edge of the coast, and a very small private beach for guests.

Southern West Coast
UNDER 1,500B

A great budget option in Karon is the **Pineapple Guesthouse** (261/1 Patak Rd., Karon Plaza, tel. 07/639-6223, www.pineapplephuket.com, 700B), with very clean, basic guest rooms just a few minutes' walk from the beach. The outside is unimpressive and blends in with the overly aggressive signage in Karon Plaza, but the owners have added some little extras inside, including colorful walls and decorations, to make the guest rooms stand out among so many competitors in the area. There are also shared dorms for those who want to save some cash or solo travelers looking to meet people.

Karon Café Inn (526/17 Patak Rd., Karon Beach, tel. 07/639-6217, www.karoncafe.com, 800B) is a typical Karon Beach guesthouse—set inland a few minutes on foot from the beach on the upper floors of a commercial shophouse. Rooms are clean and well-furnished and come with hot-water showers, air-conditioning, cable TV, and refrigerators. There's a restaurant on the lower floor and Wi-Fi Internet access. There are also larger family rooms available if you need to sleep more than two people.

Karon Living Room (39/119 Patak Rd., Karon Beach, tel. 07/628-6618, www.karonlivingroom.com, 900B) is what an inexpensive guesthouse should be—clean, comfortable, and very friendly. Guest rooms are spotless and have simple but attractive wooden furnishings, and baths are modern and very clean too. Rates include a basic but sufficient breakfast, although there are plenty of places to eat a few minutes away. The location, a few minutes inland from the beach, isn't perfect, but you probably won't find a better value in Karon.

Tony and Eak Guest House (213-215 Khoktanot Rd., Kata Beach, tel. 07/633-0425, www.kataguesthouse.com, 1,200B), just a few minutes on foot to Kata Beach and the center of Kata, has basic, modern, comfortable guest rooms, very clean baths, and friendly owners. Those who want no frills but require some style and good service will love this property. The guesthouse is very small, and there is no bar or restaurant on the premises, but everything you'll need is very convenient.

1,500–3,000B

The ⦿ **3rd Street Cafe and Guest House** (4 Kata Rd., Karon Beach, tel. 07/628-4510, www.3rdstreetcafe.com, 2,200B) is almost too stylish for the neighborhood and the price. With hardwood floors, concrete bathtubs, flat-screen TVs, and modern, urban furnishings, this six-room guesthouse is a great choice in this price range if you want to feel like you're staying in a boutique hotel without breaking the bank. The guesthouse is less than 10 minutes from the beach.

3,000–4,500B

The **Phulin Resort** (10/2 Patak Soi 18, Karon Beach, tel. 07/639-8327, www.thephulin.com, 3,300B) is a great-value property if you want the amenities of a larger resort but are looking for the more reasonable prices of a three- or four-star property. The compound offers many of the things you'll find in the big brand-name spots, such as a nice large swimming pool, a spa, well-landscaped grounds, and Thai-themed design throughout, but the guest rooms are a bargain—especially during the low season. The property is set back about a 20-minute walk from the beach, but there is a frequent shuttle to bring you to Karon Beach.

Metadee Resort (66 Kata Rd., Kata Beach, tel. 07/633-7888, www.metadeephuket.com, 3,500B), a modern, full service resort a 10-minute walk from the beach, has a stunning, massive, free-form central swimming pool. The modern, spacious villas and guest rooms are clustered around the pool, and some have direct access from their balconies, though some have their own smaller, private pools. The overall design at the resort is clean, light, and minimalist, with some small Thai details. There is a fitness center, a spa, and a restaurant on the premises, and it's just a short walk to town. This is not quite a five-star property, but if you're able to book it at a discount, it's a great value in a great location.

For a larger family-friendly property near Kata Beach, try **Kata Palm Resort** (60 Kata Rd., Karon, tel. 07/628-4334, www.katapalmresort.com, 3,500B). The resort is just a few minutes on foot to Kata Beach but also has a very large pool area with a funky little artificial waterfall and a bar in one of the pools, should you wish to remain at the resort for the day. Guest rooms are a mix of traditional Thai with a nondescript large hotel; it's nothing stunning from a design point of view but definitely nice-looking, clean, and comfortable.

OVER 4,500B

Set on a small lagoon close to Karon Beach, the **Front Village Resort** (566 Patak Rd., Karon, tel. 07/639-8200, www.frontvillage.com, 4,500B) is a great choice for families because of the large swimming pool and the extra-large family rooms available. Although it's close enough to Karon Beach and Karon village to walk, it's not in the center of all the action, though you will hear the busy main road, depending on which way your room is facing.

The ⦿ **Evason Phuket & Spa** (100 Vised Rd., Rawai Beach, tel. 07/381-1010, www.sixsenses.com/Evason-Phuket, 5,000B) has its own stretch of private beach right near Rawai, and airy guest rooms with minimalist furnishings and beautiful views. The property is a full-scale resort with beautiful tropical grounds, three swimming pools, its own spa, and even its own small private island off the coast, where you can hang out for the day or just have lunch. There's nothing much to do right around the resort, and if you want to go out exploring, you'll need transportation.

Mom Tri's Boathouse (Kata Beach, tel. 07/633-0015 to 07/633-0017, www.boathousephuket.com, 6,500B) is a beautiful small hotel in a fantastic spot right at the end of Kata Beach. The comfortably appointed guest rooms are decorated in a modern Thai style, and many have views looking right out onto the ocean. There is an excellent restaurant on the premises, and a spa and small swimming pool too. This is a great place to stay if you're looking for something a little more upscale right on Kata Beach.

Phuket Town and the East Coast

Staying in Phuket Town has its benefits and drawbacks. You'll be in a more historic area than the beach spots, and you'll generally pay less for your accommodations. But you'll also be far from the beach, which is the main reason most visitors come to Phuket. There are buses that go from the market to the popular beaches every day, but you'll spend about 30 minutes each way, depending on traffic,, making it a good choice only if you're not interested in the ocean or have a lot of time on your hands to spend commuting.

UNDER 1,500B

If **Talang Guest House** (37 Thalang Rd., Phuket Town, tel. 07/621-4225, www.thalangguesthouse.com, 350B) were ever to be renovated, the family-owned and run guesthouse has the potential to be a lovely old Sino-Portuguese shophouse boutique hotel. For now, it's just a comfortable, inexpensive place to sleep with quite a bit of character. Some guest rooms have air-conditioning, and all have private baths, but the property is definitely wearing its decades. Nevertheless, it is a very friendly place to stay, and it is also conveniently located and very inexpensive.

If there ever was a reason to stay in Phuket Town, it would have to be **Phuket 346** (15 Soi Romanee, Thalang Rd., Phuket Town, tel. 07/625-8108, www.phuket346.com, 1,300B), an art gallery–guesthouse in an old Sino-Portuguese shophouse in the center of the city. Each of Phuket 346's three guest rooms are quirky and funky but have big, comfortable beds, TVs, and Wi-Fi. The lobby, gallery, and attached café are very modern but have incorporated Phuket Town's historic architecture.

1,500-3,000B

The **Phuket Merlin Hotel** (158/1 Yaowarat Rd., Phuket Town, tel. 07/621-2866, www.merlinphuket.com, 1,500B) is a large, modern

hotel and offers some nice amenities, including a swimming pool and a restaurant. Guest rooms are clean and comfortable but not charming or unique. This hotel seems to be very popular with tour groups. Although it's very far from the beaches, there are daily shuttles to Patong. Of course, if you're spending the money for this property, you might as well stay at their sister resort in Patong or another place closer to the beach.

OVER 4,500B

The Vijitt Resort (16 Mu 2, Vised Rd., Rawai Beach, tel. 07/636-3600, www.vijittresort.com, 6,000B) on Phuket's southeast coast, has beautiful spacious stand-alone villas scattered in the mountains overlooking Rawai Beach. The villas are elegantly furnished with modern minimalist furniture made mostly from natural materials, are airy and spacious, and take advantage of surrounding views of the ocean and grounds. The only downside is that Rawai is lovely but really isn't a swimmable beach, so guests will have to travel to the west coast for the beach.

Nearby Islands

Rayaburi Resort (Racha Yai, tel. 07/629-7111, www.rayaburigroup.com, 3,000B) is one of just a few hotels on the island of Racha Yai, and though it's a little bit of a hassle to get here, it definitely has the relaxed desert-island feeling most find lacking in bustling Phuket. Bungalows are clean and well-designed, with simple but pretty Thai furniture and lots of lush foliage in the surrounding gardens. Some but not all of the spacious guest rooms have access to a semiprivate swimming pool, and some guest rooms are designed to accommodate families with children.

FOOD

You'll find that although the island is packed full of beautiful resorts and beaches, food offerings are simply not up to par with what you'll find in Bangkok and other urban areas in the country, although things have been improving over the past few years. Nearly all restaurants in tourist areas offer some sort of hybrid menu combining Thai food and Western food, whether it's German, French, Italian, Swiss, or just cheeseburgers and french fries to go with your pad thai or fried rice. Unfortunately, most places do neither cuisine particularly well but manage to stay in business because they're located on the beach or because visitors are happy enough to be in such beautiful surroundings that they're not so bothered by the lack of excellent food.

Patong and Vicinity

Patong Beach has everything, and lots of it. Hundreds of guesthouses, hotels, and resorts, hundreds of little shops to spend your money in, and hundreds of places—from small street stalls to sit-down restaurants and familiar Western-brand fast food—to find something to eat. Quantity aside, Patong is unfortunately not known for quality dining. To find the best places, you'll have to venture out a little bit. If you're looking for some authentic Thai food and are not too picky about where you eat, venture over to the **night market** on Rat-U-Thit Road, parallel to the beach, between Soi Bangla and Sawatdirak Road. You'll find plenty of seafood and other stalls set up, catering to hungry visitors and locals alike.

Right in the center of all the action, across the street from the beach, is the **Ban Thai Restaurant** (94 Thaveewong Rd., Patong Beach, tel. 07/634-0850, 11 A.M.–1 A.M. daily, 500B). The outdoor dining area is lovelier than one would expect in the middle of Patong Beach, and the seafood is fresh and well prepared. The restaurant is great for people-watching, but it's not a place for a quiet romantic dinner: There's often loud live music playing in the background and plenty of commotion to be heard from the streets of Patong.

Unpretentiously serving up solid Thai food, **Kaab Gluay** (58/3 Phrabaramee Rd., Patong Beach, tel. 07/634-0562, 5 A.M.–2:30 P.M. daily, 200B) is always a favorite among local residents. The simple restaurant up the road from Patong Beach has many of the Thai dishes you'll see all over the country, including

tom yam kung, but also fresh local fish dishes, all for very reasonable prices.

An excellent choice for high Thai cuisine is **Baan Rim Pa** (223 Prabaramee Rd., Patong, tel. 07/634-0789, noon–10 P.M. daily, 600B), in the cliffs adjacent to Patong Beach, overlooking the ocean. The view is wonderful, and the food is solid, although the menu may feel a little touristy. The atmosphere is relaxed but much more formal than most beachfront restaurants. It's not the type of place to walk into in flip-flops after a day at the beach, but it's a great choice for a special night out on the island.

If you're in the mood for Indian, **Navrang Mahal** (58/11 Bangla Rd., Soi Patong Resort, tel. 07/629-2280, noon–midnight daily, 300B) off Soi Bangla is unpretentious and relaxed but has fantastic food. They have both northern and southern dishes on the menu and you'll find good curries and dals as well as many dishes with fresh seafood.

For something a little more chic, with a great view and a relaxed vibe, **C Joe's Downstairs** (223 Prabaramee Rd., Patong, tel. 07/634-4254, noon–1 A.M. daily, 600B), right below Baan Rim Pa, is a fun tapas bar–cocktail lounge–restaurant with an international menu. The modern white interior is a nice backdrop to the view of the ocean and the colorful, artfully arranged dishes.

White Box (247/5 Prabaramee Rd., Kalim Beach, Patong, tel. 07/634-6271, noon–11 P.M. daily, 800B), a slick modern restaurant just north of Patong Beach, has great views of the ocean from the glass-enclosed indoor dining room or the terrace. The trendy restaurant's menu, which includes French, Thai, and fusion dishes, is a bit pricey, but the atmosphere, views, and attentive service make it worth the price. Those who don't want to dine here can stop in for rooftop cocktails and live jazz instead.

At the southern end of Kamala Beach is **C Rockfish** (33/6 Kamala Beach Rd., tel. 07/627-9732, 8 A.M.–10 P.M. daily, 500B), one of the most popular restaurants on the islands. No wonder it gets kudos: The menu, split into Thai, Western, and fusion sections, has something for everyone but does everything well, apparently a difficult task considering the quality of fare served up at many tourist-oriented restaurants in the area. The restaurant-bar also has a nice casual atmosphere and, set right on the beach, a beautiful view of the Andaman Sea.

White Orchid (18/40 Mu 6, Kamala Beach, tel. 08/1892-9757, 11:30 A.M.–11 P.M. daily, 250B) offers inexpensive but well-prepared classic Thai dishes in a pleasant setting on the beach. The restaurant, essentially a large thatched-roof roadside shack on Kamala Beach, also has tables on the sand. Service is very friendly and relaxed. Eating here feels a little like Phuket used to be—full of character and less crowded and commercialized.

Sure, you're not in Cabo, but if you're in the mood for some Mexican food, head to **Coyote** (94 Beach Rd., Patong Beach, tel. 07/634-4366, 11:30 A.M.–11 P.M. daily, 350B) on Patong. Like their locations in Bangkok, the decor is bright and colorful, the margarita menu huge, and the food surprisingly good considering how far you are from Mexico.

Northern West Coast

Tatonka (382/19 Mu 1, Srisoontorn Rd., Cherngtalay, Thalang, tel. 07/632-4399, 6 P.M.–midnight Thurs.–Tues., 600B) just outside of the Laguna Resort area, offers innovative global cuisine in a Native American–themed restaurant with an open kitchen where you can watch chefs prepare your Thai bouillabaisse or Peking duck pizza. This is some of the best fusion food you'll find on the island, and the dining room and outdoor dining areas have a casual elegance to them.

C **Silk** (Andara Resort and Villas, 15 Mu 6, Kamala Beach, tel. 07/633-8777, www.silkphuket.com, 6 P.M.–1 A.M. daily, 600B) recently relocated from its Surin Plaza location to more central Kamala Beach, but it's still as swanky and chic as ever. No wonder: It's owned by the same group that owns the popular bar area Lan Kwai Fong in Hong Kong. The interior is stunning, with soaring ceilings, red silk, and dark wood throughout, and you can have

your meal served at one of the dining tables or, if you're feeling indulgent, lounging on one of the opium beds. The menu has many typical Thai dishes with a little extra flair, such as the panang curry with duck and asparagus.

Right on Surin Beach, there are a number of small restaurants serving up seaside meals and offering menus of both Thai and Western food. Everything is pretty much predictably decent and inexpensive. If you come around dusk and sit at one of the tables on the beach, you'll feel like you're dining like royalty regardless of what you're eating—the view from the tables is magnificent during sunset. In the parking lot of the beach, a number of **street vendors** begin setting up in the late afternoon, and there is plenty to choose from there if you're looking for something more casual.

Twin Brothers (Surin Beach, tel. 09/591-1274, 11 A.M.–10 P.M. daily, 200B) is a little fancier than most of the choices on the beach. They have a mixed Thai and Western menu, including pizza. In addition to the food, they've set up a free Wi-Fi zone, so you can surf the Net and eat at the same time.

For something a little more upscale right on the beach, **C** **Catch Beach Club** (Surin Beach, directly across from Twin Palms, 11 A.M.–11 P.M. daily, 500B), the beach restaurant of the Twin Palms, has indoor and outdoor seating that opens right onto the beach. The restaurant, done in stark white with an amazing array of cocktails and a good wine list, is more Miami Beach than Surin. They also have live-music performances on the weekends. It's a jet-set spot on an otherwise totally unpretentious beach. But despite appearances, it is a laid-back and friendly place to have food or drinks.

In keeping with the upscale urban trendiness that characterizes many of the best resorts in Surin, **Kindee** (71/6 Mu 5, Mai Khao Beach, tel. 07/634-8478, www.kindeephuket.com, noon–11 P.M. daily, 250B) offers authentic, flavorful Thai dishes in an unpretentious, relaxed outdoor restaurant. The atmosphere, basic bamboo furniture in lush surroundings, is casual but very pretty. The vast menu includes familiar dishes such as pad thai and some, such as banana flower salad, that new visitors to Thailand may not have tried before. The owner also offers cooking classes.

The attractive, high-end **Thai@Siam** (82/17 Mu 5, Nai Yang Beach, tel. 07/632-8290, 11:30 A.M.–11 P.M. daily, 450B) features mostly Thai seafood dishes served in a lovely setting—an expansive old wooden Thai house surrounded by lush gardens. In addition to Thai classics such as fried spring rolls and *yam talay* (seafood salad), there are also some Western dishes and fusion dishes. This is really a restaurant for travelers, so those who want more intense flavors should make that clear when ordering.

Southern West Coast

Set inside the Aspasia Phuket, **Malina's** (1/3 Laem Sai Rd., Kata Beach, Karon, tel. 07/633-3033, 7 A.M.–11 P.M. daily, 500B) has a chic contemporary feeling thanks to lots of stainless steel and glass, and it offers a Thai menu as well as Mediterranean fare. The food is less edgy than the decor, but expect the Thai dishes, such as seafood in tamarind soup, to be more interpretive than what you'll find at traditional restaurants. The best part of the place, aside from the view to the sea from the outdoor seats, is the desserts.

The Boathouse (Kata Beach, tel. 07/633-0015, www.boathousephuket.com, 10:30 A.M.–11 P.M. daily, 800B), right on Kata Beach, is the restaurant next to Mom Tri's and has one of the best wine selections on the island. This is definitely a place to trade the flip-flops for nicer garb. The kitchen serves both Thai and Western food, and although the restaurant is technically indoors, it opens out onto the beach, and there's a wonderful view to accompany your meal.

Locanda (Bougainvillea Terrace Resort, 86 Patak Rd., Kata Beach, tel. 07/633-0139, www.locanda-phuket.com, 2 P.M.–2 A.M. daily, 1,000B) in Kata is part Argentinean *churrascaria,* part Thai restaurant that is owned by Swiss people and has an Italian name, but the combination works well. It's one of the best

places on the island to get a steak. A big plus for those balking at the sorry selection of wines on the island, there's also a wine cellar with Old World and New World wines to choose from. If you're not totally stuffed by the grilled meats, the restaurant has a small but well-prepared Thai menu.

The entrance to **Kampong Kata Hill** (4 Karon Rd., Kata, tel. 07/633-0103, 6–11 P.M. daily, 500B), in the center of Kata, is easy to miss, but if you walk up the hill on the (many) outdoor stairs, you'll find one of the nicest Thai restaurants in the area. The decor, filled with Thai antiques and Buddha images, might seem a bit over-the-top to some, but it's pretty and pleasant. The menu includes just about every Thai dish imaginable, from Thai salads to curries plus plenty of seafood.

Two Chefs Bar and Grill (526/7-8 Patak Rd., Karon Beach, tel. 07/628-6479, www.twochefs-phuket.com, 8 A.M.–11 P.M. daily, 450B) probably comes the closest to American chain-restaurant dining on Phuket. The restaurant serves a mixed menu of Tex-Mex, Thai food, sandwiches, and burgers in a comfortable, modern setting. Though the Thai food is definitely toned down for Western palates, it's consistent, and most find the flavors plenty intense. They also serve some hearty breakfast dishes in the morning. In addition to the Karon location, there are two locations in Kata.

Phuket Town and the East Coast

The **night market** in Phuket Town, on Ong Sim Fai Road near the bus station, probably has the best casual food in the vicinity. Although Phuket Town attracts a number of travelers, the diners here are mostly locals, and the food is consequently reasonably priced and freshly prepared.

Raya Thai (48 Deebuk Rd., Phuket Town, tel. 07/621-8155, 10 A.M.–11 P.M. daily, 300B) is a must if you're anywhere near Phuket Town around lunch or dinnertime and prefer excellent local food and charming atmosphere to Westernized menus and slick decor. The elegant yet unpretentious restaurant is in an old Chinese-style home, and there's also outdoor seating in the small courtyard. Madam Rose (as the restaurant is sometimes called) has been running things for decades, and she offers deliciously prepared traditional Thai cuisine, with lots of fresh seafood on the menu. The *tom yam kung* is particularly good. This is one of those gems that's more popular with out-of-town Thais on vacation than with hordes of Westerners. It is a very family-friendly restaurant too.

Even if you're not staying in Phuket Town, **Siam Indigo Bar & Restaurant** (8 Phang Nga Rd., Phuket Town, tel. 07/625-6697, www.siamindigo.com, 6:30 A.M.–11 P.M. daily, 500B) is reason enough to make the trip. The restaurant, set in a nicely restored old Sino-Portuguese building, offers a mixed menu of Thai and French fusion dishes as well as creative cocktails. The decor is fresh and modern, and the space also doubles as a modern art gallery to showcase local artists' work.

The stately, expansive **Baan Klung Jinda Restaurant** (158 Yaowarat Rd., Phuket Town, tel. 07/622-1777, 11 A.M.–2 P.M. and 5–10 P.M. Mon.–Sat., 350B) is set in an old colonial-style house, complete with porticoes and shuttered windows, a definite step up from most of the dining options on the island. Inside, the menu is deliberately traditional and typical, although there are some more exotic ingredients such as venison. Expect to find lots of curry and seafood dishes, all well prepared and presented. The restaurant also has a good wine selection, another plus if you're looking for a special place to dine.

Blue Elephant Cooking School and Restaurant (96 Krabi Rd., Phuket Town, tel. 07/635-4355, 11:30 A.M.–10:30 P.M. daily, 650B), set in the old Phuket governor's mansion, has been serving royal Thai cuisine to patrons for years. Dishes, including curries and *tom yam kung,* will seem familiar to most who know Thai food, but presentation here is meticulous. The physical setting, another old colonial mansion, is stunning and makes for a very special spot for lunch or dinner. Like the Bangkok location, the Blue Elephant in Phuket also offers cooking classes.

There are several seafood restaurants along Chalong Bay, but **Kan-Eang Seafood** (9/3 Chofa Rd., Chalong Bay, tel. 07/638-1323, 10 A.M.–midnight daily, 400B) is a favorite among returning visitors to the island. Originally opened in the 1970s as a small fish stand, Kan-Eang has grown into a large open-air restaurant facing the bay. Try the steamed fish with lime and chili sauce and crab-fried rice for an authentic local seafood meal. This restaurant is insanely popular with large tour groups, but don't be put off by the big buses in the parking lot.

Wood-fired pizza, fresh seafood, Thai food, and a great view are what draw travelers and expats to **Nikita's** (Rawai Beach Rd., tel. 07/628-8703, 10 A.M.–1 A.M. daily, 250B) night after night. You might not get that cultural experience you've been craving if you come for dinner, but you'll definitely satisfy any pizza urges. The view from the tables on Rawai beach, the cold beer on tap, and the relaxed atmosphere only add to the experience.

INFORMATION AND SERVICES
Tourist and Travel Information
The **main island tourist office** (191 Thalang Rd., Phuket Town, tel. 07/621-2213 or 07/621-1036, www.tourismthailand.org) is located in Phuket Town and offers maps and general information about the island. There's also a Tourism Authority of Thailand office right in the airport, and it's a convenient place to grab some maps and get general information.

There is also a noticeable presence of tourist police in Phuket, especially during the high season. If there's ever a need, dial 02/678-6800, 02/678-6809, or toll-free 1699 from any phone in Thailand.

Banks and Currency Exchange
As long as your local bank is on one of the international networks, such as Cirrus, you should have no problems getting access to money anywhere on Phuket, although many of the outlying islands don't have ATMs or banks.

There are ATMs and currency-exchange kiosks in the Phuket International Airport.

You will get the best rate if you use your ATM card instead of changing currency or traveler's checks. The ATMs will all have an English-language option. Remember that Phuket is a pretty casual place, and you'll most likely be spending a lot of time swimming, away from your valuables or on a boat with other travelers you don't know, so it's better not to carry wads of cash with you. If your hotel doesn't have a safe that you feel confident with (and most casual bungalows don't), take out only as much as you need for a day or two.

Branches of all of the major banks offer currency-exchange services in Phuket Town and the larger beach areas. Rates are always posted, and after you calculate in fees and commissions, they will be better than anything you'll get from someone offering to exchange money for you on the street or out of a shop front. You may be required to show your passport, so make sure to bring it with you. If you want to exchange traveler's checks, you will be able to do so at any of the bank branches as well.

As in Bangkok, international hotels and restaurants will take American Express, MasterCard, and Visa cards, but smaller guesthouses and virtually all casual restaurants are cash-only.

Communications

The best place to get stamps is at your hotel, and even the smallest guesthouses will arrange to send postcards home for you.

The region abounds with **Internet cafés,** so unless you're out hiking in the rainforest or on one of the smaller islands, you will be able to check in from anywhere for 100B per hour and up. Increasingly and conveniently, cafés and inexpensive guesthouses are offering **free Wi-Fi** on their premises. Even if you're staying in an 800B-per-night guesthouse, you may find a solid Wi-Fi signal in your guest room.

Emergency and Medical Services

Phuket has two major private hospitals with English-speaking staff. While the level of service may not be as high as in the swanky international hospitals in Bangkok, these institutions do cater to foreigners, and staff are well trained and professional. If there is an emergency or you need to be seen by a doctor before you head off the island, do not hesitate to stop into one of these hospitals. Both have 24-hour walk-in services for a fraction of what you'd pay back home. **Bangkok Hospital Phuket** (2/1 Hongyok Utis Rd., Phuket Town, tel. 07/625-4425) is located in Phuket Town. **Phuket International Hospital** (44 Chalermprakiat Ror 9 Rd., tel. 07/624-9400) is on the airport bypass road. Both hospitals have emergency services. If you want help from Bangkok Hospital, dial 1719 from any local phone. The Bangkok Hospital has a 24-hour emergency response, including ambulance service. The emergency number for Phuket International Hospital is 07/621-0935, and they also have 24-hour emergency service. If you are using Phuket as a base and heading out to one of the surrounding islands, remember that you may be hours away from medical care.

There are small **pharmacies** all over the island if you need a prescription filled. If you need something that isn't commonly used in Thailand, you may have trouble getting it. Antibiotics and oral contraceptives are very easy to find, but make sure you know the generic name of the drug you need, as many pharmaceutical companies brand their products differently in different countries.

The American (tel. 02/205-4000), British (tel. 08/1854-7362), and Australian (tel. 02/344-6300) **embassies** do not have consular offices on the island, but each can be reached by phone in case of emergency or to provide guidance.

Laundry Services

There are no real wash-and-dry launderettes on the island, but there are plenty of places to get your laundry done inexpensively. If you are staying in any of the popular beach towns, including Patong, Kamala, Kata, or Karon, there will be plenty of shops offering laundry services, sometimes as a side business to a convenience store or even a coffee shop, so keep an eye out for little signs, and ask if necessary. Nearly every hotel, even cheap bungalows, will have some laundry services too. Take advantage of this when planning your packing. Expect to pay 50–100B per kilogram. Prices will be substantially higher in larger resorts, however.

Luggage Storage

There is luggage storage at the Phuket airport at a rate of 60B per day per item; it's to the left just after you exit the baggage-claim area.

GETTING THERE

Although Phuket is an island, it is connected to the mainland by a short bridge, making boat travel unnecessary unless you are coming from one of the smaller islands in the region (such as Phi Phi or Lanta). Many people take advantage of the inexpensive flights from Bangkok, but it is also easy to travel overland to the island.

Air

Phuket has one international airport, the **Phuket International Airport** (tel. 07/632-7230 to 07/632-7237) located in the northwest part of the island on Thep Kasattri Road, serving passengers arriving from all over the world.

If you're coming from Bangkok, it's cheap and easy to get to Phuket by air. Between regular and low-cost airlines, there are more than 20 flights per day, and even during peak travel it is unlikely you won't be able to find a flight on the day you want to leave (although you're better off making reservations in advance if you are traveling in December–January). The low-cost carriers, including **Nok Air** and **Air Asia,** often have same-day flights available for less than 2,000B each way. Unless it's peak season or Sunday night (when Bangkok residents are returning from weekend getaways), you can literally show up at the airport and ask for the next available flight. Flights are just over an hour from the city, making Phuket an easy place to go even for a weekend.

Flights from Bangkok to Phuket and Krabi are still running from both the new

Suvarnabhumi airport and the old airport, Don Muang, which was supposed to be decommissioned after the new airport was built, but was reopened for domestic flights while repair work was being done on the new airport and seems to be lingering. The situation is supposed to be temporary, and the old airport feels makeshift, with very limited food or modern airport comforts. There is only one terminal open, so you won't have to worry about going to the wrong place, but if you're taking a taxi to the airport in Bangkok, make sure the driver understands which one you are going to. Make sure you understand too. It's not uncommon for carriers to book you on a flight from Don Muang going to Phuket but returning to Suvarnabhumi.

Train

Phuket does not have rail service, but you can take a train to Surat Thani (actually Phun Phin, about 10 minutes by car outside of Surat Thani), and then switch to a bus for the remainder of the journey. An overnight second-class sleeper to Surat Thani will cost around 650B, and there are also a couple of trains leaving during the day. The train ride is around 14 hours, then you'll switch to a bus, which you need to pick up in town, although there are cheap buses from the train station to Surat Thani. The bus from Surat Thani to Phuket is about five hours and costs under 200B. The whole journey will take around 20 hours, making taking a bus directly from Bangkok a little more appealing (and less expensive).

Bus

There are frequent buses to Phuket from Bangkok and other parts of the country. If you're coming from Bangkok, you can take a bus straight from the **Southern Bus Terminal** into Phuket. The journey takes around 12 hours and costs 625B baht for the air-conditioned luxury bus run by **Phuket Central Tour** (tel. 02/434-3233 or 07/621-3615). Other air-conditioned government express buses cost around 500B. If you're heading to Phuket from Bangkok, watch out for tour companies running their own buses, especially those originating in the Khao San Road area. They can be cheaper than government buses and seem more convenient since they leave from the center of the city. But oftentimes you'll arrive at the departure point at the scheduled time only to have to wait another hour or more as other passengers arrive. Government buses leaving from the Southern Bus Terminal are generally prompt, and the air-conditioned buses are surprisingly pleasant. Seats are comfortable and recline, there is a bath on board, and you'll be given a blanket if you take an overnight bus.

If you're coming from Krabi, there are frequent daily buses to Phuket; the cost is less than 200B, and they take about four hours. You can also travel between Phuket and Phang Nga by bus. The ride is about 2.5 hours and it costs under 150B.

Car

Depending on where you're coming from, it's easy to drive into Phuket (the island is connected by bridge to Phang Nga), and since getting around once you're there can be expensive, a car could come in handy. Phuket is best reached from Highway 4, which runs north–south down the peninsula. To get to Phuket, you have to travel through Phang Nga Province to get to the Surin Bridge, and the turnoff from the highway is at Route 402, which is well signed in English indicating that it's the route to take to get to Phuket. Route 402 is called Thep Kasattri Road; it runs inland down the island and is where the airport is located.

GETTING AROUND

Transportation on the island is the one thing that's relatively expensive and can sometimes account for more of your budget than your accommodations.

Taxi

Metered taxis are generally hard to come by in Phuket, but you will be able to find them at the airport, and they will probably be cheaper than any car service you're offered. Expect to pay 400–700B to get from the airport to your hotel. The **official taxi stand,** which is on the right of the arrivals terminal once you exit the building, has posted estimates of the cost to various beaches. Although there will be many people offering you taxis the minute you step out of the terminal, just walk to the taxi stand and take one from there, as it's almost always a better deal. Once outside the airport, though, there are no metered taxis.

In every beach village, there are taxi stands for unmetered taxis with prevailing prices posted. These prices are somewhat negotiable but are always shockingly expensive compared to Bangkok. Expect to pay at least 300B for any trip you take with one of these cars. If you're traveling farther than the next beach town, prices will be higher. To get back to the airport from your hotel will generally run around 700B if you're in the southern part of the island and slightly less the closer you are to the airport.

Tuk Tuk

The most common way to get around the island is by *tuk tuk*. Not quite like the three-wheeled version seen all over Bangkok and Chiang Mai, the Phuket version is more like a small pickup truck with seats in the back facing backward and forward. They're often painted in bright colors or carry advertisements for local businesses, and some of them also have bright neon lights. You can't miss them—they look like mini disco buses. In Patong, you'll find rows of *tuk tuks* lined up on the main road waiting for customers. When none are waiting, you can just flag one down. It's best to settle on a price before you get into the *tuk tuk,* and generally it's around 200B to get to a nearby beach, more for farther destinations. They don't have seat belts—nor doors, for that matter—so if you're traveling with small kids, be advised.

Motorcycle Taxi

Motorcycles are less common in Phuket than in Bangkok, but they can be found in very developed areas such as Phuket Town and Patong. Drivers wear brightly colored vests, often with white numbers on the back, and will negotiate fares to take you where you need to go. Prices range anywhere from 50B to get from one part of a beach to another to a few hundred baht if you are traveling farther.

Motorcycle Rental

Many people rent motorcycles to get around Phuket. Mostly you'll find 100 cc and 110 cc Honda Waves, which have a clutchless shift system (you still have to change gears with your left foot, but you don't need to squeeze a clutch to do so), but there are also lots of places renting newer scooters that are totally automatic. At around 250B per day (slightly more in high season or if you're in a remote area), it's the cheapest form of transportation you'll be able to find on the island. It's also a great way to see the island, since you're totally mobile and you can come and go as you please. The downside is that some of the roads are windy and hilly, which can be challenging or scary for new riders. Also, riding a motorcycle anywhere is dangerous. If you rent one, make sure you know what you are doing, and always wear your helmet. You may feel like the only person on the island with one on, but you'll be the safest. You will also avoid potentially expensive and inconvenient traffic tickets, as the Phuket police occasionally crack down on helmetless riders.

Car Rental

There are numerous international and local car rental companies on the island. While a car isn't necessary, this is a great option if you have children. Although not all of the agencies will require this, it's best to go to a auto club office at home to get an international driver's license before arriving. You can legally drive in Thailand without one, but for insurance reasons some companies will ask that you have it anyway.

Avis (arrival terminal, Phuket International Airport, tel. 07/635-1243, www.avisthailand. com, 8 A.M.–9 P.M. daily) has a rental counter right at the airport, and you can book online and pick up your car when you arrive.

Andaman Car Rent (51/11 Mu 3 Cherngtalay Rd., Surin Beach, tel. 07/632-4422, www.andamancarrent.com, 9 A.M.–9 P.M. daily) is located on Surin Beach and has a good selection of Jeeps and other sport vehicles as well as regular cars. They'll pick you up from the airport if you arrange it ahead of time.

Via Phuket (120/18 Rat-U-Thit Rd., Patong Beach, tel. 07/634-1660, www.via-phuket.com, 8 A.M.–5 P.M. Mon–Sat.) has off-road vehicles in addition to normal cars and will pick you up and drop you off wherever you are staying.

Braun Car Rental (66/29 Soi Veerakit, Nanai Rd., Patong Beach, tel. 07/629-6619, www.braun-rentacar.com, 9 A.M.–9 P.M. daily) is on Patong Beach and will do pickup and drop-off at the airport or at your hotel. Braun also rents baby seats for a small fee.

Phang Nga Province   จังหวัดพังงา

Phang Nga Province, north of Phuket on the mainland, is home to the spectacular Phang Nga Bay, which overlaps with Phuket and Krabi. But aside from this well-known tourist spot, traveling north along the west coast, the region has beautiful beaches and a mountainous, forested interior. It's also home to the Surin and Similan National Marine Parks off the coast. With plentiful coral, this is some of the best diving and snorkeling in the country. The mainland beaches are arguably as top-notch as those in Phuket and Krabi, and the area is more visited by travelers every year. Although there are world-class resorts, and the lower part of the region is easily reached from the Phuket airport (to Khao Lak it's about the same drive as to parts of southern Phuket), it's definitely quieter. There's nothing even close to the density of Phuket's Patong Beach, so it is perfect for those looking for a slightly off-the-beaten-track experience without having to cut out any amenities.

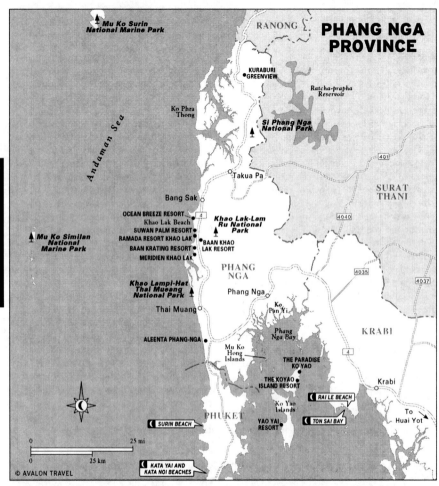

PHANG NGA BAY
อ่าวพังงา

Surrounded by Phuket to the west, Phang Nga Province to the north, and Krabi to the east, Phang Nga Bay is filled with small islands and rock formations rising out of the sea, creating breathtaking scenery that, for many, is what the Andaman coast is all about. There are more than 100 islands in the bay; some, such as Ko Yao Noi, are large enough for accommodations, and some, such as "James Bond Island," are so small that they're barely more than rocks. In addition to some sandy beaches, the bay's islands and surrounding coasts are also home to verdant mangrove swamps. You may be able to sight egrets, kingfishers, and herons. There are hidden lagoons inside some of the islands where you can snorkel or swim in sheltered waters, and caves on some of the islands from the continued erosion of the limestone material they're primarily made of. The relatively shallow waters create amazing ocean colors, from light blue when the sun is shining to deep emerald, and despite the fact that you'll probably be plying the waters and exploring the caves with thousands of visitors from all over the world, it's worth the crowds and the slightly commercialized feeling of the area just to enjoy the physical landscape.

There is only one public ferry to the bay, traveling from the east side of Phuket to Ko Yao Noi. To tour the bay, you'll either need to arrange a group tour with one of the many travel agents in the region or hire a private boat from Phang Nga. There are many agencies offering tours, and it can be a convenient way to see the area.

Islands
Ko Pan Yi (เกาะปันหยี, Sea Gypsy Island) is really a large cluster of houses, shops, and even a mosque built on stilts right over the water next to a small rocky island, a sort of Water World–esque village in the middle of the sea. The people living in the village are primarily Muslim fisherfolk, who used to make their living plying the surrounding waters but now have seen much of their existence subsidized by the thousands of tourists who visit each day and who buy food and drinks on the island. The island is quite picturesque, but it's not inhabited by the traditional sea gypsies of the region, called Moken, a nomadic people who spend months at a time at sea.

About one hour by boat from Krabi, the **Mu Ko Hong Islands (หมู่เกาะห้อง)** are a stunning group of limestone formations surrounded by coral reefs with some sandy beaches. Although the islands are too small to have any accommodations, they can be visited during day trips and for snorkeling, canoeing, or kayaking. One of the larger islands in the group, Ko Hong, has a small hiking trail.

The **Ko Yao** islands (เกาะยาว) are the largest islands in Phang Nga Bay and comprise the larger **Ko Yao Yai** and the smaller **Ko Yao Noi** to the north. Just a couple of hours by ferry from the mainland, the Ko Yao islands are amazingly untouched by the rampant tourism that seems to have changed even the smallest

islands from places supported by local industry and quiet refuges for indigenous animals to bungalow- and bar-laden resort spots. Here it's dirt roads, water buffalo, and dense green forest. Perhaps this is because the beaches are not as beautiful as some of the others in the area—at low tide it's just too rocky to swim. Still, if you are looking to get away somewhere quiet and feel like you're actually in Thailand, these islands are a truly special experience. The local culture is primarily Muslim Thai, and there's much less of a party scene; it can even be hard to find a beer at the handful of small restaurants. Both islands have accommodations, even a couple of luxury resorts, although the smaller Ko Yao Noi has the most options for places to stay. So far, there are no ATMs on the island (although this may be changing soon), so bring plenty of cash from the mainland if you're planning on hanging out here. To get to Ko Yao, you can take a longtail boat from the Bang Rong pier on the east coast of Phuket. There are daily ferries at 9:30 A.M., noon, and 5 P.M.

Sea Kayaking
Phang Nga Bay is a great kayaking destination. You can explore the smaller islands that have lagoons, caves, and no beaches to land on. Many kayaking trips originate from Phuket, where you can make arrangements for a day-long or multiple-day trip to the area.

Accommodations and Food
If you want to stay on Ko Yao but are looking for something in the budget category, the **Yao Yai Resort** (Mu 7, Ban Lopareh, tel. 08/5784-3043, www.yaoyairesort.com, 1,000B) has some very cheap little wooden bungalows with their own small outdoor sitting areas. The guest rooms are not spectacular, but they are clean, and many of them have air-conditioning. There's no pool, but there is a small restaurant on the premises and a nice beach.

The Paradise Ko Yao (24 Mu 4, Ko Yao Noi, tel. 07/623-8081 or 08/1892-4878, www.theparadise.biz, 7,500B) is a contemporary but casual bungalow resort with very well-

JAMES BOND ISLAND

When the James Bond thriller *The Man with the Golden Gun* came out in 1974, Phang Nga Bay was barely known by anyone outside Thailand. The tiny island where Roger Moore stood is formally called Ko Phing Kan, but it's often referred to as James Bond Island. Like many of the islands in Phang Nga Bay, it has spectacular karst topography and a small but beautiful beach.

Fast-forward three decades, and little Ko Phing Kan has become a staple on the tourist trail. During high season, literally hundreds of people visit the island each day, a trip that's often combined with a visit to Ko Pan Yi to see the "sea gypsies" of Thailand. Instead of a deserted beach in paradise, as seen in the film, the beach is now crammed full of vendors selling postcards and other tourist items. And everyone, it seems, wants to have their picture taken on the island, against a backdrop of the spectacular Ko Tapu. Ko Tapu, which means "nail island" in Thai, is a beautiful karst formation towering about 180 meters straight out of the water; it can also be seen in the film.

Many tour companies will encourage visitors to take this day trip, and if you're a big James Bond movie buff, you might enjoy it despite the crowds being herded on and off the island. But bear in mind that although the islands of Phang Nga Bay are beautiful and worth visiting, marine ecosystems are fragile. There are plenty of stunning islands to see, and it's better to spread the impact of our visits around instead of piling it all onto one tiny island.

designed, open, airy guest rooms, many with their own sitting rooms that open to the surrounding landscape of Phang Nga Bay. Some of the guest rooms even have whirlpool tubs. The grounds are set in the hills, which are speckled with the thatched roofs of the bungalows, and they also have a very chic infinity swimming pool.

This is the place to go if you want to experience that secluded desert-island feeling with a little luxury. **The Koyao Island Resort** (24/2 Mu 5, Ko Yao Noi, tel. 07/659-7474 to 07/659-7476, www.koyao.com, 8,000B) has some beautiful villas set right on the beach, each with a charming rustic feeling but without compromising on amenities such as airconditioning or nice baths. There's also a small spa and a beautiful swimming pool.

If you want a lot of luxury, **Six Senses Yao Noi** (56 Mu 5, T. Ko Yao Noi, A. Ko Yao, tel. 07/641-8500, www.sixsenses.com, 12,000B) is an indulgent, beautiful, discreet five-star resort set on massive lush grounds. Most accommodations are spacious private pool villas; there are also some larger villas available or groups or those who want even more room. Like other Six Senses properties, the decor looks very understated and blends with the surrounding environment but is luxurious at the same time—thatched-roof bungalows done in mostly natural fibers but with amazingly comfortable beds, ice-cold air-conditioning, large baths, and private swimming pools. The resort has several restaurants and bars to choose from as well as staff to prepare meals in your villa if you prefer.

Since most of these islands are visited as day trips, the only food you'll find is very casual beach dining. Ko Pan Yi, a popular lunch stop for boat tours, has some reasonable restaurants right on the water, serving seafood and other Thai dishes, and Ko Yao has some similar spots to eat.

If you're staying at one of the resorts, meals are not included, but each of the accommodations listed has a reasonable restaurant on-site.

Getting There

As Phang Nga Bay is bordered by Phuket, Krabi, Phang Nga, and Trang to the south, there are a number of different launching points from which to see the islands. If you are flying into Phuket airport, it's actually easier to get a boat from Phuket than to drive to Phang Nga and seek sea transportation from there. Phuket is so heavily visited that many of the tours around Phang Nga Bay will originate at one of the Phuket marinas. Krabi is also a very popular launch point, and if you fly into Krabi, you'll most likely be taking a boat from Ao Nang.

If you are staying at one of the island resorts, they will advise you of the best way to get there (the nicer ones will arrange transportation for you). If you're going for a day trip, you'll most likely do it as part of an organized tour leaving from Phuket or Krabi; these tours almost always pick you up from your hotel and bring you back in the evening. Tours advertising trips to Ko Pan Yi or "James Bond Island" are good for viewing the bay, and if they don't include snorkeling or other activities, they will cost around 500B pp. Many of the small islands don't have consistent ferry service, so if you want to spend the day on one of them without a tour, you will have to hire a boat to take you out. You can hire a boat from Phuket marina, but you'll probably pay hundreds of dollars, since the only boats that can access the bay from there are speedboats. If you're coming from Phang Nga, you'll be able to hire a private boat for a couple of hours from the Ao Phang Nga Marine National Park visitors center in Tha Dan. Expect to pay around 1,000B for two hours.

If you're driving, the only island in the bay you'll be able to access is Ko Lanta. Otherwise, plan on driving to Tha Dan, Krabi, or Phuket and leaving your car there to switch to sea transportation.

KHAO LAMPI-HAT THAI MUANG NATIONAL PARK
อุทยานแห่งชาติเขาลำปี-หาดท้ายเหมือง

The Khao Lampi-Hat Thai Muang National Park (Mu 5, Amphoe Thai Muang, Phang Nga, tel. 08/4059-7879 or 07/641-7206, 8:30 A.M.–6 P.M. daily, 400B) is a small national park on just over 7,200 hectares of land and water that is best known for some spectacular waterfalls, including the **Namtok Lampi,** a three-tiered waterfall that runs all year. The waterfall is about 13 kilometers from the park headquarters on the beach; to get there you'll

need to drive most of the way along the main road (there are plenty of signs for the waterfall) and then take a short walk to the falls.

Another great waterfall to explore is **Namtok Ton Phrai,** the largest in the park (although like most waterfalls in the country, it will be less impressive during dry season). These falls are about 11 kilometers from the park's headquarters on the beach, and there are marked roads from there. There is also a ranger station here and a canteen, as it is one of the most popular spots in the park. If you're looking for a quiet beach, **Hat Thai Muang** is a 13-kilometer stretch of sandy beach with clear blue waters. If you visit November–February, you may see **sea turtles** coming to lay their eggs on shore at night, and park rangers collecting the eggs to incubate them safe from poachers or predators in their nursery (this is the main reason the beach is a protected national park). In March there's a festival in which locals and visitors watch the little baby turtles make their way to the sea after hatching.

The park has both bungalows for rent and camping areas where you can pitch a tent. There are some small food vendors around during the day in addition to the canteen at Namtok Lampi.

Getting There
By car from Phuket airport or anywhere on Highway 4, head straight north to Phang Nga on Highway 4 for about 56 kilometers to the Tai Muang Market, where you'll see a sign for the national park. Turn off the main road onto Route 401 for about 6.5 kilometers.

There are frequent buses from Bangkok to Phang Nga, which often traverse the popular Highway 4 and terminate in Phuket; they cost 400–500B for an air-conditioned bus. From Phang Nga to the park, you can pick up a normal local bus for about 30B or an air-conditioned bus for 45B.

BO DAN HOT SPRINGS
น้ำพุร้อนบ้านบ่อดาน

If you want a hot-spring experience without going to a spa, the Bo Dan Hot Springs

(6 A.M.–9 P.M. daily, 10B) are hot mineral springs that locals swear will relieve arthritis and mental and physical stress. Even if it's not the cure-all it's hyped to be, bathing in the springs is a fun experience, and the surrounding greenery is relaxing.

Getting There

The springs are on a side road a few kilometers off of Highway 4. When you reach Khok Kloi, look for the turnoff; there will be a sign for the hot springs. A taxi from Takua Pa costs at least 1,000B.

TAKUA PA
ตะกั่วป่า

Just an hour's drive from the Phuket airport is Takua Pa Province, although it's often referred to as Khao Lak (the name of a part of the province). Despite being literally washed away by the 2004 tsunami, the area is once again an up-and-coming resort area with beautiful beaches, scenic mountain ranges with rainforest in the background, and some luxurious resorts and quaint bungalows. Although more travelers are visiting the area every year, especially in Khao Lak, and you'll see some big brand-name accommodations, it still feels much quieter and more relaxed than any beach you'll find on Phuket.

Khao Lak-Lam Ru National Park
อุทยานแห่งชาติเขาหลัก-ลำรู่

Spanning four provinces, the Khao Lak-Lam Ru National Park (8:30 A.M.–6 P.M. daily, 400B), named after the large mountain within its borders, Khao Lak, has kilometers of pristine beach and thick forest. There are a number of small waterfalls, including the Lam Ru waterfall, a five-tiered waterfall hidden amid thick trees. During the day the park is populated not only with visitors but also with beautiful butterflies and exotic birds. If you feel like camping, there is a campground with some limited facilities and just a few bungalows available for rent. Khao Lak Beach is also part of the park, and although parts of the beach are too rocky for swimming, there are some sandy patches

where you can lay out a towel and enjoy the view of the Andaman Sea.

Beaches and Islands

The **Khao Lak Beach** region, close to the bridge connecting Phuket with the mainland, offers clean, quiet stretches of beach with amazing crystal-clear waters. From north to south, there are three beaches in the stretch called Khao Lak—Bang Niang, Nang Thong, and Sunset—and together they take up about eight kilometers of coastline. Khao Lak has traditionally been a hangout for divers, since it's an easy place to set off to the Similan or Surin Islands, and thus remains a laid-back, rustic place to visit. There are lots of dive shops, a handful of restaurants, and the Andaman Sea to keep you occupied.

About 32 kilometers north of Khao Lak is **Bang Sak,** even less developed than its neighbor to the north, which has attracted some luxury resorts in the past few years. There's no nightlife in the area, but if you're looking for a place to be based for some diving or looking to enjoy the water and the convenience of the Phuket airport without dealing with crowds, this is a great spot. The beach is really spectacular: The shore is wide and flat, and the white sands are smooth and relatively unmarred by rocks.

Accommodations

Ocean Breeze Resort (26/3 Mu 7, Kuk Kak, Takua Pa, www.gerdnoi.com, tel. 07/648-5145, 1,800B), formerly called Gerd & Noi Bungalows, isn't very fancy, but it is located right on the beach and has clean, very family-friendly accommodations. The larger bungalows can easily sleep a small family, and there's a small swimming pool and a restaurant serving Thai and European food. The vibe is like old Khao Lak—laid-back and unpretentious.

If you plan to spend some time doing a live-aboard diving trip to the outer islands, the **Kuraburi Greenview** (140/89 Mu 3, Kura, Kuraburi, tel. 07/640-1400, 1,900B) has some charming cabins in which to base yourself at super-budget prices. The cabins and guest rooms look like they would be more appropriate in New England than Southeast Asia, with lots of exposed wood and rocks along with views of the grounds. The hotel runs lots of dive and snorkeling trips and can arrange liveaboards on their boats, but the hotel itself is not right on the water.

Just south of Bang Sak, **Baan Khao Lak Resort** (26/16 Mu 7, Phetchakasem Rd., Kuk Kak, Takua Pa, tel. 07/648-5198, www.baankhaolak.com, 3,500B) is a great value, even during the high season. All of the guest rooms and villas are modern, stylish, and well maintained, and the grounds of this resort on the beach are lushly landscaped and have lots of amenities you wouldn't expect for the price, including a pool right on the beach, restaurants, and an outdoor beach bar. This is a family-friendly property and also one of the rare resorts in the country that have wheelchair-accessible rooms and grounds.

Set on Bang Niang, **La Flora** (59/1 Mu 5 Kuk Kak, Takua Pa, tel. 07/642-8000, 5,500B) is a surprisingly large resort, with over 100 guest rooms and villas set on a quiet stretch of beach. The guest rooms are spacious and designed with a modern Thai theme, and the best are the villas on the beach. While the area may be quiet, the resort's restaurants, spa, gorgeous swimming pool, and even free Wi-Fi will keep you occupied.

For a smaller resort experience, **Baan Krating Resort** (28 Mu 7, Kuk Kak, Takua Pa, tel. 07/648-5188 or 07/648-5189, 2,000B), next to Khao Lak National Park, has rustic grounds set in the cliffs overlooking the ocean and peppered with wooden bungalows connected via walkway. Each of the guest rooms is individually decorated, but you won't have to do without nice sheets and decent baths if you decide to stay here, as the bungalows, although not brand new, are definitely not in the budget category. The pool and common areas are small, as is the resort, but there's a restaurant on the premises, and the view of Khao Lak Bay is amazing. This is definitely a place for the young and agile: Depending on where your bungalow is, you may be climbing stairs.

The **Suwan Palm Resort** (30/27 Mu 7, Kuk Kak, Takua Pa, tel. 07/648-5830, www.suwanpalm.com, 3,000B) is on the same beach as some of Khao Lak's most expensive properties, and although it's not a luxury chain, it does offer guests clean, modern guest rooms, a nice swimming pool, a bar and restaurant on the premises, and even a small spa. The facilities are small but sufficient for those whose primary goal is to enjoy the beach. Low season rates can be an excellent value.

The **Ramada Resort Khao Lak** (59 Mu 5, Kuk Kak, Takua Pa, tel. 07/642-7777, 3,500B), though not quite as nice as Le Meridien, is a nice new resort set on a beautiful strip of beach. The guest rooms are large and modern, and some have unobstructed views of the Andaman Sea. Pool villas are compact but a great value for those who want some privacy. The property's main swimming pool, which is just behind the beach, is massive. There is also a spa, a fitness center, and an activity program for kids.

《 Le Meridien Khao Lak (9/9 Mu 1, Kuk Kak, Takua Pa, tel. 07/642-7500, www.starwoodhotels.com, 5,000B) is one of the nicest resorts in the area. The nine-hectare grounds are lush and well manicured, with a large child-friendly pool and direct beach access. The guest rooms are modern, airy, and comfortable, with dark-wood details and crisp linens. The villas are spacious, although they can cost significantly more than the rooms. There's a beautiful spa on the premises and a charming Thai restaurant. Although this is a large chain resort, there's no generic feeling here.

The small, luxurious **Sarojin** (60 Mu 2, Kuk Kak, Takua Pa, tel. 07/648-5830, www.sarojin.com, 7,000B) resort, located right on the beach, has large, comfortable guest rooms and suites filled with modern Thai-style furnishings. The grounds are lush and spacious and include shaded *salas* for lounging at the large modern pool as well as a high-end spa. The resort's restaurant and bar options are a little pricey, but the breakfast, included in most rates, has lots of variety and is served till late. Service in general is excellent and attentive, and this is a great choice for a romantic getaway or honeymoon.

Just south of the Khao Lak area, and only a few kilometers from the Sarasin Bridge to Phuket, is the **⬤ Aleenta Phang-Nga** (33 Mu 5, Khok Kloi, Takua Pa, tel. 02/508-5333, www.aleenta.com, 12,000B), at the top of the class of small boutique resorts in Thailand. The villas are swanky and contemporary, with a blend of Mediterranean and Thai styling; some are full apartments with living areas and small private pools. The common areas are small, but the restaurant has an excellent East-West menu. Little touches, including iPods in every guest room and scented oil burners, will make you feel pampered. This is definitely a place you're likely to find incognito movie stars.

Getting There
The easiest way to get to Phang Nga is to fly into Phuket International Airport. Since the airport is in the northern part of the island, it's less than an hour's drive from the Sarasin Bridge to Phang Nga. Metered taxis from the airport will drive you to Phang Nga for 300–1,000B, depending on where you're going. If you're heading for Khao Lak, expect to pay around 700B.

If you're driving, Phang Nga is best reached by car by driving along Highway 4 until you reach Phang Nga, which will be well signed in English.

Buses running from Bangkok to Phuket will always stop in Phang Nga along the way as long as you let the driver know that's where you're going (since Phang Nga is the only land crossing to the island).

KO PHRA THONG
เกาะพระทอง
Separated from the mainland by a channel, mudflats, and mangroves, this little island, just 90 square kilometers, is named Phra Thong, or golden Buddha, based on a legend that shipwrecked pirates buried a gold statue of the Buddha somewhere on the island. These days, there are no pirates around, and the treasure

has never been found, but the island is home to a handful of fishing villages and just a couple of ecofriendly resorts. The beaches on the west side of the island are beautiful, serene, and relatively untouched by commercialism. In addition to the mangroves, sea grass, and patches of rainforest, the island is home to macaques, otters, and lemurs, to name just a few of the small animals you might run into. It's also home to sea turtles that come to bury their eggs on the shore every year. Although the island and neighboring Ko Ra together form one of the newest national parks in the country, there are no national park amenities.

Sports and Recreation
There are plentiful opportunities to hike and walk the island, although there are no established marked trails. If you are staying on the island, the resort will provide you with a map of the areas you can safely explore.

Accommodations
The Golden Buddha Resort (tel. 08/7055-4099, 3,500B) is a small, quiet, ecofriendly resort on the west coast of the island. Here you'll find beach yoga and wooden bungalows close to the water, without the typical crowds or prices. You have to forgo luxuries such as air-conditioning and reliable Internet access, but if you're looking for a quiet, remote place on the shore, this is a beautiful spot to relax and unwind. There are also larger houses available for groups.

You can also camp on the island, as it's a national park, although right now there are no bungalows, tent rentals, or canteens, so you have to bring everything you need with you, including water.

Food
There's really no tourism infrastructure set up on the island, so finding food is challenging. If you're staying at the island's resort, they'll make sure to feed you. Otherwise, you may be able to find someone to prepare a meal for you in the villages, slightly inland. If you're coming for the day or camping, pack food and water.

Getting There

To get to Ko Phra Thong, you'll first have to find your way to the Kuraburi pier. If you're driving, take Highway 4 to the Kuraburi district, which is south of Ranong Province and north of Takua Pa and Si Phang Nga National Park. From the pier in Kuraburi, there are no scheduled boats. You can either negotiate with a longtail captain to take you, or if you are staying at the Golden Buddha Resort, they will arrange to have someone pick you up. Expect to pay 1,000–1,500B each way, even if you arrange it through the hotel.

SI PHANG NGA NATIONAL PARK

อุทยานแห่งชาติศรีพังงา

Mostly rainforest on a rugged mountain range, Si Phang Nga National Park (8:30 A.M.–6 P.M. daily, 400B) has the 60-meter-high **Namtok Tam Nang** waterfall and a number of smaller waterfalls. There are a limited number of marked trails in the park; on them are ample opportunities to spot rare birds, including hornbills. There are small bungalows for rent as well as a camping ground, but this park, unlike most others in the region, does not have a beach. Although the names are similar, this is not the same park as Ao Phang Nga National Park.

Sports and Recreation

There are a few short marked hiking trails in the park. The nicest is actually the shortest, at just over 1.5 kilometers, starting at the **Tam Nang waterfall.** From there, you head up to a viewpoint in the forest where you can see the mangrove swamps edging out into the sea.

Getting There

The national park is located between Kuraburi and Takua Pa on Highway 4. If you're driving, you'll see signs from the highway for the national park and the Tam Nang waterfall. Follow signs for either, as the park's headquarters are right next to the waterfall. The park is east of Highway 4.

Krabi   กระบี่

With a rugged coastline and white sandy beaches, the former fishing area of Krabi is probably the most beautiful province on the mainland of Thailand if you're looking for a beach destination. Like the island of Phuket, Krabi has a mountainous green interior broken up by highlands and some plains as well as an irregular coastline creating lots of small bays and beaches. Right off the coast of Krabi are some of the most beautiful limestone rock formations in the Andaman Sea, which offer great opportunities for rock climbing, if you're feeling adventurous, or sea kayaking through some of the caves worn into the rocks, if you prefer a less strenuous approach. The best beaches in Krabi are located in the center of the province, around Rai Le and Nang, and you'll have to see them to understand just how beautiful a simple beach can be. It's not just the water and the sand, although the crystal-clear blue Andaman Sea and clean, fine sand certainly help. It's the surrounding cliffs and luxuriant tree greenery as well as the view to the small islands off the coast that create a landscape like nowhere else in the world. Krabi Province is also technically home to some of the best islands in region—Ko Phi Phi and Ko Lanta—although many people will travel to these from Phuket or Trang, as they are about halfway between those locations and Krabi. Although Krabi certainly has its share of luxury resorts catering to vacationers' every whim, the region is nowhere near as built-up as Phuket is. Getting to some of the popular beaches involves taking a boat from the mainland—although Krabi is not an island, there are many spots where no roads go. Maybe because it is slightly less accessible, Krabi also has a more rugged feel to it.

mainland Krabi

© SUZANNE NAM

KRABI TOWN
เมืองกระบี่

Most people pass through Krabi Town on their way to the beaches or skirt it entirely on their way from the Krabi airport to the boat pier. While there's no reason to stay in Krabi Town unless you're on a really tight budget, as it's not close to the beach and the available accommodations are not quite up to international standards, it's an interesting place to spend a few hours, if only to see what life is like away from the beaches. The town is set on the Krabi River, an estuary that empties into the Andaman Sea farther down, and there are some picturesque wooden houses built on stilts, although you may find some of the town less charming and appealing due to its urbanized feel. Krabi Town does have some of the most interesting and creative statues–cum–traffic lights in Thailand. If that's not enough to hold your attention for very long (they're not *that* interesting), there's also a **night market** (Khong Kha Rd., right next to the Chao Fa pier, 6–10 P.M. daily) where visitors often stop to take photos or grab a snack from one of the curry stalls or *satay* vendors. The **Maharat Market,** on Maharat Soi 9, opens at 3 A.M. and closes by midday daily. It's one of the largest indoor markets in the country, and although you probably won't be taking home any of the seafood or produce on offer, it's worth looking at.

BEACHES
Ao Nang Bay
อ่าวนาง

The large, sweeping Ao Nang Bay is the most popular beach area in Krabi, with scores of accommodations, including many large international chains. Although nowhere near as hopping as Patong, Ao Nang is nonetheless a very touristy, slightly generic resort area. Still, the physical landscape surrounding the bay is impressive—there are scores of different small islands and rock formations in view. Ao Nang also serves as a jumping-off point for day trips to the surrounding islands. Unfortunately, the beach itself is not swimmable all the time because of the boat traffic.

© SUZANNE NAM

THE ANDAMAN COAST

Rai Le Beach

◖ Rai Le Beach
หาดไร่เลย์

The small Rai Le Beach, surrounded by limestone cliffs behind and large rock formations rising from the sea in front, is the most beautiful of the beaches in Krabi and arguably one of the most beautiful in all of Thailand. Since Rai Le is an isthmus jutting off the mainland, there are actually two Rai Le beaches, one to the east and one to the west. With crystal-clear blue waters, soft sand, and only a handful of resorts and small restaurants right near the beach, **West Rai Le** is both breathtaking and totally relaxed. **East Rai Le** also has lovely surrounding scenery, but it's actually mostly mudflats, and there's no sand and nowhere to lay out a towel. But that's not a problem, as you can easily walk to sandy West Rai Le in 10–15 minutes if you're staying on the east side, where accommodations are generally less expensive.

Noppharat Thara Beach
หาดนพรัตน์ธารา

Just adjacent to Ao Nang is Noppharat Thara,

a long sandy beach that's technically part of a national park. Lined with casuarina trees and just a handful of amenities, this is a great beach for hanging out if you're looking for something quiet and peaceful but close to the more happening Ao Nang.

Tham Phra Nang Beach
หาดถ้ำพระนาง

Just a short walk from Rai Le at the end of the peninsula, this small, secluded beach is bordered by a rocky headland on one side and limestone cliffs on the other. There's also a mystical cave here—**Tham Phra Nang Nok,** or Princess Cave—believed by local fisherfolk to house a sea princess. Although so far she hasn't been sighted by any travelers, you can check out the interesting offerings that are left for her in the cave.

SPORTS AND RECREATION
Rock Climbing

Krabi has the best rock climbing in the country, thanks to the beautiful limestone mountains and the built-up rock climbing industry. There are hundreds of bolted routes that will take you as high as 300 meters at varying levels of difficulty. This is not a sport to try without some training or proper equipment, but fortunately there are at least half a dozen rock-climbing shops offering lessons, rentals, and guided tours. Total beginners can take either full-day (2,000B) or half-day (1,000B) lessons, which include on-the-ground training and climbing. Those with experience can either hire a guide to explore the many routes in the area or just rent the necessary equipment and pick up a map from any of the shops.

Wee and Elke of **Basecamp Tonsai** (Ton Sai Beach, next to Ton Sai Bay Resort, www.basecamptonsai.com), formerly Wee's Climbing School, literally wrote the book on rock climbing in Krabi. You can buy their newly updated guide at their shop or take one of the half-day, full-day, or multiple-day classes they offer. Their shop also sells and rents an extensive selection of equipment. **Hot Rock** (Rai Le Beach West, tel. 07/562-1771, www.railayadventure. com) is also highly recommended because of the professionalism and personalities of their guides. They offer instruction for beginners and tours for advanced climbers. Their shop also sells and rents equipment.

Kayaking

The uneven coastline, mangrove forests, and scores of rock outcroppings and islands make Krabi an excellent area to explore with a kayak. Many guided kayaking tours (around 1,500B for a full day) leave from Ao Nang. On a typical tour, you'll spend some time paddling through the nearby mangrove forests and also set out to explore some of the small islands and sea caves that have been created through thousands of years of erosion. **Sea Canoe Thailand** (Ao Nang, tel. 07/569-5387) is one of about half a dozen companies offering daily kayak tours.

On Rai Le Beach West, there are rental kayaks available right on the beach(400B for the day). Inexperienced kayakers should be aware that currents can be surprisingly strong and that longtail boats, speedboats, and larger vessels are frequently in the water and may not see you.

Snorkeling

The islands around Krabi, including Ko Phi Phi, have some of the best snorkeling in the country, and it's quite possible to see not only amazingly colorful tropical fish and coral gardens with just a snorkel and a mask, but you might even spot some reef sharks. While many people choose to enjoy snorkeling on one of the day tours offered by dive shops and travel agents in Krabi, it is also possible to charter a longtail boat to take you out on your own. If you're going the prepackaged-tour route, **Kon-Tiki Thailand Diving & Snorkeling Center** (61/1 Mu 2, Ao Nang, tel. 07/563-7675, www. kontiki-krabi.com) offers snorkel-only excursions (850B) instead of the usual boat tour of the area with snorkeling tacked on. Their tours will take you to Ko Phi Phi and the Mu Ko Hong islands, and since they're focused on snorkeling you'll spend as much time as possible in the water.

If you'd prefer to go out on your own, longtail boats can take you out to the smaller islands around Ao Nang and will generally know where you'll be able to see fish or coral. There are scores of private longtail captains in Ao Nang and West Rai Le available; prices for personalized trips are entirely negotiable, but you should expect to pay at least 1,000B for a few hours on the sea. Longtail boats are smaller, less comfortable, and slower than speedboats (and life preservers are generally nonexistent), so if you are planning on going out on one, it's best done for shorter distances.

ACCOMMODATIONS
Ao Nang

If you want to avoid the big properties, **The Buri Tara Resort** (159/1 Mu 3, Ao Nang, tel. 07/563-8277, www.buritara.net, 3,500B), with only 69 guest rooms, is a smart, stylish choice in the budget-luxury category. The pool isn't as large as what you'll find at other resorts, and it's a few minutes' walk to the closest beach, but the property opened at the end of 2006 and the guest rooms are nicely decorated in a modern dark-wood style with some Thai touches.

The small, charming **Alis Hotel** (125 Ao Nang, tel. 07/563-8000, www.alisthailand. com, 2,500B) has a unique Mediterranean design and comfortable guest rooms with luxurious baths. For nice guest rooms and a good location about 10 minutes from the beach, it's a good choice. There's a nice rooftop pool and a bar on the premises, but the grounds aren't massive, and the lack of things like elevators are a reminder that it's not quite a boutique resort but rather a small hotel.

Although not as beautifully kept up as the Centara Grand, the large **Krabi La Playa Resort** (143 Mu 3, Ao Nang, tel. 07/563-7015 to 07/563-7020, www.krabilaplaya.com, 5,100B) has a great pool area and roomy, well-furnished guest rooms done in a modern Thai style. It is right on the beach and an easy walk to town. Some of the guest rooms have swim-up access to the pool.

The **Cliff Ao Nang Resort** (85/2 Mu 2, Ao Nang, tel. 07/563-8117, www.k-bi.com, 8,000B) is a beautiful property with many design elements from traditional bungalows but completely modern, comfortable guest rooms. Although there are some rustic elements, they're purely aesthetic—there's not a trace of backpacker to be found. The semi-outdoor baths are spacious and have rain showerheads, the restaurant is elegant, and the pool is large and minimalist so as not to detract from the natural beauty found in the surrounding cliffs and ocean. This is definitely a hip, romantic resort designed for couples, although kids are welcome.

The **Centara Grand Beach Resort and Villas** (396–396/1 Mu 2, Ao Nang, tel. 07/563-7789, www.centralhotelsresorts.com, 8,000B) has large, beautiful guest rooms with stunning ocean views, top-class resort amenities, and excellent service, all set on its own small private bay with a small beach right next to Ao Nang. If you don't feel like leaving the compound, there are five different places to eat within Centara as well as a spa and multiple swimming pools. If you're looking for a big resort experience in Krabi, this is probably the best price you'll find in the category, and especially in the off-season, when you'll pay about half the price; it's a bargain.

Rai Le Beach

Since it's set on the mudflats side of Rai Le, you'll have to walk about 15 minutes to get to the good part of the beach from **Sunrise Tropical Resort** (39 Mu 2 Ao Nang, Rai Le Beach, tel. 07/562-2599, www.sunrisetropical.com, 3,500B), but it is a great value if you want to stay in a well-appointed beach bungalow without paying five-star resort prices. The bungalows are modern, spacious, and clean, the baths have outdoor showers and are nicely fitted, and the grounds are leafy. The larger villas are enormous for the price. Although it's a small property with only 28 bungalows, there's a pool, a small restaurant, and an Internet café.

If you can get one of the bungalows at ■ **Railei Beach Club** (Rai Le Beach, Ao Nang, tel. 07/562-2582, www.raileibeachclub. com, 5,000B), consider yourself lucky. A cluster of houses set right on the beach, this is neither a resort nor a hotel. Each of the homes is individually owned and rented out by owners when they're not in town, and they vary in size from cozy bungalow to four-bedroom house. The design of each is a little different, but they're all wooden bungalow houses with clean, comfortable bedrooms and baths. Some have elegant dark-wood furnishings; others are a little more rustic. The larger buildings have their own kitchens and entertaining space, perfect for a family or larger group, or a couple that wants to spend an extended time. There's no pool, although it is set on what is arguably the most beautiful part of the beach. Although it's not a resort, there's daily maid service, and if you want, they'll arrange to have someone come to your bungalow and cook dinner for you.

"Beach bungalow" doesn't do the **Rayavadee Premier** (214 Mu 2, Ao Nang, tel. 02/301-1850, www.rayavadee.com, 15,000B) justice. The individual accommodations are more like small luxury homes set in a quiet, secluded part of the beach. This is one of the most indulgent places to stay on Rai Le, as is clear from the hefty rates you'll pay. The property has nearly 100 bungalows, so there are lots of amenities, including tennis courts, a fitness center, and a handful of restaurants. While most people staying on Rai Le have to arrive at the pier on the east side of the beach and walk to their resort, the Rayavadee will arrange to have a private boat pick you up from Krabi Town and deliver you straight to the resort. Despite the high prices, peak season fills up months in advance, so book quickly if you're interested in staying here.

FOOD
Krabi Town

Hands down the best Thai restaurant in Krabi Town, both for food and ambience, is 🄲 **Ruen Mai** (315/5 Maharat Rd., tel. 07/563-1797, 11 A.M.–10 P.M. daily, 200B). It may be filled with travelers, but don't be put off. It's worth feeling like a lemming to enjoy a meal in this verdant garden setting. The curries and other typical Thai dishes are well executed, but for something different, try the crunchy *plai sai* fried fish snacks or *kaeng som* sour curry with fish. This is also a great place for vegetarians. Although there aren't many straight veggie offerings on the menu, the kitchen will prepare just about anything you want without meat.

For a distinctly southern-Thailand breakfast dish, head to **Kanom Jin Mae Weaw** (137 Krabi–Khao Thong Rd., next to the PTT gas station, tel. 07/561-2666, 7 A.M.–noon daily, 50B) for some *kanom chin*—curry served over thin rice noodles. This very casual place has three different varieties and serves them spicy. For Western palates it may feel more appropriate to have this for dinner, but it's a morning meal, so get there early to try it.

Ao Nang

For seafood on the beach, **Wangsai Seafood Restaurant** (98 Mu 3, Ao Nang, tel. 07/563-8128, 10 A.M.–10 P.M. daily, 300B) is a good relaxed restaurant with a view of the ocean and a large deck right on the beach. The large sign is in Thai (it's the only place with no English sign), but the menu has English translations for all the typical Thai seafood dishes, including seafood fried rice and braised fish in lime, chilies, and garlic. The restaurant is quite popular among foreign visitors.

Another popular, solid choice for seafood on the beach is the **Salathai Restaurant** (32 Mu 2, Ao Nang, tel. 07/563-7024, 9 A.M.–10 P.M. daily, 300B). The menu has both traditional Thai dishes with seafood and some Western fare. Better to stick with the local food and seafood, which you can select yourself, and enjoy the view at this charming thatched-roof restaurant right on the water. It's not very fancy, by any standard, but the food and location are just right.

Krua Thara (82 Mu 5, Ao Nang, tel. 07/563-7361, 11 A.M.–9:30 P.M. daily, 200B) has great seafood dishes, whether part of a traditional Thai meal or just plain grilled or fried with Thai sauce. Like most of the places to eat in Krabi, it's nothing fancy to look at, but the food is good.

Rai Le

While Rai Le has some of the best beachfront property in Thailand, it's definitely not a contender for best dining options, and Krabi Town and Ao Nang have much better dining. That's not to say the food is bad, but there isn't much selection—most of it is from bungalow and resort restaurants and the roti vendors on the beach in the afternoon.

GETTING THERE

When planning your trip, remember that Krabi Town is more than 16 kilometers away from the area's main attraction—the beaches.

Air

The Krabi airport has frequent flights from Bangkok and is served by **Thai Airways** and **Bangkok Airways** as well as the budget airlines **Nok Air, Air Asia,** and **One-Two-Go.** If you're coming in from Singapore, **Tiger Airways** also has direct flights from that city. Although the airport is comfortable and modern, it's very small, and the services inside, including food, are very limited. From the airport, it's about a 30-minute drive to Ao Nang; there are plenty of taxis on hand to take you (400–600B). There is also a private airport shuttle that runs at least every hour (more frequently during high season) between the airport and Ao Nang. The fare is 150B, so if you're traveling with a group, it can be more economical (and faster if you happen to be staying at the last hotel on the route) to take a taxi.

It's also possible to fly into Phuket International Airport and then make the three-hour drive to Krabi. There is a minibus from the Phuket airport that goes to Krabi Town. It leaves three times daily 9 A.M.–1 P.M. for 350B per person.

Boat

If you're coming from Phuket, there is a boat that heads to the **Noppharat Thara pier** next to Ao Nang at 8 A.M. daily and goes back to Phuket at 3 P.M. The ride is about two hours and costs 350B.

Boat connections between Phi Phi and Krabi are frequent, especially during high season. There are ferry boats from Noppharat Thara pier that are currently running once daily at 3 P.M. The ride is about three hours and costs 550B. To get to Krabi from Phi Phi, there are frequent boats during high season, leaving at 9 A.M., 10:30 A.M., and 2:30 P.M.

If you're on Phi Phi, there are also ferries that leave Phi Phi at 9 A.M. for Ao Nang in Krabi and take a little under three hours.

If you are coming from Ko Lanta, boats only run during high season; otherwise you'll have to take a minivan, which involves two short ferry crossings. During high season, ferries from Ko Lanta to Krabi leave at 8 A.M. and 1 P.M. daily, returning at 10:30 A.M. and 2:30 P.M. The cost is 300B pp and takes about 1.5 hours.

Even if you're coming by air or ground transportation to Krabi, if you're staying in Rai Le, you'll have to take a boat to get to your ultimate destination. Although Krabi is on the mainland, there are no roads to Rai Le; you have to take a longtail boat from Ao Nang or Krabi Town. There are frequent boats from the Saphan Chaofa pier that should run around 80B pp (unless you arrive after the scheduled boats have stopped running, in which case you will have to negotiate with the owner of the boat). Your hotel in Rai Le will be able to arrange the transfer for you. The short trip to Rai Le can be a little treacherous, depending on the weather conditions and what you're carrying. The boats stop on Rai Le East beach, and if the tides are in when you arrive, the pier may be partially submerged in water. You have to walk, carrying your luggage, through sometimes knee-deep water, so it is essential that you pack only what you can comfortably lift over your head while walking. Once you get onto dry land, if you're staying on Rai Le West, you'll need to walk about 15 minutes to get to your final location. There are no cars or motorcycles—another reason to pack light. If you happen to be staying at the Rayavadee, they'll arrange a private boat to take you directly to the hotel—they'll even carry your stuff for you.

Bus

There are overnight buses leaving from Bangkok's Southern Bus Terminal at 5:30 P.M. daily for the 12-hour overnight drive to Krabi. Tickets on air-conditioned luxury buses cost 850B and terminate in Krabi Town. Regular air-conditioned buses leave Bangkok at 7 A.M., 4 P.M., and 5:30 P.M. daily and cost 450–600B. There are also frequent buses to Krabi from Phuket, Ko Pha-Ngan, Surat Thani, Trang, and Hat Yai.

Car

It's relatively easy to drive to Krabi. Highway 4, which runs south down the peninsula, is the best way to go and is well signed in English for the correct turnoff to Ao Nang. Once you're in the area, many people find cars totally unnecessary, as most time is spent either on the beach or at one of the many marine sights that can't be reached by road anyway.

THAN BOK KHORANI NATIONAL PARK

อุทยานแห่งชาติธารโบกขรณี

Mostly mountainous rainforests and mangroves, the small Than Bok Khorani National Park (8:30 A.M.–6 P.M. daily, 400B) also has a number of ponds, caves, and streams that seem to disappear under the limestone mountains as well as, of course, sandy beaches. There are also more than 20 small islands, really just rocks jutting out of the ocean, that are a part of the park. The best way to visit the islands is by canoe or kayak, but most do not have beaches, so it's difficult to disembark. Camping is allowed in the park, but amenities are very limited, so you'll have to bring everything with you.

Inside the park is the **Tham Phi Hua To,** which is believed to have been a shelter for prehistoric people living in the area; it has some prehistoric paintings of people and animals. The cave got its name, which means "big-headed ghost cave," because of the number of abnormally large human skulls found in the cave. It is also used by Buddhist monks as a temple and for meditation retreats. The cave is not accessible by land; to visit you have to take a boat. If you aren't already exploring the area by boat, or just want to visit the cave, you can pick up a longtail boat to take you there from the Bo Tho pier in Ao Luek.

Getting There

If you're staying in Ao Nang, you can get to the park either by land or by sea. It's a one-hour drive to the Bo Tho pier in Ao Luek, where you'll be able either to rent a canoe or kayak or charter one of the local boat captains to take you around. If you don't have a car, you can charter a longtail boat from Ao Nang to take you to the park and tour you around the islands (expect to pay around 1,000B for the trip, regardless of the number of passengers), making it a great day trip if you're hanging out in one of the more touristed areas in Krabi.

KHAO PHANOM BENCHA NATIONAL PARK

อุทยานแห่งชาติเขาพนมเบญจา

Another small national park worth visiting for a few hours because of the waterfalls and peaks is Khao Phanom Bencha National Park (8:30 A.M.–6 P.M. daily, 400B). There are some short hiking trails, including one that will take you to the highest point in the area, at more than 1,200 meters, and another that will bring you to a three-tiered waterfall called **Namtok Huay To,** where the water collects into 11 large pools at the base. The Tham Khao Phueng cave has stalagmites and stalactites typical of caves in the region. You can pick up a map of the park at the ranger station; the trails are easy to moderate.

Getting There

Less than 32 kilometers from Krabi Town, Khao Phanom Bencha National Park is best accessed either by car, *tuk tuk,* or motorcycle. If you get a ride from Krabi Town or Ao Nang, it's better to arrange round-trip transport, since when you're done exploring the park, there may not be anyone around to bring you back. If you are driving, take Pracha U Thit Road north out of Krabi Town, until you see Ban Thap Prik Health Center, where you take a left and continue heading north to the ranger station.

KHLONG THOM

คลองท่อม

Sights

The **Khlong Thom hot spring** (10B pp) is worth a visit if you happen to be in the area, particularly for the so-called **Emerald Pool,** where springwater collects in the forest, creating a strangely deep emerald or turquoise color, depending on the time of day. To see the pool at its best, come when the light is soft, either very early in the morning or just before dusk.

Right near the Emerald Pool is the **Ron Khlong Thom Waterfall,** in a part of the forest with lots of small hot springs that flow into cold streams, creating a warm-water waterfall.

The **Khao Pra-Bang Khram Wildlife Sanctuary** (เขตรักษาพันธุ์สัตว์ป่า เขาประะบางคราม, 8:30 A.M.–6 P.M. daily, 200B), also commonly referred to as Khao Nor Chuchi, has some small trails through lowland forests and past the Emerald Pool. The sanctuary is considered the single richest site for birds in the whole region, and you're likely to spot black hornbills and kingfishers. Gurney's Pitta, of which there are less than 100 pairs estimated to exist on the planet, are known to nest in this area. There is also camping in the sanctuary, although unlike the national parks, there are no tent rentals, so you have to come equipped.

If you're interested in archaeology, the **Wat Khlong Thom Museum** at Wat Khlong Thom houses numerous items found during an excavation of Kuan Luk Pat, commonly referred to in English as the bead mound. Items on display include tools from the Stone and Bronze Ages, pieces of pottery, coins, and colored beads said to be more than 5,000 years old.

Getting There

To get to Khlong Thom, drive on Highway 4 heading south from Krabi Town; Khlong Thom will be marked at the junction of Highway 4 and Route 4038. From there, you will see well-marked signs directing you to the Emerald Pool or the wildlife sanctuary. You can also take a public bus headed for Trang from the bus terminal outside Krabi Town and tell the driver when you board that you want to get off at Khlong Thom. These buses run nearly hourly during the day, and you'll spend less than 30B to get to Khlong Thom. You'll end up in a small town area and will have to find transport to the surrounding sites, but during the day there are plenty of motorcycles that will take you. Although you can sometimes find a ride back from the sanctuary or the Emerald Pool, it's best to arrange round-trip transport at least back to Khlong Thom, where you can catch a bus heading for Krabi or Trang for the rest of your journey.

Mu Ko Phi Phi   หมู่เกาะพีพี

In recent years it seems the rest of the world has discovered what residents and intrepid travelers knew all along—the Ko Phi Phi islands, a small group of islands in Krabi Province about 40 kilometers off of the west coast of the mainland and just south of Phang Nga Bay, are lush and beautiful, the surrounding waters warm and clear, and the marinelife astounding. The discovery may have something to do with the Leonardo DiCaprio movie *The Beach*, which was filmed in the area. Certainly the movie helped put the islands on the map, but it's the physical beauty and ease with which you can go from lazing around on the beach to snorkeling or scuba diving that will make sure it stands the test of time.

The largest island of the group and the only one with tourist accommodations, Ko Phi Phi Don is shaped like two separate islands connected together by a thin strip of land with sandy beaches on each side. The beaches along that isthmus, Ton Sai Bay on the south and Loh Dalam Bay on the north, have become very popular for day-trippers and those staying on the island. The island is only about 16 kilometers long, and there are no roads or motorized transportation to take you from one part to another. Instead, there are plenty of longtail boats that function like shuttle buses and taxis. The rest of the islands in the group can easily be visited via a short ride on a longtail boat taxi from Phi Phi Don, or on a longer two-hour ferry or tour boat if you're coming from Phuket or Krabi.

Originally inhabited by Muslim fisherfolk, Phi Phi Don has changed dramatically in recent years. Ton Sai Bay is jam-packed with restaurants and small shops selling everything from sunglasses to T-shirts. Where there were once only a few simple bungalows, there are now full-scale resorts with swimming pools, spas, and anything else a traveler might be interested in, although in a much lower-key manner than you'll see on Phuket. If you're visiting Phi Phi or one of the surrounding islands for the day, you'll notice scores of speedboats and ferries moored close to the shore, all bringing in visitors who can crowd the beaches during high season. Residents and enlightened guests do their best to keep the island clean, but at times you will notice some wear and tear from the hundreds of visitors that come to the island every day. It's a shame, because Phi Phi is probably one of the most beautiful islands in the Andaman region, and it increasingly feels like its beauty is on the edge of being spoiled by overly eager tour operators and irresponsible visitors.

Neighboring, smaller Ko Phi Phi Le is a stunning limestone island encircling emerald-green Maya Bay. There are no accommodations on Phi Phi Le, but it has become a huge tourist draw, with day-trippers visiting by the hundreds per day during high season. With the throngs of other people and scores of motorboats in the bay, it's amazing that the island continues to look as beautiful as it does.

BEACHES
◖ Ton Sai Bay
หาดต้นไทร

The beaches along Ton Sai Bay, including **Hin** Khom Beach and **Long Beach** (Hat Yao), are stunningly beautiful, with white sand and mountain ranges off in the distance as well as some great opportunities for viewing the coral just off the coast. This beach area, however, is the most popular, and right behind the beach there are scores of guesthouses, bungalows, and even some bars and shops. If you want a budget backpacker experience in paradise, this is where you'll probably end up. This is also a popular place for day visitors to hang out, meaning it can become very crowded during high season.

Ranti Beach
อ่าวรันตี

Off the east coast of the larger part of Phi Phi Don, this beach has fewer accommodations and can only be reached from Ton Sai Bay on foot, or by speedboat or longtail, so pack light if you are planning on staying here. The beach itself is as beautiful as the rest of the island, and there is plentiful coral to view right off the coast. If you're looking for budget bungalows but want to avoid Ton Sai, Ranti is a great place to stay.

boats along Ton Sai Bay

© SUZANNE NAM

MU KO PHI PHI

© SUZANNE NAM

Maya Bay, Ko Phi Phi Le

Phak Nam Beach
อ่าวผักหนาม

Phak Nam has the same clear blue water and soft sand but is even more secluded than Ranti, with very few accommodations, though this will probably be changing soon in light of all the development going on in the region. To get to this beach, you can either hike to the east side of the island or take a water taxi.

Laem Thong Beach
หาดแหลมตง

Way at the northern tip of the island, Laem Thong is one of the quieter areas, with a long white-sand beach and only a few accommodations. This area, at a point when the island thins out to only about 200 meters wide, has a quiet, peaceful atmosphere and a handful of high-end resorts. It can be a little difficult to get to if you're coming from Ton Sai Bay, as it's too far to walk, and you have to travel by water, but the beach has its own pier, so you can skip the crowds and commotion and head straight here from the mainland instead.

Ko Phi Phi Le
เกาะพีพีเล

On Phi Phi Le there are no accommodations but some beautiful places to visit either from the mainland or from Phi Phi Don.

Amazing emerald-colored waters and large rock formations characterize **Maya Bay** (อ่าวมาหยา), a tiny bay on the east side of Phi Phi Le. Once you enter the bay, you'll be astounded by the beauty of the surrounding physical landscape. There's a small beach for swimming with rocky outcroppings overhead and even a tiny bit of rainforest to walk around in. There are no overnight accommodations on Maya Bay, but the place gets packed with day-trippers, so try to arrive early to enjoy a bit of the beauty without the crowds. You can go by longtail boat or speedboat, or paddle over on your own. The bay itself is not great for snorkeling (especially because it's usually filled with boats), but if you walk across the island and through a small cave (you can't miss it, as there's only one path you can walk on), there's some better snorkeling off of that

DIVING ON THE ANDAMAN COAST

The waters surrounding the Andaman coast and its islands offer an amazing diversity of marine-life and dive sites from beginner to advanced, some considered among the best in the world. Hundreds of dive shops offer courses, equipment rental, day trips, and live-aboards (where you live aboard a boat for a few days). If you're planning on diving in the region, don't worry too much about where you are staying relative to the areas where you want to dive; most diving shops (especially in Phuket) offer dives to all of the most popular sites in the region. When deciding where to dive, take advantage of the many resources on the Internet. One excellent resource is **Dive Guide Thailand** (www.diveguidethailand.com), which offers a free downloadable guide to diving in the region.

PHUKET AREA

The area surrounding the main island offers some good diving day trips. **Ko Racha Noi** is a popular place to visit on a day trip and has a nice mix of both colorful coral and challenging, rocky terrain. Another very popular destination is **Shark Point,** about 32 kilometers east of Chalong Bay. There are three rock outcroppings that attract — as the name implies — sharks (mostly leopard sharks). Just under one kilometer away is **Anemone Reef,** with lots of anemone, coral, and plenty of colorful small fish. If you're interested in wreck diving, close by is **King Cruiser Wreck,** a sunken car ferry in Phang Nga Bay. This site is appropriate for most divers and attracts lots of fish. Other wrecks near Phuket, including **SS Petaling, HMS Squirrel,** and **HMS Vestal,** are considered technical dives and can only be visited by experienced divers.

KO PHI PHI AREA

The waters surrounding Ko Phi Phi offer both nice diving and excellent snorkeling. The biggest attraction here is the colorful coral and vibrant fish. Most of the dives are not difficult, but divers looking for more of a challenge can check out the wall diving at **Ao Nui.**

KO LANTA AREA

South of Ko Lanta are some excellent (and con-venient) dive sites. The Mu Ko Lanta National Marine Park is a group of 15 small islands, many with good diving in surrounding areas. You'll find lots of rocky terrain attracting colorful fish, some underwater caves to explore, and beautiful coral. The **Ko Kradan Wreck** is now an artificial reef.

MERGUI ARCHIPELAGO

This archipelago, technically in Burma's waters, has only been open to international visitors for a decade and offers some interesting off-the-beaten-path diving opportunities. The draw of these islands is in the very rocky underwater terrain and interesting marinelife. You'll have lots of opportunities to swim with sharks, including hammerheads, reef, nurse, and bull sharks, as well as plenty of rays. These dive sites are only accessible on live-aboard trips.

SURIN ISLANDS

These islands are part of the Mu Ko Surin National Marine Park and are best known for the excellent coral surrounding them. The biggest draw is **Richelieu Rock,** a rock pinnacle jutting out of the ocean that's known to attract giant, gentle whale sharks. These islands are accessible by live-aboard trips from Phuket, but if you're staying in Khao Lak, you can visit on a day trip.

SIMILAN ISLANDS

These nine granite islands make up the Mu Ko Similan National Marine Park and are considered by most to offer the best diving in Thailand and some of the best diving in the world. Here you'll find plenty of colorful reefs and plankton blooms (during the hot season) attracting sharks, rays, and plenty of tropical fish. Other parts of the island grouping are more rugged, with boulder formations offering more adventurous diving. There are also great night-diving spots where you'll see squid, crustaceans, and other creatures. These islands can be visited on day trips from Phuket and Khao Lak, but many people choose multiple-day live-aboards.

CERTIFICATION

In Thailand most diving instruction courses offer

PADI (www.padi.com) open-water diver certification. These courses take 3–4 days, at the end of which you'll be certified to dive all over the world. You'll spend time in the classroom first learning about safety and dive theory, take your first dive in a swimming pool, and advance to supervised open-water dives. Expect to pay 10,000–15,000B for the full course, including equipment and dives. If you can't imagine wasting hours inside a classroom while you're on vacation, and assuming there is a PADI training center where you live, you can do the classroom and pool-diving components of your training at home and bring your referral paperwork with you to Thailand, where you'll be able to complete the open-water portion of the certification.

Certified divers looking to advance their skills can also take **dive master** courses, become certified diving instructors, and arrange training internships at some of the larger training centers. These programs are at least two weeks long and cost 30,000–40,000B.

DIVE SHOPS AND CENTERS

When choosing a company to go diving with, first check the PADI website, which lists all of the PADI-certified dive shops across the globe and is searchable by country. There are many excellent dive shops and training centers throughout the Andaman region, and Thailand in general has an excellent safety record when it comes to diving. Instructors and dive masters are both local and foreign, and all are fluent in English. To pick a dive shop, it's best to drop in to some in your vicinity and spend a few minutes talking to staff before deciding who to dive or train with. The following dive centers are all certified by PADI to offer open-water diving certification, dive master training, and instructor training. All also offer one-day trips and multiple-day live-aboard diving trips.

- **Ao Nang Divers** (Krabi Seaview Resort, 143 Mu 2, Ao Nang, Krabi, tel. 07/563-7242, www.aonang-divers.com)

- **Dive Asia** (24 Thanon Karon, Kata Beach, Phuket, tel. 07/633-0598, www.diveasia.com)

- **Kata Diving Service** (Kata Garden Resort, 121/1 Mu 4, Thanon Patak, Karon Beach, tel. 07/633-0392)

- **Marina Divers** (45 Thanon Karon, Karon Beach, Phuket, tel. 07/633-0272)

- **Moskito Diving** (Tonsai Bay, Ko Phi Phi, tel. 07/560-1154, www.moskitodiving.com)

- **Oceanic Divecenter** (30 Thanon Karon, Karon Beach, Phuket, tel. 07/633-3043, www.oceanicdivecenter.com)

- **Pro-Tech Dive College** (389 Thanon Patak, Karon Beach, tel. 07/628-6112, www.pro-techdivers.com)

- **Sea Dragon Dive Center** (5/51 Mu 7, Thanon Khuek Khak, Khao Lak, Phang Nga, tel. 07/648-5420, www.seadragondivecenter.com)

- **Sea Fun Divers** (Katathani Beach Resort, 14 Kata Noi Rd., Kata Noi Beach, tel. 07/633-0124, www.seafundivers.com)

- **Sea World Dive Team** (177/23 Soi Sansabai, Patong Beach, tel. 07/634-1595, www.seaworld-phuket.com)

- **Sunrise Diving** (49 Thanon Thaweewong, Patong Beach, Phuket, tel. 07/629-2052)

- **Visa Diving** (77 Mu 7, Ko Phi Phi, tel. 07/560-1157, www.visadiving.com)

- **Warm Water Divers** (229 Thanon Rat-U-Thit 200 Pee, Patong Beach, Phuket, tel. 07/629-2201, www.warmwaterdivers.com)

- **West Coast Divers** (120/1-3 Rat-T-Tit 200 Pee Rd., Patong Beach, tel. 07/634-1673, www.westcoastdivers.com)

RECOMPRESSION CHAMBER

Although accidents and the bends are quite rare, **Badalveda Diving Medical Center at Bangkok Hospital Phuket** (2/1 Thanon Hongyok Utis, Phuket Town, tel. 07/625-4425, 24-hour emergency hotline tel. 08/1989-9482) has a hyperbaric chamber and medical staff who specialize in diving injuries.

coast, including views of sea urchins and tropical fish.

Monkey Beach (Hat Ling, หาดลิง) is a fun place to visit if you want to hang out with the scores of monkeys populating this pretty little strip of sandy coast that can be reached by canoe, speedboat, or longtail boat. If you go, make sure you bring something for the monkeys to snack on—as a result of thousands of tourists visiting every year, they've grown to expect some compensation in exchange for the entertainment they're providing, and they can get a little surly and even aggressive if you disappoint them.

SPORTS AND RECREATION
Diving
Phi Phi has some of the best diving in Thailand, made even better by the fact that it's so accessible and inexpensive. There's no need to set out on a boat for days or even to stay on Phi Phi. With all of the organized dive trips from Phuket, you can easily schedule full-day trips and return to the main island at night. Most of the outfitters listed for the Andaman coast offer trips to Phi Phi.

Boating
Most of the boating that goes on around Phi Phi is through chartered speedboats that take visitors from island to island during the day. These trips are hugely popular, as evidenced by the number of charter boats that line the coast of Phi Phi. Many of these tours include some snorkeling as well as lunch and depart from either Phi Phi or Phuket. There are a handful of companies that offer tours, although they sell almost exclusively through third-party tour agents, and you can arrange a tour through any travel agency on the mainland or Phi Phi, or from your hotel. Because of the intermediaries, prices for the trips can vary and are negotiable, although the agent may not tell you that it's not actually their company putting together the package. Prices for a day trip around Phi Phi should run about 1,200–2,000B, depending on the type of vessel you're on and the number of other passengers.

If you want to cruise around the surrounding islands at your own pace, at almost any beach you can hire a longtail boat to take you from one place to another. It's quite an experience to sit back and take in the view of the Andaman Sea from one of the long, thin, colorful boats while the captain steers from behind. Compared to speedboats, longtail boats are a lot smaller and less agile in choppy waters, so they're best enjoyed if you're only doing limited island hopping. When longtail boats are used as taxis, prices are usually fixed, and you should expect to pay 40–100B per trip. Chartering a boat for a fixed amount of time can cost anywhere from 400B, depending on the number of people and the time of year.

Kayaking
The area around the Phi Phi islands offers excellent opportunities for sea kayaking to explore the hidden bays and mangrove forests surrounding the islands. If you're just looking to paddle around close to shore, there are plenty of kayaks on the beaches available for rent. More-experienced kayakers can rent boats and arrange to have them pulled by longtail from Phi Phi Don to Maya Bay on Phi Phi Le. You can also request that the boat's captain pick you up at a designated time and place when you're ready to return. It's possible to cross from one island to another by kayak, but weather conditions can change rapidly, and only experienced kayakers should attempt the venture.

If you're kayaking, bear in mind that Phi Phi is a very popular destination for speedboats and larger tour boats, and by midday in high season the whole area can get very crowded with larger vessels. What may seem like just an annoyance can become dangerous if you're not seen by another boat, so pay close attention to the waters around you. The quietest time for kayaking is early in the morning, before the rest of the world arrives.

ACCOMMODATIONS
Phi Phi Don was long a favorite of travelers on a budget, thanks to the cheap bungalows,

especially along Ton Sai Bay, that had few amenities but the prime real estate on the island. The island was devastated during the tsunami in 2004, and most of the bungalows, resorts, and hotels have had to rebuild. Like everywhere else in Thailand, tourism is moving upscale, and the rebuilding seems to have shifted the island's focus from budget backpacker upward. Although there are still opportunities to sleep in a small shack on the beach without air-conditioning or hot water for just a few hundred baht per night, you'll find those accommodations increasingly packed together in smaller and smaller areas (namely Ton Sai), with mid-range hotels and more expensive resorts popping up on the island in their place. On the luxury front, the island is increasingly getting its share of high-end resorts too. Perhaps because Phi Phi is so beautiful and so popular, hoteliers don't seem to be trying too hard to compete with one another or to woo guests. The most common complaint that travelers have about the island is that where they stayed was overpriced and mediocre, regardless of whether it was a cheap bungalow or a high-end resort.

Ton Sai Bay

With scores of guesthouses in the area, Ton Sai Village, the small strip of flat land in the middle of the island, is a popular spot for visitors to stay. Here's where you'll find most conveniences; the majority of the island's restaurants and small shops are here, but you'll find less peace and calm.

J. J. Guesthouse (Ton Sai Village, tel. 07/560-1090, www.jjbungalow.com, 700B) offers very basic fan-cooled guest rooms in their small guesthouse. Guest rooms are clean and comfortable, and definitely good value for the money. There is a small restaurant on the property. For a little more money, you can stay at one of their bungalows, which are all air-conditioned and spacious, though simple.

If you want to stay right near Ton Sai Bay but still feel a little pampered, the **Phi Phi Island Cabana Hotel** (58 Mu 7, tel. 07/560-1170, 4,200B) is a nice choice for a not-too-expensive resort. The guest rooms are well maintained, and the grounds are nicely designed. The guest rooms are all decorated in a modern Thai style and feel much less rustic than bungalows you'll find scattered along the beach, and there's a nice large swimming pool with comfortable chairs. The hotel is also very well located on Ton Sai between two beaches, so visitors can take advantage of the more inexpensive longtail boats in the area to hop from place to place. The only trade-off is that with more than 150 guest rooms, it's not quite a small resort.

Laem Thong Beach

At the northern tip of the island, in secluded Laem Thong Beach, is **Phi Phi Natural Resort** (Mu 8, Laem Tong Beach, tel. 07/561-3010, 3,300B). The standard guest rooms and cottages have a rustic feel to them, with lots of exposed wood and simple, basic furnishings. It's nothing luxurious or fancy, but there's air-conditioning and a small swimming pool with an ocean view. The resort is tucked away from any crowds and feels secluded and relaxed, more like a summer vacation at camp. There are also larger cottages that are great for families.

For something a little more predictable, if with slightly less personality, the **Holiday Inn Phi Phi Island** (Mu 8, Laem Tong Beach, tel. 07/562-7300, www.phiphi.holidayinn.com, 4,000B) has nice individual bungalows, many with ocean views. The swimming pool is not huge but opens onto the beach. Bungalows are decorated in a modern, somewhat generic style but have some small Thai details. Many have their own small balconies or porches.

Ao Lo Bakao

This beach's only resort, **Pee Pee Island Village** (Ao Lo Bakao, tel. 07/621-5014, www.ppisland.com, 6,500B), is definitely on the higher end of the beach bungalow experience, although it's not quite a five-star luxury resort. The bungalows and villas are done in a traditional Thai design with thatched roofs that fade into the surrounding palm trees and are designed to let in as much light and ocean view as possible. There is a spa and a few restaurants on the premises as well as a fantastic swimming pool looking out onto the Andaman Sea. This is a great place to stay if you're looking for seclusion and are happy to idle your vacation away reading books and listening to the waves, although at low tide the shore is too rocky and shallow to swim. Getting off the resort during the day can be a little tricky—the resort has infrequent shuttle boats running to Ton Sai Bay, but if you miss them and need to charter a private boat from the hotel, the prices are steep.

Ao Toh Ko

Ao Toh Ko Bungalows (Ao Toh Ko, Phi Phi Island, tel. 08/1731-9470, 350B) offers super-cheap, basic sleeping accommodations with lovely beach views in a quiet, secluded beach on the east coast of the island. If you're on a budget, or just want to experience what Phi Phi was like before all the other travelers came, these little bungalows will feel charming and quaint, and the little bar and inexpensive restaurant on the premises will feel like an added extra. If you're higher maintenance, this is not the place for you, however: There's no air-conditioning or hot water in most of the guest rooms.

FOOD

Come nighttime, Ton Sai Bay is ground zero for food and entertainment, and if you're staying on one of the more remote beaches, the action can be a welcome change from all that peace and quiet. Almost all of the resorts on the island have small restaurants serving Thai food. Western food tends to be more than well represented at the stand-alone shops, perhaps to feed all the hungry Americans, Europeans, and Australians who flock here.

Even if you'll feel a little guilty eating baked goods on a tropical island, ◖ **Pee Pee Bakery** (Ton Sai Bay, 7 A.M.–8 P.M. daily, 40B) is hard to resist. The shop's glass display cases of doughnuts, breads, and cakes seem to beckon every traveler, especially around breakfast time. The bakery also serves Thai food, sandwiches, and pizza, all of which are well prepared.

During the day, the seafood restaurants right on the edge of the beach overlooking Ton Sai Bay are usually filled with day-trippers on arranged tours. At night, these restaurants feel less like food conveyer belts and are pleasant places to drink a cold Singha over dinner and enjoy the view. **Chao Koh** (tel. 07/560-1083, 11 A.M.–9 P.M. daily, 250B) is one with good seafood and a nice view. Cuisine here is traditional Thai seafood dishes. The food is good, but don't expect anything too creative.

Although some visitors, particularly the over-30 crowd, seem perplexed as to the reason, **Hippies** (Hin Khom Beach, tel. 08/1970-5483, 8 A.M.–late daily, 200B) is a wildly popular restaurant, bar, and party spot right on Hin Khom Beach. The menu, which features Middle Eastern food, pizza, and plenty of Thai dishes, seems designed to offer something for everyone. The food is actually pretty good (although if you want authentic Thai food, make sure to ask for it extra spicy), but it's really the beachfront location, charming thatched roofs and bamboo furniture, and laid-back vibe that are the draws here.

GETTING THERE

The only way to get to the island is by water. In the past, intrepid tour operators have tried using seaplanes for the short flight from Phuket airport, but they have not managed to make that business model work.

Boat

Phi Phi Don is easily reached by ferry boat or speedboat from Phuket or Krabi. There are no public ferries per se, only private operators, and when you buy a ticket, most will include a ride from your hotel in Phuket or Krabi to the pier. Schedules change frequently, especially in the low season, but during high season there are least two boats from Chalong Bay in Phuket to Ton Sai Bay on Phi Phi Don, one in the morning and another in the afternoon, and returning boats on a similar schedule. The trip should take around two hours, depending on the weather conditions. From Krabi, there are boats leaving from Ao Nang and Rai Le

© SUZANNE NAM

Ko Phi Phi Le's streets are lined with shops and stalls that cater to tourists.

THE ANDAMAN COAST

Beaches daily, also in the morning and after-noon. Fares run from 350B upward, depending on the time of day and the season. If you're with a large group of people, it can sometimes be more economical to charter your own speedboat from Chalong Bay or Krabi to Phi Phi. In a small, fast vessel, the trip can take half as long as the larger boats, but you should expect to pay a few thousand baht per journey.

Given the cost of the trip, if you have some time to spare, it may be worthwhile to take one of the package tours that will not only bring you to Phi Phi but also provide a tour of neighboring islands and sights while you're on the way. Just make sure the boat will stop at Ton Sai Bay (if that's where you're going), as some tours skip this spot entirely.

Many of the hotels on Phi Phi can arrange your transport from either Krabi or Phuket for you if you're staying on their property. Otherwise, you can buy tickets from any travel agent, but when purchasing, make sure to ask about the size of the boat and the number of passengers if you have a preference for the type of vessel. Larger ferries and speedboats generally take 90 minutes from either Krabi or Phuket. During the low season, it's fine just to show up at the pier and buy a ticket, but during high season ferries can sometimes sell out, so the best bet is to find a travel agency and buy a ticket as soon as you can.

GETTING AROUND

There are no taxis or *tuk tuks* on Phi Phi; for the most part there aren't even any roads. Most of the getting-around involves walking or traveling from Ton Sai Bay to other spots on the island by longtail boat, the area's taxi service. You'll pay 40–100B pp per trip from one part of the island to another, depending on the distance and whether you are traveling alone. From one island to another, expect to pay around 100B pp for the boat trip. Your hotel will be able to arrange a boat for you, but if you're picking one up from the beach, make sure you agree on the cost in advance.

Ko Lanta   เกาะลันตา

Just off the coast of Krabi is Ko Lanta, really two adjacent islands—**Ko Lanta Yai** and **Ko Lanta Noi.** Ko Lanta Yai, generally referred to just as Ko Lanta, is a large, thin island with limestone cliffs, a jungly interior, mangroves, and some good coral beaches. Although there are mangroves along much of the coast, there are also some great sandy beaches on the west side of the island, and that's where you'll find plenty of bungalows and small resorts. The interior has some great hiking trails through rainforests and some waterfalls worth checking out in Lanta's national park, which covers nearly half the island. Ko Lanta is arguably nearly as blissfully beautiful as Phi Phi, but Ko Lanta has yet to explode with the same popularity as its neighbor, and it has a strange half-backpacker, half-luxury vibe to it that some visitors find a perfect balance. You'll see this interesting dichotomy in the choice of accommodations as well—there are some great choices at both the upper and lower ends. Ban Saladan, a small village on the northeast corner of the island, functions as Ko Lanta's Main Street. This is where many of the ferries arrive, and there are also some limited amenities such as ATMs, Internet cafés, and supermarkets, but some of the more popular beach areas will have similar amenities as well. Ko Lanta Noi, adjacent to Ko Lanta Yai, has no beaches and has therefore not become a big destination, but depending on how you get to Ko Lanta, you may end up passing through the island.

SIGHTS
Lanta Old Town
หมู่บ้านเกาะแก่เกาะลันตา

Located on the east side of southern Ko Lanta, Lanta Old Town is a quaint fishing village that now serves as the island's capital. It's picturesque, with little teakwood houses on stilts above the water and brightly colored fishing boats set against the backdrop of an enticing blue ocean speckled with islands that seem to emerge as you watch. But Lanta Old Town is

also a fascinating place to observe the cultural diversity in southern Thailand that's often difficult to discern in heavily touristed areas. The town, once a major fishing port in the middle part of the 20th century, is home to Chinese immigrants, descendants of nomadic seafarers, and Thai Muslims who've created a comfortable, peaceful town blending all of their cultures together.

BEACHES AND SURROUNDING ISLANDS
◀ Khlong Dao Beach
หาดคลองดาว

Khlong Dao, closest to Ban Saladan, is a long stretch of wide, sandy beach on the southwest tip of the island backed by casuarina and palm trees. The waters in this crescent-shaped beach are generally quite calm, but this is the island's most popular tourist spot, so expect more of everything—more accommodations, more places to eat, and more people. It's still Ko Lanta, though, so even during peak season, you won't see any overcrowding at Khlong Dao.

Pra Ae Beach
หาดพระแอะ

Also called **Long Beach,** Pra Ae is another stretch of wide, sandy beach, with a nice selection of bungalows and resorts right on the water nestled among the trees. Just a few kilometers down from Khlong Dao, Long Beach is rarely crowded.

Khlong Khong and Khlong Nin Beaches
หาดคลองโขง และ หาดคลองนิน

As you move farther down the island, there are still plenty of bungalows right on the coast, but the beaches become less crowded with accommodations or people. Both Khlong Kong and Khlong Nin Beaches are served by a little village called Ban Khlong Nin, where you'll find all the basics, including an ATM, some places to eat, and small shops.

Kan Tiang Bay and the Southwest Coast
อ่าวกันเตียง

With less usable beach in relation to mangrove or rocky shore, this is where the island starts to feel remote. Kan Tiang Beach, with white sands and just a scattering of resorts, is nearly deserted in the low season, making it a great choice if you're looking for a quiet, romantic getaway. **Mai Pay Bay** is sometimes nicknamed "Last Beach" because it's at the end of the island and feels like the last beach in Thailand that hasn't been discovered. With simple bungalows and little going on other than the beautiful scenery and warm blue waters, Mai Pay Bay feels off the beaten path, and it attracts the backpacker crowd and other adventurers seeking scenery as well as peace and quiet.

Ko Ha
เกาะห้า

A group of five small rocky islands off the coast of Ko Lanta, Ko Ha is a popular place for diving and snorkeling due to the abundant coral and exotic sealife surrounding the islands as well as the excellent visibility in the water. There are no accommodations on the island, but it's often visited on day trips. To get to Ko Ha, you'll need to charter a speedboat or sailboat or go with an organized tour.

Ko Hai (Ngai) Lanta
เกาะไหง

With just a handful of resorts and very limited amenities, Ko Hai offers the quintessential desert-island experience if you're willing to give up a few luxuries in exchange for a laid-back, secluded vacation. The small island, mostly hilly rainforest, has a stretch of beautiful beach with views of karst rock formations rising from the sea and some great coral snorkeling just off the coast. The island is in Krabi Province just south of Ko Lanta Yai, but it's more convenient to get there by taking a boat from Trang instead. If you're staying on the island, the resort will arrange transportation for you.

Ko Ta Lebeng and Ko Bu Bu
เกาะตะละเบ็ง และ เกาะบูบู

Off the east coast of Ko Lanta, Ko Ta Lebeng is a limestone island with dramatic limestone cliffs and lush mangroves as well as a small bit of sandy beach. The island is very popular among sea kayakers and is a great place to go if you're not confident in open waters—the smaller Ko Ta Lebeng is protected by the main island, and the waters are a little calmer.

If you want to stay on a small island, Ko Bu Bu has only one resort with a handful of bungalows and clear warm waters for snorkeling. "Chilled-out" might be too exciting to describe the place—there's some great sandy beach and not much else to occupy your time other than sitting in a hammock and reading a book. The island is even too small for any long hiking.

NIGHTLIFE
Club Ibark (Khlong Nin Beach, Ko Lanta Yai, tel. 08/3507-9237, www.ibarkkrabi.com, 6 P.M.–late daily, no cover) bills itself as the country's freshest and funkiest club and, while that's definitely not true, it is the hottest thing going on Ko Lanta. Of course, Ko Lanta is a small island, and the nightlife pickings are pretty slim. Still, during high season the club pulls in a good crowd, and the DJs spin music that's head and shoulders above the typical Western pop classics you'll hear at most venues. There's a casual, fun vibe at this open-air dance club, and since everyone is on vacation, the partying can go on till late at night.

SPORTS AND RECREATION
Ko Lanta National Marine Park
The National Marine Park covers Hat Hin Ngam and Hat Tanod Beaches at the southern tip of Ko Lanta as well as a handful of surrounding small islands and rock formations. There are no resorts on the beaches, and like the other national parks with beaches, there are some camping amenities. **Tanod Beach,** at the bottom of Ko Lanta, is covered in rugged mountain terrain and sugar palms, giving way to a beautiful beach. There are hiking trails throughout this area filled with birdlife,

and at the end is the Lanta lighthouse, where you can climb up and view the island from above. There are campgrounds as well as many bungalows that can be rented from the parks authority. Approaching the lighthouse and surrounding area by road can be really tough without a 4WD vehicle, and depending on the weather, it may be easier to charter a longtail boat to take you.

Snorkeling

If you're looking to do some serious snorkeling, the area surrounding Ko Lanta has some great coral reefs and marinelife to see. You can swim out on your own, but to really see what's going on in the sea, arrange a boat trip around the island and neighboring islands. **Freedom Adventures** (70 Mu 6, Khlong Nin Beach, Ko Lanta Yai, tel. 08/4910-9132 or 08/1077-5025, www.freedom-adventures.com), based on Khlong Nin Beach, runs group day trips for about 1,500B from Ko Lanta on their charming wooden motorboat and can also create a personalized itinerary for you depending on your interests and abilities. This is a great excursion for nondivers who are interested in seeing the coral and tropical fish, as these folks specialize in snorkeling and not diving, so they'll only take you places you can enjoy viewing the underwater world without need of breathing gear.

ACCOMMODATIONS
Under 1,500B

Bu Bu Island Resort (Ko Bu Bu, tel. 07/561-8066, 350B) is a throwback to the days when simple bungalows on quiet beaches dominated the now mostly built-up Andaman coast. Guest rooms are very basic thatched-roof bungalows with private coldwater baths. There's also a small restaurant here, making it a great place to just chill out and enjoy the view.

1,500-3,000B

If you want to pay backpacker prices but don't want to forgo things such as a swimming pool and a restaurant on the premises, the **Andaman Lanta Resort** (142 Mu 3, Khlong Dao Beach, Ko Lanta, tel. 07/568-4200, www.

andamanlanta.com, 2,100B) is a decent mid-range option. The guest rooms are clean, if a little weary, but the resort is relaxed and child-friendly. Located on the north part of the island, it's definitely in a more crowded neighborhood, but the nearby beach stays mellow even during high season. It sort of looks like a group of IHOP restaurants, since all of the buildings have similar blue roofs.

Right nearby, at the southern end of Khlong Dao Beach, **Lanta Villa Resort** (14 Mu 3 Saladan, Ko Lanta, tel. 07/568-4129 or 08/1536-2527, www.lantavillaresort.com, 1,900B) is a similar property with clean, basic guest rooms and a nice swimming pool right on the popular beach. The bungalow-style rooms are a little too close together to feel secluded, but for this price and this location, it really is a bargain.

Ancient Realm Resort & Spa (364 Mu 3 Saladan, Ko Lanta, tel. 08/7998-1336, www.ancientrealmresort.com, 1,800B) is a solid mid-range beach resort with excellent service and good-value guest rooms. Some might be aesthetically offended by the liberal use of Buddhist and Southeast Asian images in the decor, but if you can get past that, the guest rooms are very comfortable and clean, and the beach location is excellent. All guest rooms have air-conditioning and hot water. The resort also feels less businesslike than some other properties, so staff and guests are more relaxed and friendly.

LaLaanta Hideaway (188 Mu 5, Ko Lanta, tel. 07/566-5066, www.lalaanta.com, 2,800B) is quiet, secluded, and relaxing, and though the bungalows are not at the five-star level, they are clean, nicely furnished, and comfortable enough that you won't miss much. There is a hotel restaurant and bar, plus a large swimming pool overlooking the Andaman Sea. The beach the resort is located on feels very secluded, and those who are looking for a place that feels like a deserted island will enjoy their time here.

3,000-4,500B

The small **Baan Laanta** (72 Mu 5, Kan Tiang Bay, Ko Lanta Yai, tel. 07/566-5091, www.baanlaanta.com, 3,500B) resort has only 15 bungalows, which straddle the line between rustic and luxurious. Terra-cotta tiles and lots of wood and bamboo give the guest rooms a very natural feeling, but things like a minibar, bathrobes, and private balconies with excellent views add bits of pampering and indulgence. The dark-tiled pool, spa *sala,* and outdoor bar are small but swanky-feeling and well maintained.

A boutique resort of the best kind, **◖ Sri Lanta** (111 Mu 6 Khlong Nin Beach, Ko Lanta Yai, tel. 07/566-2688, 3,800B) is both aesthetically pleasing and geared toward connecting visitors to the beautiful surroundings of Ko Lanta. This is not a place designed to make you forget where you are: The individual thatched-roof villas have wall-length shutters that you can open out onto the grounds, and the interiors are rustic but comfortable and deliberately don't have TVs. But things like the amazing black-tiled swimming pool, Wi-Fi, and good iced coffee mean you won't feel like you're missing out on much during vacation.

Over 4,500B

With bright, beautiful guest rooms set on a property that creeps into the surrounding rainforest along with lots of things to do, the **Rawi Warin Resort & Spa** (139 Mu 8, Ko Lanta, tel. 07/560-7400, www.rawiwarin.com, 7,800B) has more personality and charm than most large resorts. The guest rooms are modern but have an airy, clean tropical style to them, and the stucco exteriors give the resort a more Mediterranean feel than a Southeast Asian island feel. Some of the gigantic villas have their own swimming pools, but the common areas, which include multiple swimming pools, tennis courts, and a gym, are more than sufficient to keep you occupied. One of the restaurants also has free Wi-Fi. The property is very child-friendly, although some of the guest rooms are located up in the hills and will require a little bit of walking.

If you're looking for more amenities, the **◖ Pimalai Resort** (99 Mu 5, Ba Kan Tiang Beach, Ko Lanta, tel. 07/560-7999, www.pimalai.com, 12,000B) is a larger property with more than 100 guest rooms nestled in the hilly

rainforest above a beautiful, quiet stretch of white-sand beach. All of the guest rooms are in small bungalow buildings, giving the property a less crowded feeling despite the fact that there may be hundreds of guests and staff around during peak season. Inside, the guest rooms are a little more generic but still have some nice Thai design elements. The 35-meter infinity swimming pool overlooking the ocean is nearly as beautiful as the beach below.

FOOD

If you're just looking for casual food, you'll find lots of roti vendors around, selling the traditional Muslim rolled and flattened pancakes. They're traditionally served with savory curries, but these guys will stuff them with all sorts of sweet treats, including chocolate and bananas, for around 30B.

Gong Grit Bar (Khlong Dao Beach, 176 Mu 3, T. Saladan, A. Ko Lanta, tel. 08/9592-5844, 8 A.M.–10 P.M. daily, 300B) is one of the many places you'll find on Khlong Dao Beach serving up local fare and seafood dishes on the beach. This one isn't very fancy—none of them are—but the food is well done and the service is good. Gong Grit is at the southern end of the beach.

GETTING THERE
Boat

During high season, there is a twice-daily ferry boat from Krabi's new pier on **Tharua Road,** just outside Krabi Town. Remember that there are two piers in Krabi: **Chao Fah** pier, which is now used for travel immediately around Krabi, and the new pier, which is used for larger vessels. The ferry for Lanta leaves at 8 A.M. and 1 P.M., takes about 90 minutes, and costs 300B. It's best to arrange transport to the pier through your hotel in Krabi. There are also daily boats during high season from Ko Phi Phi to Ko Lanta, departing at 11:30 A.M. and 2 P.M. daily. That trip takes 90 minutes and also costs 300B.

Bus

Although Ko Lanta is an island, you can do much of the journey there by land, using two ferry crossings that can accommodate vehicles. In the low season, this is the only option, and there are numerous minivan services that will take you from Krabi to Ko Lanta. If you take one of the scheduled vans with **Lanta Transport** (tel. 07/568-4121), which run every few hours and take about 90 minutes, you'll pay 250B pp. You can also arrange to have a private minivan with any tour company, which should cost around 1,000B.

Car

If you're driving to Ko Lanta, head south on Highway 4 toward Trang (if you're coming from the Phang Nga area). Turn off at Route 4206 at Khlong Thom, about 32 kilometers from Krabi Town, and follow that road heading south all the way to the Hua Hin pier on the mainland. That leg of the journey is about 29 kilometers. From there you'll take your first ferry crossing to Ko Lanta Noi. The second ferry, about eight kilometers after the first, will bring you to Ko Lanta Yai; each will cost 100B.

GETTING AROUND

Ko Lanta does not have a public transportation system; to get around you'll have to rely on occasional motorcycle taxis and the shuttle buses and trucks run by the island's resorts. If you're driving on your own, by car or motorcycle, the island has a main road on the west coast that runs north–south and will allow you access to those beaches.

Trang and Satun Provinces จังหวัดตรัง และ จังหวัดสตูล

The two southernmost provinces on the Andaman coast before Thailand becomes Malaysia, Trang and Satun have not yet become popular tourism destinations, although direct flights from Bangkok to Krabi and Trang make them readily accessible for those looking for something off the beaten path. Both share much of the topography of neighboring Krabi—limestone cliffs, beautiful beaches, mangrove swamps, and a verdant interior, but are less commonly visited by travelers, most likely due to the plethora of amazing places to see so close to Phuket and its well-maintained tourism infrastructure. If the idea of flying into a big international airport and staying in a place where you'll most definitely see other foreign travelers is unappealing, these two provinces are worth the extra effort it takes to get here, if only for the chance to see what Thailand is really like while at the same time enjoying beautiful beaches and islands. The provinces are home to some spectacular small islands off the coast, most protected by two large national marine parks and easily accessible from the mainland either for day trips, if you're in a hurry, or extended stays, if you're looking for a desert-island experience. Off the coast of Trang is the Mo Ko Phetra National Park, comprising about 30 islands you can dive and snorkel around, or enjoy the gray-white sandy beaches and do some bird-watching. Off the coast of Satun are the Tarutao Islands, which, compared to their northern neighbors, are more visited, although still nothing like what you'll see in Phang Nga Bay. The national park comprises more than 50 islands where you can see coral and go snorkeling and scuba diving.

The mainland also has its share of natural beauty, and although there are scant tourist sights to see, there's still plenty to keep you busy should you decide to stay here for more than a day or two. Trang was the first area in Thailand where rubber trees, now an important part of the economy of the south, were planted, and Satun is home to a majority Muslim population, making both provinces culturally and historically interesting places to visit in addition to their physical beauty.

Compared to Phuket or Krabi, you won't find the same number or quality of accommodations on the mainland of either Trang or

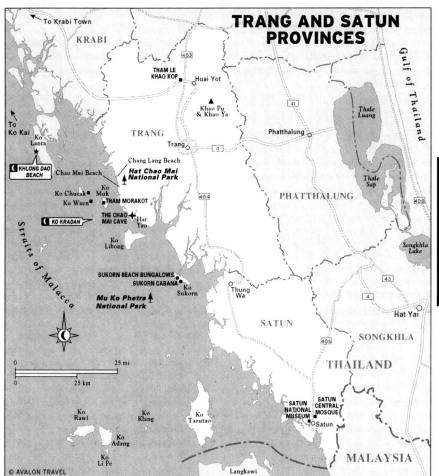

THE ANDAMAN COAST

Satun, although a couple of resorts have sprung up in the area as well as some very budget, very simple beach bungalows.

TRANG
Trang Town
เมืองตรัง

Trang Town isn't so much a tourist town as just a small town going about its daily business: Although there are travel agencies that can set up dive expeditions to the nearby islands,

hardware stores and noodle shops are the rule instead of tailor shops and bars. It's not a physically beautiful town, and most travelers will see it only in transit from the mainland to the beaches, but if you're interested in what semi-urban life looks like in this part of the world, it's a pedestrian-friendly place where you can wander around for a while observing the mundane without fear of getting lost. While it's sometimes difficult to discern small cultural differences among regions in foreign countries,

Trang feels distinctly different from more northern areas of Thailand. Like other parts of southern Thailand, the distinct mix of Thai-Chinese and Malay cultures can be fascinating to observe, plus there is some Sino-Portuguese architecture. Other than that, there isn't too much to see except for the markets and the governor's house, set on one of the area's hills.

Here you'll also find some of the best coffee shops. Say goodbye to instant and order a *kopi* instead. Just like the coffee you'll find in cafés in Malaysia and Singapore, this is the strong cloth bag–filtered version with a generous helping of sweetened condensed milk to make it go down smoothly. Trang is also known for two other culinary specialties—dim sum, which you can find at many coffee shops and which is especially popular for breakfast, and *mu yang Trang,* Trang-style crispy roasted pork. **Ton Noon Dim Sum** (202 Pad Sathani Rd., 6 A.M.–9 P.M. daily, 30B) and **Khao Chong Coffee** (Phatthalung Rd., tel. 07/521-8759, 6 A.M.–9 P.M. daily, 30B) are two traditional *kopi* shops with excellent dim sum choices.

Nok Air is the only airline offering flights to Trang from Bangkok, currently leaving from Don Muang airport. If you book far enough in advance on Nok Air, tickets are as cheap as 2,800B round-trip with tax. Otherwise, you may pay a little under 4,000B for a ticket.

There's an **overnight train** from Bangkok to Trang that leaves Hua Lamphong Station at 5:05 P.M. and arrives in Trang at 7:55 A.M. the next day. The tickets cost under 800B for a first-class sleeper ticket, so if you're comfortable sleeping on trains, it's a really economical and adventurous way to get to the region.

There are buses for Trang that leave the Southern Bus Terminal in Bangkok around 6 P.M.; call 02/435-1199 for the latest schedule. Buses take 12–14 hours. Expect to pay in the neighborhood of 800B for a ticket on an air-conditioned luxury bus, less than 550B for an unair-conditioned bus.

If you're driving from the surrounding areas, Highway 4 cuts through Trang in a zigzag pattern, making it the most accessible route for inland travel in the province. For the beaches in the southern part of the province, however, you'll have to turn onto secondary road 404. Although Trang is close to Phuket, Krabi, and Phang Nga as the crow flies, the drive can take hours due to the mountainous terrain. The drive from Krabi Town to Trang takes two hours; from Phuket to Trang, it takes 4.5–5 hours, so plan accordingly.

Mu Ko Phetra National Park
อุทยานแห่งชาติหมู่เกาะเภตรา

Mu Ko Phetra, a marine park in Trang, is a small grouping of islands just north of the Ko Tarutao area that feels even more remote than the rest of the province. The scenery, including the craggy limestone rock formations jutting out from the ocean and rainforest-covered islands, is spectacular. Under the surface of the sea surrounding many of the islands there's coral at relatively shallow depths, making this a great destination for snorkeling. The only way to stay in the national park is either to camp or to rent one of the national park bungalows on Ko Phetra.

Ko Khao Yai means "large mountain island." Although that could adequately define many of the islands in the Andaman Sea, Ko Khao Yai stands out because, thanks to erosion and tectonic forces, one of the large chunks of limestone jutting off the island has been worn through and forms a sort of natural bridge that can be rowed under during low tide.

The much smaller **Ko Lidi,** which covers less than 10 square kilometers, doesn't have great beaches for swimming, but it has some caves within the limestone cliffs that are nesting grounds for swallows, along with a campground where you can rent tents.

Ko Muk
เกาะมุก

Just off the coast of Trang, across from Chang Lang Beach, Ko Muk is a small inhabited island with some beautiful beaches backed by limestone cliffs on the west coast, coral clusters to snorkel around (particularly nearby Hat Sai Yao), and a scattering of bungalows and resorts catering to travelers. To the south, the eastern part of the island is mainly a fishing village, and the local economy is also dependent on the rubber plantations in the center of the island. But to the north, on the west coast, lies one of the coolest physical attractions in the region—the **Tham Morakot** (Emerald Cave). If you visit during low tide, you can access the cave and interior lagoon by boat, but the more fun way to go is during high tide, when the entrance to the cave is nearly filled with water and you have to swim through the limestone passage. When you reemerge, you'll be in a beautiful emerald lagoon surrounded by cliffs. During high season this is a popular place, so don't expect to have it to yourself.

To get to Ko Muk, you can take a longtail or speedboat from the Kuan Tungku pier, which is about 30 minutes from Trang Town. If you're flying into the Trang airport, there are frequent *song thaew* traveling this route during the day; expect to pay around 50B pp. At the pier, you'll have to negotiate with the captain, but a trip to Ko Muk will take around 30 minutes on a longtail boat and will cost around 400B.

Hat Chao Mai National Park
อุทยานแห่งชาติหาดเจ้าไหม
The Hat Chao Mai National Park (Mu 5, Ban Chang Lang, Amphoe Sikao, tel. 07/521-3260, 8:30 A.M.–6 P.M. daily, 200B) is a large protected area covering 19 kilometers of rocky and sandy coastline north of Hat Yao and south of Krabi Province. The interior of the park includes mangrove swamps, mountains, and rivers. The park also technically extends to the adjacent islands of Ko Muk, Ko Kradan, Ko Waen, Ko Cheaung, Ko Pring, and Ko Meng, although you won't necessarily notice that you've entered the park or even have to pay an entrance fee if you're visiting one of these islands. Although the park is a beautiful nature preserve and includes some amazing coral reef offshore, what Hat Chao Mai is best known for is the **dugong,** or sea cows, that live in the ocean territory covered by the park. This endangered species, similar to a manatee, was once hunted but has now been adopted by the locals as the region's unofficial mascot. The

sweet, awkward-looking dugong can sometimes be spotted during snorkeling or diving trips along the coast or islands covered by the park. If you're looking to explore the mainland part of the park, there are simple bungalows for rent as well as areas to camp with restrooms and canteens serving up tasty, casual local food.

Ko Kradan
เกาะกระดาน
Partially under the protection of the Hat Chao Mai National Park, Ko Kradan is often called the most beautiful island in Trang. It's no surprise, given the beautiful view of Ko Muk and other neighboring islands that seem to emerge magically from the Andaman Sea, the pristine soft-sand beaches, and the surrounding coral reefs. For snorkelers it's particularly alluring: The water is clear, and you'll only need to swim out to shallow depths to see some amazing coral and tropical fish. Although there are some rubber plantations on the island, it's largely undeveloped and usually visited by tourists as part of a tour to Ko Muk. If you want to stay over, there are a few bungalows on the island, and you can also camp on the island through the parks department.

Hat Yao and Surrounding Islands
หาดยาว
The longest stretch of beach in the province, Hat Yao has some clear sandy swaths punctuated by rock formations and rocky cliffs backed by pine and palm trees. Off the coast in the warm, clear-blue waters of the Andaman Sea are some islands and rock formations where you'll be able to do some snorkeling and diving away from the crowds a little farther north. There are very limited accommodations on the beach; it's definitely quiet and secluded. For budget travelers it's a great option if you feel like you've been squeezed out of the more popular tourist areas as they've gone upscale— you can still find accommodations for less than US$15 per night in the area.

Just off the coast of Hat Yao is **Ko Libong.** The largest island in Trang is a very short trip by longtail boat from the pier at Yao Beach and has a handful of small fishing villages and rubber plantations populated by the mostly Muslim Thais living in the area. The island itself has some beautiful sandy beaches and rugged, hilly rainforest in the middle, and there is snorkeling right off the coast, although not as much coral to be seen as you'll find in and around Phi Phi. Ko Libong also has a handful of quaint resorts if you're looking to stay on the island overnight.

South of Ko Libong is **Ko Sukorn,** one of the southernmost islands in Trang Province. This island has a handful of small villages mostly engaged in fishing and working on small rubber plantations on the island. The brown sandy beaches are surrounded by clear waters, and the island is mostly flat and without many of the rock formations characteristic of the region. The island is small enough that you can walk around it in a few hours, and close enough that it only takes about 20 minutes in a longtail boat from the mainland; you'll get a chance to see how people in the region make a living while enjoying the laid-back atmosphere on the island.

There are some relaxed bungalow resorts here, although nothing is fancy. If you're looking for an off-the-beaten-path island getaway, this is a great place to stay for a few days. **Sukorn Beach Bungalows** (Ko Sukorn, tel. 07/526-7707, www.sukorn-island-trang.com, 1,000B) is casual and unpretentious. This is definitely a place to stay for the location and the price, and for now you won't have to worry about being overrun by other travelers, since Ko Sukorn hasn't made it big yet. The guest rooms are filled with simple bamboo furniture and are a very short walk to the beach; most have air-conditioning. There aren't many amenities available here, but there is a small restaurant serving Thai food.

Sukorn Cabana (Ko Sukorn, tel. 07/511-5894, www.sukorncabana.com, 1,000B) has airy, basic, but pretty bungalows. This is not a high-end resort—many of the bungalows don't have air-conditioning or hot water—but they're just minutes from the beach.

Ko Chueak and **Ko Waen,** just adjacent to each other off the coast of Trang, are two very small islands with some of the best casual snorkeling in the region. Aside from some exotic, colorful fish, there is plenty of deep and shallow-water coral to view.

On the mainland, the national park area covers **Khao Pu** and **Khao Ya** mountains, which have thick forest cover, caves, and plenty of waterfalls to hike around in. Tha Le Song Hong—Lake of Two Rooms—is a fascinating and beautiful physical phenomenon to view. The large, clean lake is nearly divided by a mountain rising from the middle, creating two separate bodies of water. To get there by car, take Phetchakasem Road (Huai Yot–Krabi) to Ban Phraek, then turn right and drive about 13 kilometers. There will be signs in English pointing the way. If you want to rough it a little, there's a Boy Scout campground (tel. 07/522-4294) nearby. When it's not filled with kids, they rent out the houses.

Chang Lang Beach
หาดฉางหลาง

This beach has all of the spectacular scenery typically found along the Andaman coast—limestone cliffs, sandy beaches, and casuarina pine trees. One of the campsites, as well as the main headquarters for Hat Chao Mai National Park, is located on the beach.

At the tip of a forested headland is **Chao Mai Beach,** a wide stretch of sandy beach covering about three kilometers of coastline. Both of these beaches are beautiful and feel much more remote and less populated by visitors than the national parks to the north; if you come during the low season, you may well be the only person around.

The **Chao Mai Cave** is one of the larger caves in the region, with extensive stalactites and stalagmites, fossils, and multilevel chambers. There's also a spring inside one of the chambers, and some of the stalactites and stalagmites have joined, creating strange-looking pillars and an altogether otherworldly feeling inside. Although the cave is on the grounds of the national park, it's easier to access from Yao

Beach. From here, you can rent a rowboat to row into the cave from the ocean.

Another cool cave to visit is **Tham Le Khao Kop,** which has pools of water and a stream flowing through it as well as steep interior cliff walls, plus more than three kilometers of stalagmites and stalactites. During the day there are guides who'll row you through the cave in a little boat. At one point the passage is so low you have to lie on your back in the boat, which feels like a bit of adventure. To tour the cave with a boat and guide, the fee is 200B per boat or 30B pp. Take Highway 4 from the Huai Yot district heading toward the **Wang Wiset district** (อำเภอวังวิเศษ). After about six kilometers, you will see Andaman intersection; continue for 460 meters, and you will see another intersection with a temple on the right; turn left, drive about 640 meters, and you'll see a bridge to the cave.

SATUN
Satun Town
เมืองสตูล

As untouristed as Trang Town is, Satun Town is even more so. The center of the southernmost province on the Andaman coast before Malaysia, the town of Satun, as with the whole province, is primarily Muslim, having been a part of Malaya until the early 19th century. Sectarian violence has infected the three southernmost provinces on the east side of the peninsula, but even though Satun is nearly right next door, there have been no reports of insurgent activity here, and it's a great opportunity to catch a glimpse of a culture different from what you'll see to the north. To better understand Islam in Thailand, visit the **Ku Den Mansion,** the Satun National Museum. Housed in a colonial-style former palace that once housed King Rama V, this museum for Islamic studies has interesting displays on the lives of Muslims in the area through the ages. There's also the large **Satun Central Mosque.** Although it's not going to win any architectural awards, having been completed in the late 1970s, you can visit to pray or watch others do so.

If you're heading to Satun, you can take a train to Hat Yai (there's no train station in Satun), but then you have to travel by land for the remaining 95 kilometers.

Satun is on the same bus line as Trang. Buses leave the Southern Bus Terminal in Bangkok around 6 P.M.; call 02/435-1199 for the latest schedule. Buses will take 12–14 hours to reach Satun. Expect to pay in the neighborhood of 800B for a ticket on an air-conditioned luxury bus, less than 550B for an unair-conditioned bus.

If you're driving through Satun, Route 416 travels down the coast slightly inland, and from there you'll turn off onto country roads depending on your destination. Although Satun is close to Phuket, Krabi, and Phang Nga, keep in mind that the drive can take hours due to the mountainous terrain. If you are driving from Krabi Town to Satun, it will take three hours. From Phuket to Trang, the drive will take 5.5–6 hours.

Ko Tarutao National Park
อุทยานแห่งชาติหมู่เกาะตะรุเตา

Ko Tarutao National Park in Satun is the highlight of region if you're looking for a place to do some diving and snorkeling. The park comprises more than 50 islands off the coast of Satun and just north of Malaysian territorial waters, some barely a speck on the map and some, such as Ko Tarutao, covering dozens of square kilometers of land. Within the island group you'll find rainforests, clean quiet beaches, mangroves, coral reefs, and plenty of wildlife. Many people visit these islands on chartered tours from the mainland. As in other parts of the region, these tours are generally done on speedboats with other visitors from around the world and include lunch, a chance to enjoy the scenery, and some snorkeling. On the larger islands, there are a small number of decent accommodations, if you are looking to hang out in the area for a few days as you island-hop from one sight to the other. If you're on a budget or really want to enjoy the natural environment unfettered by modern distractions, try camping at one of the many campgrounds or renting a bungalow from the national parks department.

The largest island, **Ko Tarutao,** is a mountainous, forested island with limestone cliffs, mangrove swamps, and white-sand beaches. The island formerly housed a detainment center for political and other prisoners, but these days it's home to some of the national park facilities as well as the biggest selection of bungalows and resorts. If you're interested in seeing the darker side of the country's history, you can visit the old prisons at **Talo Udang Bay** in the southernmost part of the island and Talowao Bay in the southeastern part of the island. They're connected by a trail that was built by prisoners before the site was abandoned during World War II.

Mu Ko Adang Rawi comprises two islands, **Ko Adang** and **Ko Rawi,** both characterized by light-sand beaches, verdant interiors with limestone cliffs, and some coral reefs offshore that can be easily viewed when snorkeling or diving. Many people visit these islands as part of a day trip, but if you want to stay overnight, there are some bungalows available through the parks department, or you can rent a tent from them or bring your own to camp on the beach.

Ko Kai and **Ko Klang** in the center of the marine park are also both popular spots for snorkeling and hanging out on the clean sandy beaches. There are no accommodations here, and tour groups will often add these islands to a multiple-island day tour.

Ko Li Pe
เกาะหลีเป๊ะ

Just below the national park is Ko Li Pe, a small, charming island just 40 kilometers from Malaysia's Langkawi Island. Populated by sea gypsies and a smattering of unpretentious resorts and bungalows, every year the island is becoming more popular with adventurous vacationers looking for something a little off the beaten path. Still, it's small enough that you can tour the whole island in two hours,

and you won't find any big partying or even ATMs on Ko Li Pe, just a handful of beautiful beaches and some dive shops catering to those who want to enjoy the underwater life around the island.

There are three beaches on Ko Li Pe, which is shaped roughly like a boomerang pointing northeast. The eastern beach is called Sunset Beach, the northern beach is Sunrise Beach, and the southwestern beach (the inside of the boomerang) is called Pattaya Beach. Sunrise Beach and Pattaya Beach are connected to each other by a road that functions as the island's main street.

Many resorts close up shop during low season, but there are some that remain open year-round. **Idyllic Concept Resort** (Sunrise Beach, tel. 08/8227-5389, www.idyllicresort. com, 3,500B) features modern, funky guest rooms and bungalows right on the beach, plus a resort restaurant. The resort is only a few years old and is very clean and well-maintained.

Sita Beach Resort and Spa Villa (Pattaya Beach, tel. 07/475-0382, www.sitabeachresort. com, 3,500B) is a full-service mid-range resort with a swimming pool, a restaurant, a bar, and a small spa. Guest rooms are comfortable and have flat-screen TVs and vaguely Thai decor. The pool area is spacious and surrounded by guest rooms and villas. The resort is very family-friendly too. It's the location, and the view of the beach, though, that are the big attraction here.

The cool, popular, and ecochic **Castaway Resort** (Sunrise Beach, tel. 08/3138-7472, www.kohlipe.castaway-resorts.com, 2,000B) is a collection of stand-alone bamboo bungalows on the beach, plus an outdoor bar and restaurant. The accommodations are basic—there's no air-conditioning or hot water, although because the bungalows are right off the water, ceiling fans keep everything cool enough. Most bungalows have an upstairs and a downstairs plus a small balcony for lounging and enjoying the view.

www.moon.com

DESTINATIONS | ACTIVITIES | BLOGS | MAPS | BOOKS

MOON.COM is ready to help plan your next trip! Filled with fresh trip ideas and strategies, author interviews, informative travel blogs, a detailed map library, and descriptions of all the Moon guidebooks, Moon.com is all you need to get out and explore the world—or even places in your own backyard. While at Moon.com, sign up for our monthly e-newsletter for updates on new releases, travel tips, and expert advice from our on-the-go Moon authors. As always, when you travel with Moon, expect an experience that is uncommon and truly unique.

KEEP UP WITH MOON ON FACEBOOK AND TWITTER
JOIN THE MOON PHOTO GROUP ON FLICKR

MAP SYMBOLS

▦ Expressway	◖ Highlight	✗ Airport	⚲ Golf Course
Primary Road	○ City/Town	✗ Airfield	▣ Parking Area
Secondary Road	◉ State Capital	▲ Mountain	⬟ Archaeological Site
Unpaved Road	✹ National Capital	✚ Unique Natural Feature	⌂ Church
Trail	★ Point of Interest		⌂ Temple/Pagoda
Ferry	● Accommodation	⟨ Waterfall	▲ Wat
Railroad	▼ Restaurant/Bar	♠ Park	Mangrove
Pedestrian Walkway	■ Other Location	◙ Trailhead	Reef
Stairs	Λ Campground	⛽ Gas Station	Swamp

CONVERSION TABLES

°C = (°F - 32) / 1.8
°F = (°C x 1.8) + 32
1 inch = 2.54 centimeters (cm)
1 foot = 0.304 meters (m)
1 yard = 0.914 meters
1 mile = 1.6093 kilometers (km)
1 km = 0.6214 miles
1 fathom = 1.8288 m
1 chain = 20.1168 m
1 furlong = 201.168 m
1 acre = 0.4047 hectares
1 sq km = 100 hectares
1 sq mile = 2.59 square km
1 ounce = 28.35 grams
1 pound = 0.4536 kilograms
1 short ton = 0.90718 metric ton
1 short ton = 2,000 pounds
1 long ton = 1.016 metric tons
1 long ton = 2,240 pounds
1 metric ton = 1,000 kilograms
1 quart = 0.94635 liters
1 US gallon = 3.7854 liters
1 Imperial gallon = 4.5459 liters
1 nautical mile = 1.852 km

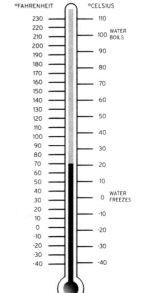

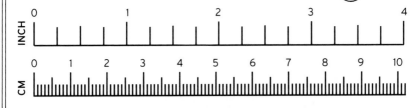

MOON SPOTLIGHT KO SAMUI
& THE ANDAMAN COAST
Avalon Travel
a member of the Perseus Books Group
1700 Fourth Street
Berkeley, CA 94710, USA
www.moon.com

Editor: Elizabeth Hollis Hansen
Copy Editor: Christopher Church
Graphics and Production Coordinator:
   Lucie Ericksen
Cover Designer: Kathryn Osgood
Map Editor: Albert Angulo
Cartographers: Kat Bennett, Chris Hendrick,
   Kaitlin Jaffe

ISBN: 978-1-59880-970-1

ABOUT THE AUTHOR

Suzanne Nam

Suzanne Nam moved to Thailand in 2005 for a one-year stint as a newspaper reporter – and she hasn't left since. Like all meaningful things, Suzanne's career was more a product of evolution than of planning: She grew up in Cambridge, Massachusetts, went to law school after college, and practiced law for five years – enough time to produce a rain forest's worth of corporate paperwork – and then she gave it all up to work toward a journalism degree at Columbia.

Next the world pulled Suzanne east – first to London, then the Middle East, and finally Bangkok. She is now a reporter for Forbes magazine, a reformed corporate lawyer, and a dedicated travel writer.

Suzanne met her future husband during her first year in Bangkok. In 2009 they adopted a street dog named Sam; in 2011 their twins, Bix and Ella, were born. Raising children in a foreign country brings plenty of adventure and challenges, but daily life in Thailand is surprisingly stable and comfortable. Suzanne couldn't imagine living anywhere else.

CPSIA information can be obtained at www.ICGtesting.com
Printed in the USA
LVOW13s0845150714

394413LV00009B/21/P